THE NOVEL OF ADULTERY

THE NOVEL OF
ADULTERY

Judith Armstrong

'Tragedy is the vindication of a universal Order, when it is in the interests
of the Spectator to see that Order
justified.'

G. W. Ireland

BOOKS
10 East 53d St.. New York 10022
(a division of Harper & Row Publishers. Inc.)

First published 1976 by
THE MACMILLAN PRESS LTD
London and Basingstoke

Published in the U.S.A. 1976 by
HARPER & ROW PUBLISHERS, INC.
BARNES & NOBLE IMPORT DIVISION

ISBN 0–06–490203–X
LCN 76–15793

Printed in Great Britain

With gratitude to
Nina Christesen and
Richard Coe

Contents

Acknowledgement

This publication has been assisted by a grant from the Committee on Research and Graduate Studies of the University of Melbourne.

1 The Establishing of the Order

A proper understanding of a society's ideas on adultery necessarily involves an understanding of its ideas on marriage. The aim of this introduction therefore is to provide an account of the legal, social and religious attitudes to both marriage and adultery in France, England, America and Russia in the second half of the nineteenth century. However, chronological cut-off points being the most arbitrary of divisions, I have begun by tracing, however briefly, the way in which each of these nineteenth-century societies has emerged from its own immediate past, and from the common remote past of Europe as a whole. I have also found it helpful to bring this historical perspective into focus by including scholarly reaffirmations of what is vaguely felt to be the case about marriage by most people in the Western world – for example, the belief that marriage is a universal institution. The anthropologists confirm that nowhere in the world and at no time in the history of man has a durable human community existed without it. 'To achieve order and regulation in sexual behaviour', says Henriques in explanation of the phenomenon, 'some form of marriage is necessary. Marriage assures the sexual rights of the partners in each other, and ensures the creation and care of a family to inherit property and to help perpetuate the society.'[1] It may be, as, for example, Henriques believed, that there are many forms with an equal right to be regarded as marriage properly so called – monogamy, polygamy, polyandry and group marriage – or it may be that 'Monogamy is, has been, and will remain the only true type of marriage',[2] but it seems agreed among anthropologists that some things about marriage are virtual constants in all societies whether primitive or advanced. In few, if any, cultures is pairing off in marriage a matter of an entirely free choice by the two partners, although our own culture may be one of the rare exceptions. Adultery is almost always regarded as a grave offence, even though there are a few communities which permit extra-marital intercourse in circumstances regulated by tribal law and many in which unmarried boys and girls are free to mate in temporary unions. Further, as

Malinowski dispassionately reports, the penalty inflicted on an adulterous wife is invariably greater than that inflicted on an adulterous husband.

The nuclear family (consisting of mother/father/children) is another institution whose universality has frequently been asserted,[3] and one to which marriage is inextricably linked; it has four defining functions : sexual, economic, reproductive and educative. If we set aside the last two functions as not *essential* to marriage (since most societies are willing to regard a couple as married even when they have no children), we arrive at one reasonable attempt to define marriage. As the anthropologist G. P. Murdock puts it, 'Marriage exists only when the economic and sexual are united in one relationship, and this combination occurs only in marriage.'[4] The breaking of the combination in the individual case may be seen as anything from sensible to tragic, but it is rarely regarded as trivial.

The early history of marriage in Western Europe

In an examination of the original basic pattern of the marriage contract in Indo-European society, around the seventh century B.C., Father E. Schillebeeckx O.P.[5] describes in both Greek and Roman mores a family-based society, with the life of each family centred around its own hearth and its own household gods. The religion of the hearth, depending uniquely and exclusively on the perpetuity of the family, contributed to the notion of marriage as essentially monogamous and indissoluble except in cases of barrenness. The essence of the marriage was for the woman the transference from one religion – that of her parents – to another – her husband's, which involved a religious, though priestless, and legally valid ceremony.* Once married, she was subject to the authority that the husband, as head of the household, wielded over her as well as over the children and servants; but it is significant that the wife enjoyed equal dignity with her husband, and was a copriestess in the family religion. The ethics of this household religion were also naturally family centred and adultery was considered to be a transgression of the utmost gravity.

In the immediately pre-Christian era the customs of Rome and Greece began to diverge. In both cases the girl's father or brother chose the husband from amongst the suitors, but in Rome both priestly authority and temporal powers were excluded from the marriage ceremony, which was an essentially personal and family matter and only

---

* It is interesting to note that the bride and groom celebrated their union with the eating of a loaf which has now become the familiar wedding cake and that the carrying of the bride over the threshold is symbolic of the pretended abduction by which the girl was removed from her own hearth.

required valid witnesses. In Greece religious rites usually accompanied the making of the contract, though the presence of a priest was not legally necessary. Moreover, harsh laws preserved Greek marriages. The repudiation of an unfaithful wife was obligatory, and there were sanctions against adulterous women, though not against her guilty partner. A very clear distinction was drawn between the three categories – women of pleasure, who were beneath morality; domestic women, who must be subservient to their husbands and unimpeachably virtuous; and the intellectual women of the *hetaerae* who were usually foreign and outside the normal strictures of morality.

Roman law during the pre-Christian era had at first contributed to the lowly status of women, so that they, like Greek women, could not exercise public or civil office, act as witnesses, sign wills, own more than half an ounce of gold, or wear parti-coloured clothes, as laid down by the Lex Oppia of 215 B.C. But gradually, and for largely indirect economic reasons grounded in the fact that even married women continued in tutelage to family-appointed guardians whose rights overrode those of their husbands, these laws evolved to allow married women greater and greater independence, and finally to produce the era of the great Roman matriarchs.

Nevertheless, adultery was, until the time of the Christian emperor Justinian, still a capital offence for a woman, and for a man also if his partner was married. Divorce, however, was always relatively easy to obtain, on the grounds of mutual consent. After Justinian a husband could divorce his wife for adultery.

Thus the concept of marriage had evolved considerably even before the influence of Christianity, from a 'sacral' event drawing its significance from the 'religion of the hearth' through a secularisation process which resulted in the acceptance of a partnership based on 'mutual consent', or, alternatively and more commonly, the selection of a bride by the prospective groom's family. However, both Greece (which had always retained the religious significance attached to marriage) and Rome had developed marriage ceremonies distinctive and solemn enough to be recognised as rites by the Christian Church after both civilisations had embraced that faith.

During the ensuing centuries of the Christian era marriage tended to follow local secular and civil custom as far as the ceremony was concerned, but was provided with additional pastoral care by the Church. Whether the parents or partners made the choice depended on custom. For some time clerical intervention was considered unnecessary, though perhaps desirable. By the fourth century a priestly blessing was often sought, though the marriage was still solemnised within the family circle; this development grew up into a non-obligatory ecclesiastical liturgy of marriage. However, not only was this not a requirement, it was actually forbidden to those who were not exemplary Christians and could only apply to civilly valid marriages.

From the tenth to the twelfth centuries there was a move towards ecclesiastical control of marriage, although surveillance was not deliberately sought by the Church. It came about through the loss of power of the various Christian kings, and the transfer of their jurisdictional power to the bishops. With the natural disappearance of the ancient ceremonies, the role of the priest tended to become more influential. Feeling the weight of its new responsibilities in this area, the Church pressed for the declaration of mutual consent to be made public – for example, to take place at the church porch rather than in the family circle.

During the eleventh, twelfth and thirteenth centuries the sacramental nature of marriage, having hitherto been somewhat neglected by the early fathers, received attention from the scholastics. Both churchmen and pagans were united in seeing marriage primarily as a means of founding a family and in their horror of the thought of an illegitimate child in the family circle. But pagans recognised a husband's right to repudiate an adulterous wife, whereas there was no doubt in the minds of the Church Fathers that marriage was indissoluble no matter what the provocation. Their convictions were based on the belief that marriage was a sign of a more profound reality, a mysterious union as profound as that between Christ and His Church; but within this definition there arose a debate as to the precise meaning of the sacramental nature of marriage.

The debate arose in a situation where the Church had not – and surprisingly perhaps has still not – provided a dogmatic definition of the word 'sacrament'. Its Latin form, *sacramentum*, is a rendering of the Greek word for 'mystery' which itself refers to both Jewish and Christian teaching in relation to the divine plan for man's salvation. In early ecclesiastical writings the word contained two basic concepts, being used to refer to a sacred secret, and to the manifestation of that secret. Thus Augustine talks of sacraments as sacred signs, whereas Aquinas interprets a sacrament as 'the sign of a sacred thing, in as much as it sanctifies man'.[6] (Matrimony is the manifestation of the loving union between Christ and His Church.) All the sacraments involve element and word, or matter and form, or more simply still objects, such as oil, bread, or water, and the recitation of some prayers.

It is clear then that the idea of a sacrament as a visible sign of the mysterious relationship between man and God was an indispensable aid to the presentation of religion, as well as a necessary component of the fully devout life. And it is equally evident that the solemnity, to put it at its lowest significance, of marriage was vitally affected by the definition of its status in regard to the teaching on sacraments.

In the previously mentioned debate, St Thomas Aquinas declared marriage to be a sacrament (*a*) because it constituted an indissoluble bond of sacral obligation, i.e. a moral obligation brought about by the contract, and (*b*) because it was reinforced by the sacred symbolism of marriage as a sign of the mysterious relationship between Christ and His Church. Dissolution of this bond was, in his view, not permissible. However the scholastics, taking up his idea of sacrament, extended it still further and interpreted a marriage not just as a symbol, but as an *efficacious* sign bringing about an unbreakable objective bond. Dissolution in this case was not simply not permissable, but actually not possible.

During the fourteenth century there took place a systemisation of the legal aspects of marriage earlier summed up by Thomas Aquinas, who recognised the full secular status of marriage, but also its strictly sacramental character as a 'saving instrument' through which the mystery of Christ and of His Church were active in the marriage of baptised partners.

The scholastics having also defined that marriage must consist of both mutual consent and consummation in order to be valid, the Council of Trent (1545–63) finally insisted upon the presence of a priest as a further necessary condition of validity, and condemned the view of the Reformist Churches that the Roman Church erred in regarding a valid marriage as indissoluble even in the case of adultery. Thus all Christian marriages were brought completely into the Church's orbit, and to marriage itself was officially conferred the solemn status of being a union in which the partners were bound to each other as intimately, permanently, and mysteriously as Christ was to His Church.

Church attitudes to women

In the Old Testament women were subject and inferior beings; the Decalogue includes a wife amongst a man's possessions. They could be repudiated, but could not themselves claim a divorce. They could not inherit, nor make a valid vow without the consent of husband or father, and they were severely punished for sexual misconduct, while men were punished only if they violated another husband's rights. The Genesis account of the creation of Eve and of the Fall 'established' women's physical, intellectual, and moral inferiority.

The New Testament reflects the anti-feminism of Jewish society, overlaid with the positive misogynism of the early Church Fathers. St Paul, concerned for order and the moral impeccability of the Christian communities, insisted upon the subordination of women and the superiority of the celibate state; nevertheless, he upheld the sacred symbolism of the marriage relationship.

The scholastic asceticism of mediaeval theology perpetuated the Pauline respect for virginity to the extent of arousing considerable guilt in the male over his sexual susceptibility; it is the argument of feminism that these guilt feelings were transferred to the female sex, thus endowing women with a taint beyond their 'naturally' lowly status. It also allowed for a double standard of morality which showed itself in such instances as the fact that an adulterous husband *had* to be received back by his faithful wife, while a guilty wife could be repudiated by her husband. (In the delicate matter of repudiation, which had been widely accepted in common law, the Church was bound to uphold the durability of the married state, but separation and dissolutions were often granted on the production of sometimes tenuous evidence of consanguinity (blood-ties), affinity ('in-law' connections), or spiritual affinity (godchild/godfather relationships), all of which were bars to marriage. This made the Church to some extent a defender of women, though frequently a weak one.)

The Church also showed its concern over questions related to and arising from the debate over the validity and indissolubility of marriage. For example, the legal marriageable age was set at twelve, which was actually an improvement over the then not unknown five. There was an attempt to insist on 'free consent', though this was still ambiguous given the strength of paternal authority.

In fact, the Church often found itself powerless in any attempt to oppose the deeply entrenched tenets of feudalism, though of course, when allied to them, its hand was greatly strengthened. The powerful group-cohesiveness, which under feudal law centred around the ancestral name and made united claim to ancestral land, found itself at one with the Church's prohibition on adultery, for with the growth in importance of property, the reaction against adultery intensified. It was no longer a question, as in ancient times, of betrayal of the household religion; fear of the bastard as a usurper of name and land became an obsession which could join with the Church to the point of vilifying the adulteress but was prepared to go a great deal further in the matter of punishing her. Repudiation was an effective retribution, since women were totally dependent on their husbands, fathers and even sons, if they were widowed. The husband, father, son or lord held responsibility not only for the woman's person and property, but even for the state of her soul before God. Failing blood-kin, women became subject to the lord of the fief, who could use his power to enforce their marriage or remarriage in the interests of increasing his own property. The importance to the feudal lord of the true line can be gathered from the fact that to be illegitimate was not in itself a crime at all – i.e. someone else's bastard was not particularly offensive. Nevertheless illegitimate children were legally disadvantaged in that they were not allowed to inherit.

However, the end of the eleventh century saw changes in regard both to church and to social relationships which were observable long before they were explained. The status of the noblewoman and the rights of femininity were elevated. Piety ceased to be a masculine prerogative, and in the newly founded convents abbesses had both autonomy and authority, sometimes even over clerics. They were also granted juridical power, while laywomen were allowed to administer manors during their husbands' absence.

At the same time, much more attention was given to female religious figures such as the Blessed Virgin and St Mary Magdalene. For whereas, in the Byzantine church, the growth in the number and solemnity of Marian feasts had been marked during the period prior to the middle of the eleventh century, the development of similar liturgical rites in the Roman Church had been much slower, and in the tenth century was quite stagnant. This state of affairs was ascribed to the controversy surrounding the doctrines associated with the Virgin Mary – her immaculate conception, her assumption, and her role as mediatrix, all of which had long been assimilated in the Orthodox teaching.

However, from the eleventh to the sixteenth centuries the situation was reversed. While there was no further development in the Eastern Church, in the West there was a renewal and development of Marian theology, which reached a peak in the first half of the twelfth century. (Commenting that popular enthusiasm for the Virgin demanded artistic expression in forms which slid from the mysterious to the naturalistic, and from naturalism to artifice, a theologian has stated that the Virgins of this era are inclined to display their smile rather than their son, who is pushed to the sidelines. This fact will become all the more interesting when read in conjunction with the conclusion to this chapter.)

Of this period of unforseen change, John Langdon-Davies writes: 'The fusion between the Roman–Christian civilisation and the barbarians produced two great social institutions, feudalism and chivalry; and nothing in women's history has been of such supreme importance as the way these affected it.'[7]

The effects of chivalry and the cult of courtly love

The deeply radical change in the status of the noblewoman, and the respect newly accorded her, was intimately bound up with the appearance of chivalry and courtly love. It was a phenomenon which also bred a new attitude to adultery, with far-reaching effects. However, not the least of its many fascinations is that a full explanation of its origins is still not available. The strange gap in historical detection is acknowledged by many writers, but most significantly in the two most profound and detailed studies of courtly love available to us: C. S.

Lewis's *Allegory of Love*, and Denis de Rougemont's *L'Amour et l'Occident*.

Both of these writers make some attempt to explain the origins of the cult : Lewis refers to the abnormal circumstances which arose in feudal France during the time of the Crusades, when, in the absence of husbands and other men of equal rank, a small number of elegant ladies were shut up in a castle with numerous inferior nobles, landless knights, restless squires and young pages. The transference of vassalic devotion from the lord to the lady was plumped out with the romantic love-lyrics of the troubadours and exaggerated and intensified by the confusion with the concurrent upsurge in religious devotion to the Virgin. De Rougemont dwells upon the mutual influence on each other in Southern France of courtly love and Catharism – the neo-Manichean cult also known as the Albigensian heresy, which glorified chastity, despised marriage and loved death for its liberation of the spirit from the trammels of bodily life.

However, the essential point is that while these writers patently hesitate to make definitive statements explaining absolutely the advent of courtly love, both are agreed that it appeared quite suddenly at the end of the eleventh century in Languedoc, having been absent from classical antiquity, the literature of the Dark Ages, and the Norse saga; that it brought with it a new conception of relations between men and women, including an image of woman as *superior* to man – an idealised creature unrelated to the situation of most women; and that it located the interplay of the persons involved in the male adoration of the idealised female firmly outside Christian marriage.

Suzanne Lilar, in her *Aspects of Love in Western Society*, alone denies that passionate love was an invention of the twelfth century, citing as proof the love of Héloïse and Abelard. But her objection would appear to be answered by Henriques' sensible and balanced judgement : 'Romantic love in Europe appears to have been unknown prior to the appearance in late eleventh century France of the troubadours and trouvères. That is not to say that attachments of this kind did not exist between individuals before that time, but that it was not accepted and formalised as a popular conception.'[8] Henriques also looks at contemporary non-European societies, and finds extremely conflicting evidence – for example, while suicide for love is known in all types of societies, including the Pima Indians of North America, the Tahitians and some Australian aboriginies, Margaret Mead declares that the Samoans were reduced to laughter at the story of Romeo and Juliet since romantic love does not occur in their civilisation. Henriques concludes that romantic love *exists* 'wherever men and women meet each other', but that its incidence and intensity vary considerably according to the society considered. Under this aegis he supports Lewis's claim of a 'rise' of eleventh-century romantive love, in a form extra-ordinarily intense and widespread within its defined geographical limits.

Lewis himself, having reiterated his conviction that the now familiar erotic tradition of modern Europe is neither derived from nature, nor universal, but really a 'special state of affairs which will probably have an end, and which certainly had a beginning in eleventh century Provence'[9] tells us that before this period 'the world was bare of successful romantic love', knowing only merry sensuality, domestic comfort and the 'tragic madness'* experienced by Medea, Phaedra, Dido and others.

He goes on to argue that adultery was logically necessary to the whole notion of courtly love for the following reasons: courtly love essentially involved an idealisation of passionate sexual love; but passionate love was regarded as evil, or at least suspect, by the Church, and declared not to be a proper component of conjugal love; indeed one church view widely held was that to love one's own wife passionately was adulterous. Thus the idealisation of sexual love, in a society in which marriage was a utilitarian affair, had to begin by being the idealisation of adultery.

At the same time the mediaeval courts of love were defining 'love' in terms which could not be equated with marriage, firstly because the church explicitly *required* conjugal love of marriage partners, thus precluding the essential element in courtly love of continuing free choice, and secondly because love was awarded by the (superior) lady to her (inferior) vassal-lover. But wives were never considered to be superior to husbands – hence the confident assurance of the decree in the Countess of Champagne's Court of Love on the third day from the Calends of May, 1174: 'Love cannot extend its powers over two married persons ...'

---

* It is clear that erotic love amongst the philosophical élite of Plato's day was not directed to either marriage or adultery, but rather to homosexual relationships. However, since the term was used by later centuries almost, though not exclusively, in connection with adulterous or romantic love, it will be useful to be acquainted with the theory behind this understanding of erotic love.

According to Plato, the soul retains a memory of God, which can be awakened by a 'divine' face or body, and which can then fill the mind with the desire to possess true beauty. This is his 'divine madness', a state of intense desire leading ultimately to purification after passing through various stages: these include attraction to, first of all, an individual, beautiful body; then to beauty of a depersonalised kind; and finally, via appreciation of the non-corporeal beauty of the soul, to absolute and everlasting beauty. That this system of total love, by its religious extension and homosexual application, is quite a long way removed from later uses of the term, is already acknowledged; to know the origin of the word is simply to fit one more piece into the jigsaw picture of Western marriage.

Lewis goes on to trace the story of courtly love as it was presented through the allegorical method, but shifts his locus from Languedoc to England, where he leads his reader via Chaucer, Gower and Thomas Usk to Spenser. There, at last, in the third and fourth books of the *Faerie Queene* he sees courtly love defeated by a romantic conception of married love.

We shall return to this point later, since the moment when the English allegory broke away from the French marks our introduction to the literature of adultery in England. For the present it is only necessary to retain Lewis's conviction that courtly love and adultery are intimately and necessarily linked, and to remember it in the light of Denis de Rougemont's understanding of the tradition of courtly love as an attempt to contain the fatality of passion.

In *L'Amour et l'Occident* de Rougemont works from a very detailed analysis of the Tristan and Yseult myth, which he interprets as an indirect presentation of the obscure and inadmissible fact that passion is related to death and brings about the destruction of those who give themselves to it completely. The longing for passion and death is a craving which stirs us all in spite of ourselves; but it represents such an intolerable menace to society that it must never be openly admitted. When its effects, however, become as rapidly widespread and close to the surface as they did with the practice of courtly love, with its willed opposition between conjugal union and unconsummated desire for the wife of another, then the longing must be constrained. The legitimate accommodation of the fatal attraction of passion was achieved in the rules of chivalry themselves, and by the propagation of the Tristan myth. That is, the myth was invented to combat by containment the destructive forces in society which threatened to undermine the social and moral order – in particular the breakdown of marriage, which according to contemporary chronicles, sermons and satires, was reaching critical proportions.

A résumé of de Rougemont's theory would go like this : courtly love betrays a hankering after love *for its own sake* and not for the sake of the beloved. But if love is to be continuously desired, it must never be fulfilled. Therefore, there is implicit in the desire for love a secret quest for the obstruction that fosters love. This quest is then only the disguise for a love of obstruction and frustration for its own sake, which is a symbol of our longing for the ultimate obstacle which is death. Thus it is in fact suffering and death for which passion yearns, not the fulfilment of love. Passionate love on these terms is radically opposed to marriage and expresses an idealism which denies earthly satisfaction and, ultimately, life itself.

This, and the spurning of marriage, are two points at which the cult of courtly love met the contemporaneous and equally new religious heresy practised by the Cathars (the name came from the Greek word for spotless). A third was the cult of unattainable love, whether the object of this love was God or lady (the ambiguity of the object of devotion in the courtly love lyric is well known). The Church was bound to oppose the heresy, and did so with fire and sword; it also countered the orders of chivalry by the encouragement of monastic orders. But even more significantly the hierarchy felt it imperative to discourage the cult of Idealised Woman, with its concomitant of a love contrary to marriage, by providing a belief and worship designed to satisfy the profound seeking after a feminine ideal expressed both in Catharism and in courtly love; this it did by repeated efforts to create a cult of the Blessed Virgin Mary. The Feast of the Immaculate Conception, for example, was established at Lyons in 1140, in spite of vain opposition from St Bernard of Clairvaux whose views were still upheld one hundred years later by St Thomas Aquinas.*

The final outcome of the struggle was the triumph of Christianity over the Cathar heretics and the stilling of the troubadours. The decline and defeat of courtly love are reflected in the two parts of the *Roman de la Rose*. The first, written by Guillaume de Lorris in about 1237, already depicts a real woman and not an ideal one, but she can only be reached by a lover undergoing suitable mental refinement; in the second part, produced by Jean de Meun in 1280, the Rose having become nothing more than a sensual pleasure is won by main force. Thus, in de Rougemont's words, nature triumphed over spirit, and reason over passion.

The end of de Rougemont's story is the beginning of this present study of adultery in the nineteenth-century French novel – an investigation which cannot ignore the light he has thrown upon the relation between adultery and passion, passion and death. De Rougemont himself comments upon the links between the mediaeval myth and the modern novel. Asserting that 'the story of passionate love in all great literatures, from the thirteenth century to the present day, is the story of the descent of the courtly love myth into "profane" life', he traces the degradation and humanisation of the myth through Petrarch, *L'Astrée* and classical tragedy to its death-blow at the hands of Racine. In the eighteenth century it is in eclipse; in the nineteenth it reappears in a secular and interiorised form in the popular novel, for it is in literature that myths reappear when they have lost their sacred nature. There the banished but never eradicated desire for passionate love finds itself in conflict

* De Rougemont argues that the twelfth-century upsurge of the feminine principle was similarly revealed by changes in the personae of the game of chess: instead of the four kings who had originally dominated the game, a Lady or Queen was made to take precedence over all the other pieces except the king, whose effective action was still considerably less than hers.

with the prevailing Christian ethic and social institution of marriage, which in Catholic France is held to be a sacrament constraining the partners to conjugal affection, but which is in practice based on material and social interests.

Thus what all declare to be an eleventh-century phenomenon shows itself to have a general significance for all times – possibly including our own. But in particular it has clarified and refined yet again the underlying menace of the adulteress. From having been first the traitor who betrayed the family religion, then the cuckoo threatening to deprive the true offspring of their rightful inheritance, she is now seen to be the invitation to passion, death, and the destruction of society. The transcendant fear of the adulteress will always be translated by the individual society into terms more immediately assimilable by its members. But the de Rougemont theory provides a haunting background to the more overt reasons cited for the condemnation of adultery by those who fear it most : the overlords who see their property threatened, the lawmakers apprehensive of the undermining of the social order, and the church leaders excoriating the souls who deviate from the conjugal path to heaven.

Marriage in France

The separation from the common trunk of Catholic Christendom occasioned by England's break with Rome was very far from being her only independent shoot, as we shall see. But for the moment we remain with the parent plant, rooted in French soil, and in particular in that of the period ranging from feudalism to the Revolution.

In the following centuries the institution of marriage, freed from the distraction of courtly love, was consolidated through its being the foundation of a family life still thought of in terms of a small kingdom whose power must be preserved and increased by the acquisition of land and subjects. Preoccupation with the amount of dowry and the suitability of the alliance, combined with a fairly general absolute paternal authority (at least in the sixteenth and seventeenth centuries) led to a large number of younger sons refraining from marriage, and a large number of girls being sent to convents. Duplessis' history, *Les Mariages en France*, says crisply, 'Within these two classes [nobility and bourgeoisie] efforts were made to place the daughters, but as concern for the suitability of the match, and the dowry, was pre-eminant, if not absolute, many girls were left unaccounted for and sooner or later were obliged to enter a convent . . .' He speaks of the 'obligation of younger sons to make their own way in life, and therefore not to encumber themselves with a family', and remarks that 'love-marriages were the exception'.[10] Only the poor were unsuspicious of love matches, and free of the fear of a *mésalliance*. The higher the social status of the family the more clearly was marriage seen to be an institution designed for the benefit of the families rather than the individuals concerned, and the settling of money and property via a legal contract to be of crucial importance.

Amongst the lower classes, where the likely material gain was less and the confusion much greater about where guilt in sexual relations began and ended, there was a more ready toleration of love marriages and of bastards. Duplessis even notes that it is uncertain at what point in history sexual relations became 'guilty'. There were, it appears, a large number of natural children in all classes of society.

In earlier centuries marriage without parental consent had been permitted by the Church but in 1629 and 1639 King Louis XIII ordered the consent of the parents or grandparents to become a requirement for prospective spouses, up to the age of twenty-five for girls and thirty for boys. The legal marriageable age was still twelve for girls and fourteen for boys, but betrothals could be arranged from the age of seven in the interests of a good match.

Since 'parental' consent in fact meant paternal consent these laws have been intepreted by two modern French feminists, Andrée Michel and Geneviève Texier, as a patriarchal attempt to extend the authority of the father. And indeed the royal declaration of 26 November 1639, which decreed that reverence of children for parents was 'natural', did in fact use the example of this relationship as a model not only for the legitimate obedience that subjects ought to have towards their king, but also for the 'natural' authority of the husband over the wife. 'The family became', write Michel and Texier, 'the group in and through which hierarchical order was to be established in society, and political power and the monarchic state consolidated.'[11] Similarly the raising of the age of majority from fourteen to thirty, and the granting of the right of the father to give his children in marriage without their consent, when marriage by mutual consent had been part of canon law since before the fourteenth century, were also seen as thrusts in the male bid for absolute political and sexual supremacy. At the same time, the wife lost her common-law right to take a new husband if the first was mad or permanently absent; and in spite of the elevated status of the mediaeval lady, by the sixteenth century the female had become incapable in the eyes of the law, unable to manage a business or even be surety for her husband. The legislators went back to Roman law to find support for their idea of *fragilitas sexus*, which appeared in France from the fourteenth century onwards, though unknown during the Middle Ages.

As for divorce, Duplessis simply says it did not exist up to and in the eighteenth century – 'but in high society both spouses enjoyed great independence, and nothing was more common than adultery'.[12] This is our first acknowledgement of what will frequently be borne out in all societies – that whatever the moral climate and law of the land, the upper classes – and perhaps the lowliest also – appear to enjoy a greater degree of extra-marital freedom than the great mass of the people. The point will be taken up again when we come to consider the social milieu of the novels.

For the aristocracy at least the practice of adultery was facilitated towards the end of the eighteenth century by the growth of contraception, and aggravated by that system of arranged contractual alliances which moved Michelet to describe married life as 'usually thirty years of boredom, and a conjugal bed cold enough to freeze mercury'.[13]

In the melting pot of the French Revolution the commonly accepted ideas about marriage underwent a transformation, and the new thinking inspired reforms of much of the Civil Law. Marriage was secularised, and, in the reforming tradition we have just looked at, its indissolubility was rejected. Divorce was permitted on certain grounds, for example adultery by the wife, or the husband's keeping of a concubine in the home; mutual consent and incompatibility were also acceptable reasons. The age until which parental consent for marriage was required was reduced to twenty-one for girls and twenty-five for boys, and the marriagable age was raised to fifteen for girls and eighteen for boys. The civil status of an unmarried woman was roughly equated with that of a man. Bastards were given the same rights as legitimate children, *except* those born of adultery. The Napoleonic Code established quite specifically the following articles, in what the *Cambridge History of Modern France* calls a successful fusion of custom and Roman Law: marriage was not a sacrament, but a contract; marital authority was vested in the husband, as head of a family based on the hierarchical model of the state (thus keeping the married woman in a state of disability); adulteresses were to be imprisoned for a period of three months to two years, while the accomplice risked the same punishment as well as a fine of 100–2000 francs. But for an adulterous husband no punishment is mentioned unless he actually kept a concubine in the conjugal home – in which case, *if* the wife complained, he could be fined a sum of the same magnitude as the accomplice mentioned above. Although legal separation on the grounds of the husband keeping a concubine at home was allowed, the legally separated woman was not granted full civil rights until 1893. Nor could a woman living on her earnings deposit them in a bank and withdraw them until the laws of 1881 and 1895.

According to those tersely succinct feminists, Michel and Texier, the Napoleonic Code simply preserved and indeed consecrated the segregation of the sexes in conjugal and family life.

Fascinating it is to note, however, that as Napoleon perceived the dangers of revolutionary ideas that had for him served their purpose, so did the concept of authority tighten both in his own outlook and in that of his successors. Nothing perhaps indicates the vital link in the imperial and governmental mind between the two stabilities of state and family than the abolition of divorce in 1816 – a proscription which was to last until 1884.

In fact, this swing between liberalisation and reaction is typical of a century in which the embattled establishment struggled for supremacy over the forces of liberalism. While the governments of the Restoration and Second Empire censored and prosecuted overbold thinkers, and while the bases of education in the colleges were 'la Religion, la Monarchie, la Légitimité et la Charte', Catholics, Hegelians, positivists, and the proponents of the 'religions of humanity' tried to provide society with an ideological synthesis. With the restoration of public worship backed by the return of the émigré bishops, 'King, Church and aristocracy were now at one in their determination to found the new régime on the "union of throne and altar" '.[14] However, this bid only increased the anti-clericalism of the early Romantics and promoted an anti-establishment reaction. Thus, there were during the nineteenth century two conflicting bodies of opinion which viewed women, marriage and family life in opposing lights. The link between a stable hierarchical state and a stable hierarchical family system was taken by the temporal and spiritual rulers of the Establishment to be axiomatic, and was no less supported and propagated by many conservative writers.

On the other side, the swirl of ideas left over from the Revolution and espoused by the younger generation of Romantics questioned these same assumptions and, finding a more acceptable ideology in the new philosophies, reflected in their imaginative and polemical literature quite different ideas about the role of woman and of the family. The Saint-Simoniens, for example, opposed the inequalities they saw promulgated between the sexes, and preached an emancipation of sorts which included a negation of marriage. Scorning orthodox religion, they tended to see woman not just as the equal of man, but as a messianic mother figure, with a mission to achieve the moral transformation of man. Another group, the Emancipationists, consisted of a small group of women* supported by such men as Fourier and Enfantin. Infuriated by establishment leaders like Proudhon (famous

---

* The most notable being Jennie d'Héricourt, author of *La Femme Affranchie* (1860), and Juliette Lamber, author of *Idées anti-proudhoniennes sur l'amour, la femme et le mariage* (1861).

for remarks such as 'man's primary condition is to dominate his wife and be the master') they reacted against the subjugation of the married woman and the exploitation of the working woman, so frequently forced into prostitution by inadequate wages and the absence of laws protecting maternity.* Few women were trained to work, and the number of trades they were legally permitted to practise was minimal. The wages they earned were kept low by the competition offered by the convents and houses of refuge, which charged little for their goods, and by the influx of men into trades normally the prerogative of women. With the liberal professions closed to the girls of the bourgeoisie, even non-working women could scarcely exist without a male support, and the illness or low wage of a husband frequently drove a wife to prostitution. Thus while heavy opprobrium was commonly directed at the *femme adultère*, the reformers and feminists, amongst them many poets and novelists, took up the theme of the hypocrisy of a society which differentiated between the wife who was faithful because she could afford to be, and the woman driven to prostitution or adultery through need.

In this very small sub-genre of pro-feminist writing, it is amusing to note that the husband is unfailingly vile, misunderstanding and too old. Indeed, if the catchcry of the broken marriage of the twentieth century is 'My wife doesn't understand me', the protagonists of the exploited wife present the reverse situation. In the nineteenth century it was rather the wife who sought love and a lover to console her for her sad married condition.

One of the most ardent writers to espouse the feminist cause was George Sand. Strictly speaking, she does not belong to this study, since she neither writes precisely of adultery nor falls within the allotted time period. However, she was an important precursor to the novelists we shall consider, being a striking example of the advocates of female liberation and also one of the few women writers of the Romantic period. But most importantly not only did she take up the anti-marriage cudgels in an outstanding fashion she finally admitted defeat or rather, a change of heart. Because, therefore, she cannot be overlooked, it is now proposed to consider, by way of a preface to the later novels of the century, George Sand's *Indiana*, with its principle theme of unhappy marriage exemplified mainly, although not solely, in the arranged union of the young, impulsive, and passionate Indiana with

* Edith Thomas's book *Les Pétroleuses* (New York, 1966) on the women incendiarists of the period, states that the average daily wage rarely exceeded five francs, and was usually about one or two francs. Since the contemporary American dollar is worth about five 1871 francs, it is not surprising that even if the woman never fell sick, prostitution was a frequent and often indispensable source of income.

a stern, uncommunicative martinet forty years her elder. Sand wrote in the preface to the 1842 edition of *Indiana* : 'I wrote *Indiana* with a deep and legitimate conviction – even though it was not reasoned out – of the injustice and barbarity of the laws ruling the marital, family, and social lives of women.' Thus the gentle Indiana, doomed to her unhappy marriage, finds her situation even more intolerable when she falls unwillingly in love with the handsome but caddish Raymond. In spite of his ardent persuasions Indiana refuses to become Raymond's mistress; he punishes her by leaving her to contract a loveless but profitable marriage. When Indiana is finally released by her husband's death, she goes off to seek faithful but unmarried love on a tropical island with her devoted and upright cousin Ralph. Ralph has also had to be released by a similar cosmic intervention from his equally unhappy marriage with the fiancée of his dead brother.

Like a companion volume, *Jacques*, the novel makes clear George Sand's conviction that conventional marriage is necessarily stultifying, loveless, and generally made for reasons of convenience or profit. But Indiana does not find happiness in her unconsummated extra-marital relationship, for her would-be lover Raymond is a child of this world, whose 'promesses d'amour n'engagent pas l'honneur' and who forsakes her for position and money. Thus a second theme emerges, claiming that the woman, be she servant or mistress (for the experience of Indiana's maid Noun bears out the point), is always exploited by the male, either sacrificed to his amorous but selfish desires or rejected because of his worldly ambitions. In taking this view, George Sand may be universalising, but she is not inventing. It must have been true, in a society where arranged marriages designed mainly to aggrandise fortunes were the rule and not the exception, that any women not in the marriage stakes were seen as fair game, a distraction from the serious business of wife-selection.* Woman did indeed become the object of a variety of male exercises, in none of which was she considered as a person in her own right.

A distinct though related point is George Sand's conviction that true unconstrained love is incompatible with civilised society. Even though, finally, no spouses stand in their way, Indiana and Ralph feel they can only achieve complete freedom and happiness on a distant island, their union untrammelled by church or state. This is partly a reflection of the romantic yearning for faraway places (the romantic tendency to bracket distance and death as alternative negations of civilised life is borne out in yet another novel, *Valentine*, in which both the hero and the heroine die, victims of their situation). But it is also an admission that the free union had no recognised place in French society of the time.

* How serious it was may be judged by the imbroglio Eugène de Rastignac was willing to engage in, in order to capture a fortune.

George Sand herself acknowledged in the 1842 preface that the escape to an island was not an adequate solution, and the post-Romantic generation of novelists rejected flight from society as any kind of answer at all. No later French writers portray the need for the female to escape, as Tolstoy did when he sent Anna off on her bitterly unsuccessful bid for happiness with Vronsky in Italy. The French novels of the second half of the century show many unhappily married couples, but they are all coping or failing to cope *in situ*. At the same time, one must look hard to find a novel celebrating free love as George Sand's did. In spite of the great popularity of her writings she herself stands intrepidly alone, without real influence in France. (Her influence in Russia was considerably greater.)

However, we cannot pretend that her daring was unlimited. Indiana in fact conforms to conventional morality in that she insists on remaining physically pure in her relations with her lovers during her husband's lifetime. (She scorns to become a mistress, and whenever the situation looks morally dangerous there is always an interruption. But the main safeguarding is done by Indiana herself; the picture stresses her chastity, purity and honour. At least in the early stages, only her heart, never her body, is stirred.) George Sand could criticise the concept of marriage, but she could not flout an existing union. Why not, when she certainly did in her personal life, is a question with no simple answer. Perhaps, in order to win sympathy for her heroines in the hearts of a conventional public, she had to endow them with conventional virtues. No doubt the novel-reading public were as yet unready to accept the unconstructed relationships proposed by Diderot in his Bougainville commentary. Certainly there was in the nineteenth century, both inside and outside France, a gallery of writers who dared not preach what they practised (witness Victor Hugo and George Eliot).

There is however, another string to the Romantic violin on which George Sand was playing her idealistic theme. Like the courtly lovers, like Frédéric in *l'Education Sentimentale*, like the hero of *Dominique*, and perhaps like many real women of her time, Indiana basically wants her love affairs to remain static at the point of an effective, emotional exchange without consummation – a situation which provides the nourishment necessary to the romantic soul without the distasteful complications. But within the dynamics of a love affair can there be such a static relationship? Must it not move on to a resolution of some sort, whether consummation, renunciation, or mere loss of interest? Certainly Indiana cannot maintain this state of permanent under-achievement with Raymond, who gives up in disgust and moves on, while Indiana settles finally for enduring monogamy. But this is only one piece of evidence. The question of whether lovers can manage without permanent relationships in situations where marriage is either impossible or undesirable is indeed one of the main topics of this whole study. George Sand argues for permanency, as opposed to constant change, so long as there is no wedding ring; *but* she sees it as normally unattainable. She thus unintentionally prompts the reader who cannot escape to a tropical island to wonder which category will be the more unhappy – those who accept marriage and its possible tedium or those who prefer the variety provided by a series of lovers (like Maupassant's Bel-Ami). Or, to go uncomfortably further, to ask whether the desire for permanence, perpetuated constantly through the happy-ever-after myth, is any more than the recognition that old (middle?) age reduces the likelihood of attracting successive lovers.

The point will be further explored in the study of the novels; for the moment we should restate the facts about marriage in France that this brief account has thrown up, in order that the contrast with the situation in England may be as clear as possible.

The most striking factors relating to French marriage are undoubtedly the stranglehold put upon it by the importance attached to the dowry, the heavy hand of the parent applied to the selection of a suitable partner, and the lovelessness of a vast number of unions. While this situation naturally invited hostile attacks upon the institution of marriage from a number of different quarters, and while *discreet* adultery provided some alternative to unhappy marriage in a society which brooked no divorce, the conventions were on the whole difficult to defy. The most ardent advocate of freer unions, George Sand, found herself unable to match her ideals to the society in which she in fact lived, given that that society was basically Catholic, conservative, and never unconscious of the value of property, despite the appearances of secularisation and reforming zeal. With this in mind, we cross to the other side of the Channel.

Marriage in England

In *Sex in History* G. Rattray Taylor gives a brief account of the behaviour of Celtic and Saxon tribes derived, in the absence of any large body of earlier writings, from the Irish literature of the first few centuries of the Christian era. His findings that virginity was not prized, nudity not shameful, bastardy not despised, and marriage itself often of a temporary nature, are supported by Schillebeeckx's claim that the Celts and Anglo-Saxons originally regarded women as merchandise, and marriage as a kind of deed of purchase. No mention of any marriage rite can be found until the eleventh century, well after the Anglo-Saxon Synod of A.D. 786 had enjoined monogamy and declared bastards unable to inherit. However, the Christianisation of Britain slowly brought marriage and morals into line with Continental Catholic teaching, though of course the *status quo* lasted only until the sixteenth-century break with Rome.

Prior to the Reformation marriage continued to be, as in Europe, a private contract between two individuals, upon which the blessing of the church was often sought but not required.

The obligation to conduct the marriage ceremony in the presence of a priest had been imposed by the Catholic Church at the time of the Counter-Reformation, but by this time England had already left the Roman communion. So, provided they were within the laws of consanguinity, an English man and woman could simply declare their intention to marry by a process known as 'spousals'. This actually constituted a valid marriage, though it was normal to follow the spousals by a Bride Mass. However, in the sixteenth century the Church of England ordained that the presence of a priest should be required, though it recognised the distinction between an illegal (priestless) marriage and an invalid one. No banns or licence were required, until the abuses produced by this casualness finally resulted in the requirement of both, under the Hardwicke Act of 1753.

However, even after the break with Rome, the English ecclesiastical courts continued to have jurisdiction in matrimonial causes. One way in which their influence was significant was their recognition of *matrimoneum per verba de future* or 'spousals' which contracted a future marriage. With parental consent the betrothed could be as young as seven. Such a contract was legal though voidable later, if copulation had not taken place, and in need of ratification when the partners were 'of ripe age'. The existence of this practice throws light on the rather obscure question of the extent to which English children and young people were subject to arranged marriages. It is thought that child marriages involved only about one per cent of the population; the degree of parental pressure exerted on older sons and daughters is difficult to assess – but it was certainly stronger in aristocratic circles where the question of property was more crucial.

In their work *Children in English Society* Pinchbeck and Hewitt quote many of the Books of Domestic Relations written for the 'education and edification of the middle classes' in their attempt to define contemporary opinion; they are convinced that in Tudor times love was not regarded as a sufficient reason for marriage, although it was recognised that once married, the husband and wife had a duty to love each other. 'The romantic view of marriage was heavily at a discount', they write, while the wife, in spite of a new opinion about women which began to gain favour after the break with Rome, was still enjoined to be obedient. This is interpreted as part of the Elizabethan concern with the necessity for 'order and degree, and the consequent insistence upon authority and obedience'. It is not surprising then that the treatise writers were agreed that children should not marry without their parents' consent; but Pinchbeck and Hewitt qualify the picture : 'There is much evidence, however, to show that, particularly as regards the marriage of their daughters, the interests of the child were not entirely absent when parents contrived a marriage.' And further, 'As the sixteenth century advanced there was increasing debate not so much as to the right of the parents to arrange such matches, but as to their rights to do so irrespective of their childrens' own feelings.'[15]

James I declared that 'parents may forbid their children an unfit marriage, but they may not force their consciences to a fitt', while in 1638 Lord North writes of the need to persuade parents to leave 'theer children full freedome with theer consent in so important a case'.

By the middle of the seventeenth century, it appears, most parents had conceded a right of veto to their eldest sons in the arrangement of a suitable match, though the daughters continued to be subject to parental persuasion. This situation contributed to the considerable tightening of the attitude towards extra-marital relations during the Puritan revolution, of which the earlier period of more strictly arranged marriages had been more tolerant – especially as the latter had corresponded with the period of the cult of courtly love on the Continent. On the other hand, although bastards had no legal rights they were little, if at all, stigmatised.

Through the sixteenth and seventeenth centuries there had been a gradual change of attitude towards marriage itself. Quoting L. G. Wright, Pinchbeck and Hewitt record that 'After the break with Rome, with its conservative attitude to sexual relations, now no longer was virginity held to be a highest good, but a chastity of marriage was glorified by the Protestants . . . The Puritan began to concentrate his interest upon preserving the purity of the married state rather than the physiological purity of the individual.' That women were judged more severely than men during this period of hardening social attitudes towards adultery is ascribed by Pinchbeck and Hewitt to the Church's Pauline ambivalance towards women, to the greater Puritan reliance on the Old Testament with its traditional view of woman as the temptress, and to the growing insistence, as we have seen in France, on family stability as the basis of a stable society. However, the new severity did not extend far beyond the concern for marriage itself. The illegitimate children of unmarried mothers still tended to be censured only when the State recognised a duty to support them financially. Throughout the seventeenth, eighteenth and well into the nineteenth centuries, the natural children of the wealthy were openly acknowledged and provided for by their parents.*

The reason we have been at pains to elicit the comparative slightness of the degree to which arranged marriages were common in England† has been phrased by Lewis with lucid simplicity: 'Where marriage does not depend on the free will of the married, any theory which takes love for a noble form of experience must be a theory of adultery.'[16] Now, as we have seen, de Rougemont argues that in France, where arranged marriages were the norm in the middle and upper classes, the cult of passionate love, and hence of adultery, was so powerful that it had to be contained in a myth; the cult was put down, but was not exterminable; the myth went underground, but re-emerged in other literary forms, notably the novel.

In England there was a different social pattern, including greater freedom in the choice of marriage-partner. Thus we should expect a different approach to adultery – which indeed, Lewis provides.

Although Lewis's book appeared some years before de Rougemont's, so that there is no question of his commenting in it on the latter's theory, he does, however, corroborate their common starting-point – the rise of courtly love. He then shows how English literature took a different turn. 'Chaucer and his audience . . . see the common world outside the charmed circle of courtly love', he writes. And further, the loves of Troilus and Cryseide

> are divided only by the thinnest partition from the lawful loves of Dorigen and her husband. It seems almost an accident that the third book celebrates adultery instead of marriage. Chaucer has brought the old romance of adultery to the very frontiers of the modern (or should I say the late?) romance of marriage. He does not himself cross the frontier; but we see that his successors will inevitably do so . . . The wild Provençal vine has begun to bear such good fruit that it is now worth taming.[17]

The frontier is at last crossed, though in allegorical form, in the third and fourth books of Spenser's *Faerie Queene* : here courtly love is

---

* This casualness did not receive universal approval. Dr Johnson was adamant that illegitimate children must be penalised from birth, 'because the chastity of women being of the utmost importance, as all property depends on it, they who forfeit it should not have the possibility of being restored to a good character'. (Quoted by Langdon-Davies, op. cit., p.233).

† One literary application of the difference between England and France can be seen in the social conventions assumed by the English Restoration playwright, as compared with those Molière takes for granted. While he bases many situations on the projected arranged marriage of a reluctant daughter, the English dramatists find the source of their humour in a pre-marital battle of the sexes in which the hero and heroine are equal protagonists.

defeated by 'the romantic conception of marriage', which becomes 'the basis of all our love literature from Shakespeare to Meredith'. We must note that for Lewis romantic love does not die with courtly love any more than it does for de Rougemont, but it is celebrated in marriage, whereas in the French tradition it continues to be associated only with adultery. Rattray Taylor confirms the surprise occasioned by this turn of events when he says of the notion that romantic love is the natural preamble to married love, 'I can still remember the astonishment which I felt at about the age of twenty, when I first learned that this conception had never existed in any other period of history and that it was confined, for all practical purposes, to Britain and the United States.'[18]

Lewis does not continue his study beyond Spenser although he throws off a few remarks about the magnitude of Spenser's influence on the nineteenth-century Romantics, in contrast to the little he had upon his own age. To some extent – though there could scarcely be more difference between the styles of writing – his work is taken up by Leslie Fiedler, in *Love and Death in the American Novel*. Fiedler pays homage to Lewis's study of the eleventh-century rise of love, which Fiedler describes as 'the psychic breakthrough that at the same moment introduced into a patriarchal world the worship of women and into a Christian one the cult of art'.[19] He agrees with de Rougemont that the courtly love episode produced the adulterous archetypes of Paolo and Francesca, Tristan and Iseult and Lancelot and Guinevere. However, he postulates an explanation not hazarded by either Lewis or de Rougemont. The worship of the Lady in the cult of courtly love is the fruit of the 'inruption [his word] of the female principle into a patriarchal world', a vindication of the Great Mother figure officially rejected by a male-dominated church and society. The Great Mother is also the 'huge, warm enveloping darkness of unconscious life', the blind source of passion, reproduction and death. She had been worshipped in the ancient world by 'men content to be eternal sons', and rebelled against in the male bid for dominance. Without some rebellion against the female blackness, asserts Fiedler, there can be no civilisation, no proper consciousness; but denied utterly the female principle will always return in some other form, in nightmare, art, witch-cult or Romantic literature. He explains the cult of courtly love as a reaction against both the paternalism of feudal chivalry and the inadequacy of Christian conjugality, and also stresses the equally important point rather neglected by de Rougemont that European love-mythology was attracted both to consummation and to *liebestod* – to love as joy as well as to love as death.

Like the others, Fiedler rather skips over the next century or two until he comes to the rise of the novel in what he calls 'the religious marches' of Europe, the countries like France, England and Germany, where Catholicism and Protestantism met (in Spain, Italy and Greece, where this clash was not felt, the novel did not attain first importance). For Fiedler the rise of the novel represents the second 'inruption' of the Great Mother, or feminine principle, into a patriarchal world. In France and Germany it was accompanied by the reasserting of the adultery theme, but in England a different line developed. The revolutionary step taken by Spenser in identifying marriage with passion, and the disavowing of *domnei* (vassalic devotion to the Lady) in Shakespeare's sonnets, had been accompanied by the Protestant rejection of the Virgin Mother of God. But, argues Fiedler, the mother principle can never be eradicated from any culture; she was smuggled back into the early novel as a respectable woman – though not as Spenser's wife-figure, for marriage in art-form is a dull story.* The English dilemma was solved by the transformation of the feminine principle into a virtuous girl-figure, and the drama of passion into a pre-marital affair of courtship and seduction.

The audience for which the eighteenth-century English novel catered was largely middle class and feminine : the young ladies were imperfectly educated and therefore daunted or bored by traditional literature; they were also Protestant, and squeamish about the code of adulterous love. Thus the form and the mythology of the English novel were born together under the auspices of what Fiedler calls 'The Sentimental Love Religion', in which the Pure Young Girl offers moral salvation, the Seducer is the only devil, and marriage represents eternal bliss. The first tragedy of sentimental love, in which the Seducer and the Pure Maiden are brought face to face, was *Clarissa*; its first exponent was Samuel Richardson whose declared opinion was that 'The end of fiction is to promote the cause of religion and virtue', while his successors also laboured 'to inspire the female mind with a principle of self-complacency and to promote the economy of human life'; and 'to win the mind to Sentiment and Truth'.

The impregnable Clarissa however became not only an archetype and moral paradigm, but a woman deprived of freedom and self-determination, 'an attempt to imprison women within the myth of Woman'. She operated at various levels : as Persecuted Maiden – a projection of male guilt before the female treated as a sexual object; as Protestant Virgin replacing the Mother of God in a Protestant and sentimental society; and as Bourgeois Daughter, her virginity the emblem of the ethical purity of her class, and the sign that she has proved herself worthy of marriage. (Lovelace, her seducer, was significantly an aristocrat.)

The sentimental novel itself protested against the conviction in-

* Cf. de Rougemont, 'L'amour heureux n'a pas d'histoire'.

herited from the courtly love code that love must be adulterous, as well as against the aristocratic *droit de seigneur*; insisted that the pre-marital period was the proper time for love, and marriage only its drama-less consummation; and asserted the rights of daughters to choose their spouses – thus assisting the decline in English society of the arranged marriage.

In the course of his study of the Sentimental Love Novel, Fiedler discovers Clarissa's true descendants in Europe – in Goethe's Charlotte and Gretchen, and in Rousseau's Julie; but here of course they are renewed by the phoenix of passionate love. The old courtly theme was in the process of reasserting itself; seduction stood for a time beside adultery, as we see most vividly in *La Nouvelle Héloïse*. But finally the novel in France reverted completely and gave itself up to the tradition of Constant, Stendhal and Flaubert. The *Liebestod* theme also returned to the European consciousness while, as the century advanced, seduction and adultery turned from being symbols of class warfare to the struggle between the exceptional individual and conventional society.

What Fiedler means by this last dramatic but cogent statement is the following. In the original Clarissa story, the seducer Lovelace was an aristocrat, a Don Juan, while Clarissa and her virginity were the emblem of ethical purity of the class from which she sprang, the bourgeoisie. Their head-on collision represents opposition at a variety of levels, for the strategies of love and seduction are seen as warfare between the male and the female, between the aristocrat and the middle-class girl, between the devil and the potential (female) saviour, between the head and the heart, between reason and sentiment.

But unlike Clarissa, Lovelace stands at the end of a tradition, and is degraded and divided into three offsprings of himself. He becomes the stock villain of popular fiction; the Byronic hero of the Gothic novel; and most importantly the guilty artist in the middle-class world. This last guise he assumes with the help of Rousseau and Goethe, for although these writers learn from Richardson that the basic subject of the novel is the human heart, and both examine it in well-to-do but bourgeois settings, they effect some change upon their heroes. Death becomes the goal of the hero rather than the heroine (though only Werther achieves it); the Don Juan figure blurs into the exiled, sensitive soul in conflict with the husband, who now features as the man of reason (e.g. Wolmar, Albert); and the new male figure who occupies the lonely place at the centre of the stage or novel is identified more and more closely with the author. This composite artist-figure, feeling himself to be estranged from the bourgeoisie, will in his turn give birth to the alienated outsider of the modern generation : but for the moment he must be content to represent a development in the earlier novel which was strictly European.

B

In England there was no such reversion to the theme of passionate love and even the sentimental love novel was actively countered by the anti-bourgeois novel of masculine protest, fathered by Fielding and building on the Shakespearean inheritance. Here there was a hero instead of a heroine, an outdoor décor instead of a boudoir, an interest in general social relations instead of just seduction and marriage, and heartiness instead of sensibility. Other directions taken by the novel, states Fiedler, were that of the Gothic romance which petered out after *The Monk* (1796) and the more important and analytic school derived from Richardson's *Pamela*, and practised later by Jane Austen and George Eliot; but the essential is that all these variants of the novel were united in avoiding the theme of adultery and eschewing the dark heat of passion.

Many novelists, while concentrating their attention on the premarital chase, nevertheless promoted a genuinely admirable image of the married situation; inveighing heavily against the matrimonial market by scathing references to non-love matches, they allowed wives to bring to the marriage intelligence, independence of views, and an awareness of their own value. Trollope, for example, for all his acerbity, has some splendid creatures who offer their husbands a free, joyful allegiance which never fades nor wearies. Perhaps Taine was right when he wryly observed that the English character is so rooted in Puritanism, that 'in a state of adultery he is miserable; even at the supreme moment his conscience torments him'.

It was indeed the case that on the surface at least Victorian England was swathed in a blanket of official denial that sexuality had any rights at all, irrespective of its legality. The planks of this platform are so well known they need only be mentioned. They include the severity of the vehemently proclaimed Evangelical ideal, oddly abetted later by the more exclusive and refined Oxford Movement; the proliferation of societies for the suppression of vice, some of which bent vain efforts towards having Parliament impose the death penalty for adultery (in 1800, 1856 and 1857); the fire-breathing censorship campaigns which were effectively carried through into practice by the powerful puritanism of the circulating libraries, the two biggest of which were both run by rampant Nonconformists; the preoccupation with the verbal connotations of sexual activity and the determination to avoid the animal aspects of human existence which gives rise to the excessive refinement of the vocabulary; the subjection of children to an authoritarian family structure; and the opposition to birth control.*

---

* Though the ideas of Thomas Malthus had since 1798 provided a philosophical basis for the idea of limiting the population of the nation, Malthus

That much of this excessively refined morality was a mere façade, and that the public image was frequently contravened in private is in this day a truism. Books such as Steven Marcus's *The Other Victorians* and Ronald Pearsall's *The Worm in the Bud* have scotched any lingering beliefs in Victorian virtue. It was a time when 'the entire tissue of human relationships between men and women was shot through with contradiction after contradiction between overt belief and hidden practices'. And nowhere is this double standard more apparent than in the arbitrary and ambivalent attitudes shown to different classes of women. The Victorians divided the female sex itself itself into good and bad, and reserved an appropriate form of behaviour for each half, with suitably corresponding male responses.

Two quotations from *The Other Victorians* make the point without need of elaboration. One, from the Victorian doctor and author, Sir William Acton, states : 'As a general rule, a modest woman seldom desires any sexual gratification for herself. She submits to her husband, but only to please him; and but for the desire of maternity, would far rather be relieved from his attentions.'† The other, from an anonymous and privately printed account of an English gentleman's sexual activities, which first appeared in 1888, says : '[I have] probably fucked now . . . something like twelve hundred women . . .'[20] Duncan Crow in *The Victorian Woman* suggests that the double-think 'was adopted to hide the proximity of the abyss in which seethed the primitive society the Victorians were struggling away from . . . The Family was the only unit around which the defensive moat of respectability could be dug and guarded. The drawing room was the citadel.' The Victorian lady was required to seem as passionless as Acton wanted to believe she was. 'A lady's duty was to shut her eyes, grit her teeth, and as Queen Victoria is reputed to have told one of her daughters, who married abroad, "think of England".'[21]

Certainly the vast system of prostitution and the plethora of pornographic works churned out side by side with the 1857 Act banning obscene publications show that the guardians of public morality had something to contend with; the middle and upper classes were intent not just upon covering up the cracks in their own façade, they also

---

himself was inclined to rely on self-control and reason as the means to the end. However, more practical advice had been circulated with increasing frequency from the 1820s onwards. One example of the many books and pamphlets which poured out was Richard Carlisle's article 'What is Love?', printed in the *Republican* of May 1825, and reprinted under the title *Every Woman's Book* which went through 10,000 copies by 1828. The Besant and Bradlaugh republication of Knowlton's *Fruits of Philosophy* (1832) was prosecuted, but the defendants were ultimately let off.

† Though she could not act upon this with impunity, since, until 1884, a woman could be imprisoned for defying her spouse his conjugal rights.

feared the degenerative influence of the less disciplined working-classes. Crow quotes Kitson Clark in *The Making of Victorian England:*

> The uneasy Victorian snobbery was probably the result of the impact of new classes who wanted to secure their position in a traditional hierarchy, Victorian hypocrisy the result of the attempt to lay claim to new standards of conduct which proved to be too hard to maintain consistently, Victorian prudery the result of the struggle for order and decency on the part of people just emerging from the animalism and brutality of primitive society. These are the probable signs of the pressures and strains in a community undergoing the process of growth and change.

Marcus points out that the writing of a book like *My Secret Life* was in fact a betrayal of the system by which Victorian England operated, where consciousness of participation in a whole world of sexual activity was kept apart from the more general and public consciousness of both self and society.

This is not to say that there was no public debate on morals. As Victoria's reign progressed, and the disturbing impact of Darwinism was felt more generally, the earlier creeds were questioned in everything from drawing-room conversation to scholarly articles like John Stuart Mill's essay 'The Subjection of Women' (1869). The cause of women's emancipation, already passionately put forward by Mary Wollstonecroft in 1792, not only galvanised the feminists to word and deed but showed practical results such as the improvement of girls' secondary schools and the founding of womens' colleges in both Oxford and Cambridge. There was also a series of bills passed which gradually brought about some improvement in the general situation of women. In 1837 women had no vote, and upon marriage the wife and all her possessions, including the children, belonged to her husband. If she left, he could force her to return, or refuse to support her and deny her access to the children. By 1884 married women were allowed rights over property, and their own person, while deserting husbands could be forced to pay a small maintenance. There was still, however, a double standard in relation to divorce. The Act of 1857, which established a court for divorce and matrimonial causes, allowed adultery as sufficient grounds for divorce if committed by the woman, but required aggravation such as cruelty or unnatural practices on the husband's part. Unlike French law, however, and in spite of the various vain attempts at reform already mentioned, English law had never specifically prohibited adultery, i.e. of itself it has never been a punishable offence. It was, on the other hand, possible up until the 1884 Act which gave a woman rights over her own person, to bring an action for damages against a wife's lover – on the implied grounds of the wife being the husband's property.

Victorian England was not innocent of a free love movement, promoted by some though certainly not all of the emancipationists and free thinkers; but as Pearsall puts it, 'There was one great snag; even the most forward-looking had been conditioned by education, precept and upbringing . . . Beneath every emancipated cigarette-smoking woman with free-wheeling sexual views there was a lily of the field, a girlish plaything, embryo wife and mother, a rooted conservative, depositary of inconsistency and irrationality.'[22] Though one may bridle at the epithets, it is true that the best-known radicals meekly, perhaps cheerfully, accepted the matrimonial yoke. Sidney Webb did marry his Beatrice, and Bernard Shaw Miss Payne Townsend.* The Victorian marriage boat was as little rocked by the free love movement as it was by the Romantic movement, which was more inclined to idealise marriage than to undermine it.

The bases for the romantic view of marriage were an exalted mutual love combining both companionship and erotic pleasure; equal rights for both partners; and the necessity for pre-marital sexual experience in order to find the ideal life partner. It is of course true that in notable cases, such as those of George Eliot and Shelley, the notion of the ideal union transcended that of the existing marriage; but these were exceptions within a general climate which viewed marriage seriously at least, reverentially often, and sometimes with the greatest sentimentality. The English Romantic movement was a small-scale one and its more daring fringe operators were unlikely to modify the accepted values which the bulk of its adherers shared with the rest of the country.

Fiedler in fact dubs the Anglo-Saxon branch of the movement (except for the brief appearance of the Gothic tale of terror) 'White Romanticism', and elaborates its affinity with the genteel middle-class mind, its belief that the heart was superior to the head (though heart was to be carefully distinguished from viscera and genitals), and its rejection of both tragedy and sexual passion. The novels it produced steadfastly turned their gaze not just from the unsavoury or disturbing, but from any realistic examination of sexual relationships. The censorship system was more directed to blinkering the serious novelist than to repressing the flood of underground pornography. Even cheap fiction, of second-rate but non-pornographic quality, avoided adultery like the plague, as can be evidenced from the titles and contents in Louis James's *Fiction for the Working Man, 1830–50*.

* Perhaps he was influenced by his own aphorism, 'Marriage is popular because it combines the maximum of temptation with the maximum of opportunities' (Maxims for Revolutionists).

The novel wishing to deal with the periphery of sexuality concerned itself with a variety of themes such as the early days of marriage, before love had had time to change, the ideal state of wifely submission, the dying or redeemed prostitute, the seduced girl and unmarried mother (both treated with increasing sympathy still laced with moral correctiveness), and the governess who married into her employer's family, which was a favourite subject.* It was not even too difficult to overlay a picture of proper married life with tones of pleasure and enjoyment – after all, 'with maidenhood safely behind her, there is no end to the philanthropy a young matron may indulge in . . .' (Thus Florence Welford rejoiced in her novel of 1862, *A Maiden of Our Own Day*.)

As Marcus rightly points out, the sub-culture of pornographic writing represented a mirror image of the view of sexuality held by the official culture, and propagated by even the most intelligent novelists. But the two were bound by their striking similarities, one of which was the absence of any treatment, whether serious or profane, of the theme of adultery.

Indeed, in the whole of this section it has been evident that adultery fails to seize the English imagination in the way it does the French; and this would appear to be largely because the young were allowed a much greater degree of freedom in their choice of marriage partner. The historical evidence for this information is supported by the literary, for while married love is often assumed by the novel, the centre of attraction is occupied by the drama of courtship and/or seduction of the unmarried virgin. So, even before the mantle of Victorian prudery descended over the public literature of the nineteenth century, adultery was not an important theme; and afterwards it became simply unmentionable. The effect of the British situation upon her most important colony, culturally speaking at least, may be gauged as we now cross the Atlantic.

Marriage in America

It is impossible to give a blanket account of marriage laws in America, as each state has always established and kept to its own system. In general they followed English Common Law, transported to America via the liberalising 'commentaries' of Sir William Blackstone. These laid down that the husband and wife were one person in law, i.e. the very being of the woman was upon marriage consolidated into that of her husband. She was voteless and propertyless. Husbands (and

* See Patricia Thomson, *The Victorian Heroine: a changing ideal, 1837–1873* (O.U.P., 1956).

fathers) had almost unlimited power over the persons and possessions of their wives (or daughters), but they also had responsibilities more strictly defined than under English law. The colonial courts recognised a wife's *right* to husbandly love in house and bed, to be supported by him even if he abandoned her and to be protected from violence at his hands. Moreover a wife was upon her husband's death automatically heir, during her lifetime, to one third of his estate (thus giving a widow rights a mere wife could never have) and to one half if they were childless. The husband was responsible for his wife's debts – an inevitable result of having a wife unable to own property.

The laws of adultery varied from state to state, being most severe in New England. The first code of law of Connecticut, formulated in 1638–9, condemned any man or woman guilty of adultery, buggery or sodomy to death, while fornication was punished by fines, beating and (dire penalty!) marriage. In spite of these so-called 'Blue Laws' of New England, there was only one case of hanging, but branding, banishment and the use of stocks were frequently invoked. Women were generally punished more severely than men, suffering not only fines, but public whippings, while in many colonies the wearing of the scarlet letter 'A' was imposed. The Dutch in New Netherlands and the Quakers in Pennsylvania were, it must be noted, less harsh in their reproof of adulterers. There is more than one reason for the sternness with which marriage was protected, but the grounds are different from the European desire to consolidate family-held property. Firstly, since a wife was a positive essential both as a domestic co-worker and as breeder of a new generation, early marriage was an economic duty. Once achieved, it needed to be maintained – and there were only two women for every three men in the early days of the country. Conversely, it was attractive to both the locally born girl who apart from teaching had no other job outlet, and to the newly arrived emigrant woman who had otherwise to stay with relatives. Secondly, there was a Puritan 'stranglehold' as Milton Rugoff calls it, that lasted for one and a half centuries – long after Cromwell and his Roundheads had given way to the merry England of the Restoration. Thirdly, there was the close proximity to a savage environment; in the absence of an entrenched institution of marriage, the early American had to carve very firmly his own furrows. And fourthly there was the need of the child living on the verge of the wilderness to be protected. This often meant an injunction to stay close to mother.

Early marriage thus was a religious, family, and economic duty, and the wife did not exist with any economic independence until she was a widow. This is not to say that in New England, or elsewhere, the laws were never infringed. In remote situations, particularly when the husband was away for long periods, there was considerable laxness. Yet the appearances were always maintained.

A façade of a different sort was also kept up even when the wife was as virtuous as Susannah. In pioneering times women had been kept thoroughly occupied with the heavy demands of primitive house-keeping and child-bearing. Apart from the stricture of Puritan aus-terity, they simply had not the time to indulge their inclinations towards fashion or culture. But after the Revolution, there were signs among the well-to-do women living in big towns or on large plan-tations of a tendency to devote their increasing leisure to the culti-vation of their persons, their conversation and the finer arts. As the degree of idleness became, in Rugoff's phrase, an index to social position, a cult of idealisation of the American woman became a visible movement, to which all aspired, even if some could only attain it with great difficulty. The idea of the 'lady' was dominant, though it often veiled a continuing responsibility for or even participation in heavy domestic work.

Rugoff sums up the American ideal of the female during the early nineteenth century thus :

- As a mother the American woman taught her children a code of behaviour that stressed propriety, piety, and purity. As a wife she was expected to honor and obey as well as love her husband, to be submissive, gentle, innocent, tender, a haven of comfort, unquestion-ing in her allegiance, a fountain of inspiration and elevated thoughts. She must above all be a model of modesty . . . The ideal woman would not trouble her pretty head with serious study or business or politics. Whereas her husband was assumed to be by nature physical, she was spiritual; whereas he was aggressive, she should be diffident; whereas he was daring, she was timid. She was more imaginative and sensitive but less stable; more affectionate, but more senti-mental – in short, more angel and less human.[23]

- Travellers noted that American women were adored and ethereal-ised, but not all approved the code of elaborate gallantry. With that sound, sensible, and balanced attitude we have just discerned through the smokescreen of Victorian hypocrisy, one British lady after a visit in the mid-1830s declared that American women were given indul-gence as a substitute for justice; while Captain Marryat, the British naval officer and novelist, wrote after his visit in 1837–8 : 'When men *respect* women, they do not attempt to make fools of them, but treat them as rational beings, and this general adulation is cheating them with the shadow while they withhold from them the sub-stance.'

Finally a visiting English lecturer warned that in the South consideration of women went so far as to result in 'feebleness, effeminacy, helplessness and bad health'.[24]

It was in the South of course that the exaggeration of the delicacy · of the white lady was taken to its furthest extreme. The reading of novels, particularly Scott's, fostered the cult of the lady, while counteracting the emotional effect on the isolated plantation owners of the primitive wilderness around them. But Scott could not possibly have envisaged in what a complex society his novels would be devoured, nor the sexual aggressions and inhibitions modern writers (Sinclair, Rugoff and Mailer, for example) have with hindsight attributed to his readers. A brief account is offered here. Southern gentility was proof of a lady's delicacy and purity, and first and foremost its aim was to set her apart from the Negro woman. It also set her above the white male, who acknowledged her superiority in the drawing-room at least, and played along with the chivalry her refinement demanded. She also enjoyed the charm of being a new and relatively rare phenomenon in a man's rough world. However, the aura surrounding her untouchable purity, designed originally to protect her from the black man, inhibited the white man too, who soon sought less rarified relationships with black women. Anger and a desire to punish the erring husband led the white woman to exploit her *noli me tangere* pedestal, while the secret guilt of the white man was atoned for in his mind by his obsessive preoccupation with gallantry and protection. At the same time the guilt he still felt, coupled with the attenuation of his sexual relationship with white women, led him to fear the superior sexual prowess of the negro male, which in turn led back to a much more complicated and intense obsession with the idea of the rape of his woman by a negro.

The effect of this quagmire of often unsuspected motivations was revealed in the obsessive concern for female delicacy, which became an overt end as well as a hidden factor in sexual relationships.

The cultivation of ladylike qualities in young girls – a necessary preparation for ideal womanhood – was not considered to be a simple task, particularly in view of a theory of biology which was current. On this account, girls were considered to be more emotional than boys, because their personalities were controlled not by their reason but by their reproductive organs. Consequently they were actually in more need of restraint than boys, from whom they must certainly be separated, though it is not clear who would corrupt whom. Stimulating drinks – such as tea and coffee – were barred from the régime of young ladies, and the unnamed fear of lesbianism discouraged the · idea of setting up boarding schools for them. The prurience of the minds of the elders can be judged by their degree of mistrust of anything which might be a cause of sensual pleasure. Objects causing misgivings and prohibitions included warm beds, soft chairs, see-saws and hobby-horses.

• Such an upbringing was designed to prepare a girl for the duties of wifehood, from which was notably absent any notion of active participation in her husband's sexual pleasure. During the height of the reign of prudery and suppression which dominated the America of the early nineteenth century quite as much as it did Victorian England, there was a common assumption that women were mere 'passive receptacles' that 'the full force of sexual desire was seldom known to a virtuous woman'. The medal was not however without its reverse : as the Reverend McDowell's *Journal*, first published in 1833, revealed, prostitution was as common in New York as in London.

That information about contraceptive practices was peddled in America is known from works such as Knowlton's *Fruits of Philosophy*, Robert Dale Owen's *Moral Physiology or, a Brief and Plain Treatise on the Population Question* (1830), Dr H. A. Allbutt's *The Wife's Handbook* (1888), and from Dr Edward Bliss Foote, who published two books and a monthly magazine all advocating birth control. As in England there was opposition, from preachers, universities, other medical men, and all those many members of societies for the suppression of vice, of whom the most notorious was Anthony Comstock, famous for getting an anti-obscenity bill passed in Congress, which included a clause against contraceptives. Theodore Roosevelt himself believed that anyone who did not want children was a 'criminal against the race'. The opposition to birth control is certainly not difficult to understand in a country so underpopulated as to need to develop a huge immigration programme. It seems as though the protagonists of contraception looked not at the vast empty spaces, but rather at urban misery, and saw in a diminishing birth-rate the answer to poverty, residential overcrowding, maternal ill-health, the problems of the unmarried mother, the prevalence of prostitution, abortion and infanticide, and the desire to give fewer children a better education. Foote and his son, who was also a doctor and contributor to *The Health Monthly*, made use of the popularity of Darwinism to strengthen their argument : since the survival and improvement of the race were of the utmost importance, the sooner the whole business of propagation was put on a scientific level, the better we should all be.

The private use of contraceptive devices is obviously impossible to compute; the one indication that is available is the dramatic drop in both European and American birth-rate which took place in the 1880s.

As with marriage, the laws relating to divorce in America varied from state to state. While it is now legal in every state, it is interesting to note that divorce was not permitted in South Carolina until 1948;

and the grounds for divorce can vary from a mere whiff of incompatability, to the need for proven adultery – the only grounds permissible in New York State, until very recently. With different states liberalising their laws at different times one cannot say anything about America as a whole during the course of the nineteenth century; but a national investigation conducted by Carrol D. Wright in 1888 of divorces between 1867 and 1886 showed that the divorce rate had increased almost three times as fast as the population, with adultery cited in sixty per cent of the cases. Considerable social stigma was attached to the divorcee until late in the century, though not so much apparently as to completely negate the opportunities for remarriage : 'Marriage still remained the most holy of institutions in America; even the rising rate of divorce seemed chiefly to be for the purpose of re- • marriage.'[25]

The sway of marriage was indeed oddly strong amongst America's nineteenth-century feminine emancipationists. As Mary Wollstonecroft had done in earlier days, they tended to abandon their militancy whenever they fell in love, and at the best of times strove for social and economic equality rather than sexual liberation. Rugoff claims that what sexual freedom has been achieved came not from their efforts – since they were 'Victorian prudes' in this area – but from the general relaxation of sexual morality and the availability of contraceptives. While the feminists did gain the vote for women they did nothing • to free them from the responsibility for home-making and bringing up children.

What, then, happened to the novel when it crossed the Atlantic to take root in a country largely moulded by the bourgeois ideal of prudish morality and too refined gentility; where the desire to seem guiltless was even more important than the aim to be so; and where the virtue of purity was equated with the values of the civilised life, because of the popularised hand-down of Darwin's theory of our animal origins?

To return to the Fiedler framework, Clarissa's mighty labour gave birth not quite to the English line of changelings, and certainly not to a fertile *Nouvelle Héloïse* or *Werther*, but to a small and solitary offspring called *The Scarlet Letter*. Apart from this, there is before James scarcely a novel to be found dealing with the theme of adultery during the nineteenth century – and James was a hybrid Anglo-American. Did the state of affairs simply emulate the Victorian scene, or were there factors peculiar to America which arrived at the same result by a different route? Fiedler argues firstly that the novel fell into the hands of women novelists : by 1820 one third of the books written in America were by female authors, and nearly all the best sellers were contained in that third. Their influence so moulded the taste of the reading public that later, and better, male authors had to imitate them in order to attract audience attention. The lady writers themselves missed much of the point of Richardson's fine analysis, and reduced the story to a stereotype; they mistook ease for artlessness and sensibility for sentimentality; they flinched from candour, and finally rejected tragedy for tearful pathos and even a happy ending. The seducer already deprived in one-class America of his aristocratic advantage, came to be defeated every time – 'a symbol of the emasculation of American men' (Fiedler).

No other American descendant of a European prototype had the same importance as the sentimental novel of seduction. The Gothic strain, inherited from both England (where the main practitioners were Horace Walpole, Mrs Radcliffe and M. G. Lewis) and from Germany's Hoffmann, substituted terror for love as the central theme and was temporarily an important genre. Fiedler ascribes at least part of this success to the failure of love as a literary theme. However, in spite of the Gothic themes and atmosphere of *Huckleberry Finn, Moby Dick* and even, to a limited and not exclusive extent, *The Scarlet Letter*, the genre was shortlived, because its basic motive was to project the struggle of the middle classes with ecclesiastical authority – a form of class warfare, for which America could provide no suitable black-robed villains nor a décor of moonlit crypts and ancient piles.

The second strain was the historical romance of the Sir Walter Scott–James Fenimore Cooper line; but though Cooper wrote some forty-five books, he is remembered only for his Leather-stocking series – a classical children's author. From the point of view of the present study, he is interesting because of his unquestioning devotion to the sentimentalists' ideal of sacred womanhood embodied in pure, white Anglo-Saxon virgins. (In this he too may have been influenced by Darwin.)

Cora, the raven-haired and red-blooded symbol of passion in *The Last of the Mohicans*, is too dangerous to man's image of himself to be allowed to live; she dies, and all the spoils and rewards go to the golden-haired, blue-eyed, and fair-complexioned Alice. The double theme of the Pure White Girl and the Corrupt Dark Lady is one we shall return to; Cooper ought to be remembered as much by these unconscious sexual symbols as for the boyish archetypes and the all-male friendships he describes in his great books for boys. But the fact remains that he is not.

The field was thus left open to the sentimental seduction tale, whose legacy Fiedler measures by three yardsticks : the fact that it has never been quite abandoned in the United States 'though it seems for a while to have been exiled to the drama and from there to have passed to the moving pictures'; that its heroine, the Protestant Virgin, has continued to impose herself on American life and fiction even after the decline of her seducer; and that 'the long uncontested reign in America of sentimental archetypes and clichés has made it almost impossible for our novelists to portray adult sexual passion of a fully passionate woman'. Fiedler reiterates that nothing has shaken the mystique of virginity upon which the response to the threat of rape and seduction depends; and one can see that if it is indeed the case that the white man's chief obsession is the danger of the rape of his woman by a negro, then his literature will produce pre-eminently rapable archetypes : pure, white, defenceless, and preferably virgin. The constant failure of the would-be seducer is also explicable on the same grounds, for the white man is torn between his desire for sexual consummation and his need, as he sees it, to protect his woman. To make the black man the sole seducer and the white a protector only may save his ego and his sanity, while destroying his sexual confidence.

During the latter years of the century the seduction aspect was so played down as to be practically eliminated, while the protector was brought to the fore wearing high boots, chaps and a cowboy hat. The enduringly popular Western is the result of this phase – and the relationship between the schoolteacher and the good–bad guy in the film *Butch Cassidy and the Sundance Kid* its most winsome send-up.

Another evasive ploy was an expurgated version of the novel of lit social protest (which one might by a long stretch of the imagination compare with Zola). We shall see the horrors of drunkenness exposed in *Miss Ravenel's Conversion* – but its greatest stage was of course the slave plantations of the South. The novels relating to these we shall not examine, for with the creation of Little Eva, Harriet Beecher Stowe instituted a new heroine – the pure, blonde girl-child, who must expire before she could be sullied by the merest breath of sexuality. Fiedler says of the ensuing crop of Good Good Girls, Good Good Boys, and Good Bad Boys, 'It is hard to say whether the fear of sex, a strange blindness to the daily manifestations of sex, or the attenuation of sexuality itself drove the American novel back over the lintel of puberty in the declining years of the nineteenth century.' But whatever the cause, the effect was unquestionable. The reign of sentimentalism, with its various literary escape alleys, steadfastly eschewed passion and even found it impossible to portray a heroine as anything but a monster of virtue. 'As late as Henry Adams', says Fiedler, 'the figure of a woman refined to the point where copulation with her seems blasphemous possesses the imagination of the most sophisticated American writers.'

There is however, even in the American novel, a series of sinister Dark Ladies, who embody the sexuality denied the Pure White Maiden, and who represents the hunger of the Protestant, Anglo-Saxon male not only for the rich sexuality, the dangerous warmth he had rejected as unworthy of his wife, but also for the religions which he had disowned in fear, the racial groups he had excluded or despised. The black woman is typically Catholic or Jew, Latin or Oriental or Negro . . . She is surrogate for all the Otherness against which an Anglo-Saxon world attempts to define itself and a Protestant one to justify its existence.

We shall meet her in Miss Ravenel's French cousin, and in many of the novels of Henry James, where the opposition is not so much ethnic, but innocent-American versus experienced-European. Indeed, coming upon a scene almost totally bare of any reference to passion and adultery, James *needed* Europeans, particularly Continentals, to adulterate his too naïve Americans. But that belongs to our study of the novels themselves.

As far as this historical perspective is concerned it has become clear that the Puritan influence was infinitely stronger and longer-lasting than in England, and went hand-in-hand with practical reasons for the protection of the institution of marriage. At the same time, the desire to throw off the ruggedness, or roughness, of the pioneering generations engendered a concept of the female as a delicate flower which simultaneously gave rise to a very complicated balance of relationships between the white and the Negro as well as between the sexes. The situation provoked a mask of gentility and an upholding of the conventions quite as strong as in Victorian England; and the similar effect on the literature is marked. The sentimental tale of seduction reigned supreme, constantly asserting the purity of the pale heroine and the failure of the would-be seducer. It is with relief that we turn to an altogether different kind of woman, the kind brought forth by Mother Russia.

Marriage in Russia

The feminine principle, which had to wait until the eleventh century to draw the attention of Western Europe to itself, seems to have played a dominant role in the Russian consciousness from earliest times. It takes three forms during the course of the centuries: the damp Mother Earth of pre-Christian Russia; the Christian Mother of God who gazes down from every corner icon; and the, to Russia, far less important Lady we have already seen in Europe. It is the first aspect we are for the moment concerned with.

Russian folklore tells of a marriage between Heaven and Earth, who became father and mother of the great Slav family, and invested all their children with the sense of a collective identity overriding that of

the individual household. But no mate of comparable power has sur-
vived alongside Mother Earth, and she has swallowed up all vestige of
the erotic myth in her warm, dark, brooding body. She has become
the mother who never was virgin; the power of her attraction lies not
in her purity but in her fecundity; the emotion which springs from her
is maternal and not sexual; she invites filial devotion, not erotic fantasy. As G. P. Fedotov puts it, 'in the Russian Earth goddess Demeter
was more strongly expressed than Aphrodite'.[26] It would be rash to
assume anything at this point, but as we pursue the thread of the Russian attitude towards adultery, we may find ourselves asking whether
the fatherless son of such a Great Mother may not lack male aggressive-
ness and tend towards sexual indifference. For not only are purity and
virginity inessential qualities of the Russian's highest concept of woman
– she need not even be beautiful. Mother Earth tends to be rather
shapeless. As Fedotov again points out, however, she is not rivalled
by anyone else. There is no virgin Goddess parallel to Athena. Volu-
minous and all embracing, she shares in the beauty of Nature. Her
most stirring symbol, indeed her very persona, is the black, humid,
warm earth.

The strong tendency in early Russia to be passive to the sway of
destiny also minimised the importance of personal attraction. It was
supposed that everyone had present at his birth a female fairy or
deity, called a *rozhanitsa*, who presided over his entire life. Thus fate
would indicate whom one should marry (there is a saying which
affirms that 'You cannot ride past your predestined bridegroom') and
destiny was thought of as acting upon one, rather than as something
one shaped.

Further, the structure and strength of kinship ties were such as to
dampen the development of the individual personality. Within the
total collective family of Mother Earth was the kinship community
based on the cult of the deceased parents and ancestors, and called by
the Russian word *rod* (which can most closely be approximated to the
Latin *gens* or Celtic 'clan'). The *rod* is semantically older, and socially
far more important than the *sem'ya* or family. In the *Chronicle* of
Nestor (1120) for example, the nuclear family exists within a household consisting of ten to fifteen persons, and the same system is referred
to in the eleventh-century *Pravda* of Yaroslav.

The inherited concept of the *rod* is the reason why the Russians
continued for centuries after this period to use kinship names in
addressing strangers (usually rendered quite inappropriately in trans-
lation by such terms as 'little uncle' and the like) and why patronymics
are still in use today. Fedotov lifts these phenomena into a universal
statement about the Russian people : 'In this procedure all social
life is shaped as the extension of family life and all moral relations

amongst men are raised to the level of blood kinship.' The individual was seen as a transient moment in the eternal life of the *rod*, making the Romantic cult of the individual personality foreign to the Russian character; and we may postulate that adultery, in this situation, would take on the colour of incest, i.e. an occurring transgression, but lacking the special allure with which it was invested by the Code of Love.

The sense of clan would of course yield to the sense of family when combined with and gradually supplanted by the principle of inheritance of property; nor could the infiltration of Western ideas do anything but confirm this trend. But the notion of one large family with the Tsar as father persisted so obdurately that Berdyaev sees it not killed by, but rather transformed into the concept of the autocratic state. Certainly this sense of collective kinship exerted a lasting and profound effect upon the individual self-image, and the consequent development of social relationships. However, both this and, more precisely, the status of women, must be seen in the context of quite distinct phases of social evolution.

Firstly, it seems to be agreed that in the earliest times Russian society was matriarchally orientated; the tie uniting a man to his sister and her children was considered stronger than the relationship between two brothers, or an uncle and nephew. The Slavs used the Indo-European word for mother, but had no equivalent to express the paternal relationship; they had a word for a sister's son, though not for a brother's, and the descent was counted in the mother's line. As well as this semantic evidence, it also appears that women under this régime were free, influential, and independent; they were always equal with their husbands, and sometimes more powerful, since there was no bar to their right to own property, or become the head of a family or tribe. Marriage ties were not very strong; many unions were the result of abduction, apparently by either sex, or of games and contests of strength. So little was virginity prized and so greatly was motherhood valued, that preference in the choice of a marriage partner would often be given to a girl who had already proved her fertility. Brides could also be bartered for, but it seems that the bride price could be paid either by or to the bride's family, depending on whether she was considered an encumbrance or a useful helper. A late-nineteenth-century feminist, S. S. Shashkova, who has studied the historical development of the Russian woman, comments that the man was in most cases satisfied with the woman whom circumstances put in his path, being motivated by the traditional sense of destiny, as well as by a desire to avoid bother. Once married, the woman retained considerable freedom, and dissolution was easy for both partners if the desire was mutual. If a wife could not free herself in a friendly way, she would resort to knife or magic potion. On the other hand, if she did love her husband, she would often kill herself when he died. If the husband died first, the woman became head of the family and brought up the children, which leads Shashkova to make the pregnant statement : 'All the heroes and heroines of our past were educated by their mothers.'[27] In fairness we must recall that she was an ardent feminist, and no Freudian.

Early Russian women possessed not only an Amazonian degree of physical strength, they were also considered to harbour or be able to have recourse to some kind of magical or superhuman power – the *mana* associated by primitive tribes with the ability to give birth, to which even Tacitus alludes. It has been asserted that the establishment of patriarchal religions was man's attempt to secure for his own sex some rival *quantum* of supernatural power and mystery, during which process he sought to downgrade the female mysteries by declaring them unclean and/or evil. But in primitive Russia, at least, while the women were not above mixing up poisons and potions, their special knowledge was considered to be sacred and beneficial,* while they themselves were the repositories of human love and peacefulness. Maternal love was always represented as stronger and deeper than paternal affection.

However, this situation did not last; as the Russian Slavs moved further north, the work of clearing the huge forests and tilling the frozen soil became too hard for women to share in, and by comparison the importance of the male increased and that of the female diminished. Also, the work became too much for one family; and thus the practical inheritance of the marriage of Heaven and Earth was revealed in the formation of a large patriarchal family, who shared the labour and the lodging place. It was originally united by blood ties alone, but later grew to include servants and other hangers-on; and in it, Shashkova claims, the sense of collective identity engulfed that of the individual. 'No member of the ancient family was an individual, but only constituted a part of the collective personality of that family to which he belonged.'

From this time on began the transformation of the role of the woman, which nineteenth-century feminists like Shashkova refer to as their 'enslavement', to be reinforced in both religious and social terms by the introduction of Graeco-Byzantine Christianity in A.D. 988 and the Tartar supremacy which lasted from the thirteenth to the fifteenth centuries.

Under the patriarchal system, which endured until the beginning of the eighteenth century, the woman existed only to give birth to new

---

* By one tradition, for example, they would harness themselves to ploughs and furrow a circle round the village to keep it from harm.

life; her husband was acknowledged to be her lord and master.* Tra-
ditionally, a new husband whipped his bride on the way to their future
home, and having arrived and entered the bedroom, he would order
her to take off his boots – whereupon she would again find the whip
tucked into one of them. (The traditional lamentations which accompanied every wedding were not, clearly, only a matter of form and
custom!) Marriages were increasingly the result of passivity and parental domination. The husband and wife believed they stood beside each
other because they were fated to do so, but it was the father of the
family who exercised the will of God and the force of destiny. The
change in the structure of the society is revealed by the nineteenth-
century historian Kovalevsky, who comments on the fact that the
son or daughter who concluded a marriage without consulting their
parents lost all rights to inheritance and dowry. He writes: 'In a
society in which the interests of the family constantly prevail over
those of the individual . . . there is no room for marriages contracted
by mutual consent.'[28]

Another significant development was the new emphasis placed on
the virginity of the bride: as we have said, many Russian tribes had
paid small attention to the matter of virginity, to the point of actually
preferring to take to wife a girl who had given proof of her ability
to bear children. Now, with the growing conviction that the wife was
part of the man's property, for whom money must be paid, the husband was increasingly concerned to receive value for money – by which
he meant intact goods. The fact that this new concern for virginity
was not entirely accepted by the general population is evidenced by
the length gone to in simulating the breaking of already ruptured
hymens.

The centre and symbol of the whole patriarchal and Tartarish subjugation of women was the *terem*, the upper room in which all the
women of the patriarchal family were kept. Shashkova tells us that
one of their duties was to grow fat to conform with the Mongol ideal
of beauty; and because of this distortion of feminine beauty, the dis-
tain for feminine emotions, and the isolation of the women in the
terem, the Russian man seldom fell in love. The women were all of
the same monotonous and unlovely mould; there was no incentive to
anything more than a material, possibly comradely, relationship. She
writes:

> In view of such a conception of female beauty, of the disdain for
> feminine feeling and imagination, and of the isolation of the woman

---

* According to *The Domostroi*, a sixteenth-century handbook of family life
written by a priest at the court church of Ivan the Terrible, women were incapable of full mental and moral development, and therefore ought to be physically punished like children.

in the terem – there could not be, for us, that same development of Romantic love as we see in Europe. Traditional Russian love was of a coarse-grained character . . . in Muscovy . . . because of the unvaried conditions of life, women were all similar, and passion bore no individual stamp; the traditional Russian man seldom fell in love; if he felt desire, he would seek and choose a bride or lover as he would a comrade.

The almost simultaneous growth of Byzantine Christianity in Russia did nothing to relieve the female half of the population groaning under the yokes of the patriarchal family system, and the Tartar-inspired pattern of male domination. In fact each confirmed the other's interest in male supremacy.

The Eastern churches had had from the beginning a mystical and theological view of marriage, paralleled by the development much earlier than in the Roman tradition of the concept of the Church as the bride of Christ. They were equally far removed from the secular view of marriage with its emphasis on the legal and contractual aspects of the union, which had prevailed in the West until the eleventh century. Long before it came about in the West, in fact in the fourth century, the Orthodox Church's liturgy of betrothal and marriage developed out of the ancient family and civil marriage customs. But by the time the Byzantine Church was an effective force in Russia, Byzantine civilisation was already in a state of decline and depravity. Between the degeneracy of the ideal Greek woman into a courtesan, and the asceticism of the pure spirits, woman had come to be a symbol of corruption. A bad man was still better than a good woman, was the conviction.

This opinion slipped into general church teaching; the codes of Graeco-Byzantine canon law exist in several versions written from the sixth to the ninth centuries, and have been accepted to the present day in the Russian Orthodox Church. But these have been amplified by what Fedotov calls 'a mass of formless, anonymous, and pseudonymous literature of a canonical nature', which includes a number of articles relating to uncleanness connected with food and sex. The Russian clergy had become convinced that there could be no salvation in the worldly life, even of a sober variety. A vow of abstinence was supposed to be the ideal of every Christian man; the monastic spirit infected the whole of civilised society. Marriage was regarded as a mere concession to animal weakness; the hold the ascetic ideal had over the ordinary person, sometimes in excess of what the Church actually taught, is shown by the agonised question of whether it was lawful to have sexual intercourse with one's wife in a room in which there was an icon. (Bishop Niphont impatiently answered that a wife

was not given to you for sin, while a similar liberalism was revealed
in the permission given to kiss the relics of saints after coitus, without having a bath first, so long as one had washed up to the
waist.)

Other statutes make it clear that the inferiority of women was due
less to moral weakness than to the physical uncleanness associated with
menstruation and childbirth. Altogether, one can scarcely doubt what
Shashkova asserts with such bitterness, that the ascetic view of life
assisted with all the strength of its religious power that subjection
of women in which the patriarchal way of life was trying to keep
her.

However, it must not be assumed that the entire Russian population
immediately and conscientiously assimilated itself to the Byzantine culture. Firstly, a distinction must be drawn between the upper echelons
of society and the vast mass of people. For the latter, any kind of
Christian ritualism was out of the question. The common people
thought church marriage was only for the aristocracy; they rejected
the notion of ecclesiastical blessing, preferring to save the expense and
simply unite themselves in the presence of the community, to the cheerful accompaniment of dancing, music and general festivity. Secondly,
the Russian clergy were often more moved by what was traditional
than by what was officially authorised. Thus the easy dissolution of
marriage was continued long after the advent of Christianity even
though the permission had formally to be given by the ecclesiastical
courts which dealt with divorce, womens' rights to property, family
disputes and daughters' inheritances. Having united the knot a husband could free himself of an unwanted wife by sending her to a
convent, accompanied by a gift of money. Thirdly, the Byzantine
efforts to impose asceticism upon the Russian people met with a resistance which was not so much passive as unconscious. The clergy and
the spiritual élite of Moscow were one thing; but the dominant ancient
Russian ethic was based not on sacramental sanctification but on the
life of charity. Neither the letter of the law nor the ethic of purity were
particularly significant in this last framework, and thus in certain
areas the Church resignedly and realistically did not even try to bring
its miscreants to justice. For example, it was simply assumed that as
continence was an impossible state for a young man, all bachelors
were naturally in a perpetual state of sin. The Church did not legis-
late against them, but merely tried to see they avoided sacrilege –
hence the debate amongst the bishops as to whether bachelors might
kiss the cross or not. Similarly, the tolerance of what was unavoidable,
coupled with the highly developed sense of collective identity, meant
that bastards were accepted by the community, and by Peter the
Great's time cared for by the state.

In fact, in the existent warmth of human relations within the one vast family, some un-Byzantine aspects of Christianity found sturdy root, and strengthened an already robust plant. Fedotov writes :

Russian charity not only finds its strongest expression in the love between brothers or blood relatives, but it attempts to embrace, in a fictional kinship, all fellowmen. All men are brothers not in a spiritual Christian sense, as having the common Father in heaven, but in an earthly sense, of a common origin, or common blood. It imparts a certain warmth, a residuum of family tenderness in human relationships . . .

Thus the light which makes adultery appear more like incest than a product of romantic passion was still more powerful after the advent of Christianity, even though the brotherhood of man was a Russian and not a Byzantine persuasion.

Russian indifference to the virginity cult and reluctance to idealise sexual relations are also demonstrated in a way which is quite fascinating to compare with the rise of the cult of courtly love in Western Europe. Bogomilism was the name given to the beliefs of a dualistic sect which appeared in Bulgaria in the ninth century. Its tenets proclaimed it to be a branch of the ancient heresy of Manicheism, and Fedotov states that from the Slavic Balkan countries, where it had grown into a powerful rival of the established church, it 'penetrated Western Europe in the eleventh century, and began a very spectacular career under the name of Cathars, Albigenses, and others'. Considering the close cultural relationships, he argues, that existed between mediaeval Bulgaria and Russia, and the identity of their literary language, the infiltration into Russia of the Bogomils, or at least of their teaching, would have been very natural. But it did not happen. The main orientation both of Russian religious folklore, and Russian culture in general, indicated that the Russian religious mind held Nature to be good and was deeply opposed to dualism. Self-torturing denial was fundamentally alien to the Russian spirit; and ultimately even the overlay of Byzantine asceticism was shattered by Ivan the Terrible, who explicitly placed the ideal of the Christian family above the virtue of celibacy. 'The exclusive cult of sacred or divine Motherhood – from Mother Earth to the Mother of God – overshadowed the Christian value of purity.'

The juridical results of the conversion of Russia continued even after Peter the Great's secularisation of the state in the eighteenth century; the appropriation to ecclesiastical courts of all legalities connected with marriage was not rescinded, while under the almost perfect harmony which existed then between church and state, the civil code was in total agreement with canon law. Marriage was indissoluble except in four cases: adultery, impotency, total loss of rights through imprisonment or exile, and hopeless insanity, were all grounds for dissolution *(rastorzhenie braka)*. In the first case the adultery had to be proven, and the accusation could be directed against either spouse. The *civil* code even laid down that husbands were to love their wives as part of their own bodies, while wives must remain with their husbands in love, respect and obedience.

Towards the end of the seventeenth century the patriarchal system began to crumble, as the abuses within it and the influence of Western Europe both proclaimed themselves with loud voices. Peter the Great released women from the *terem*, called on them to play a part in public life, and at the same time encouraged an improved family life which he later tended to sacrifice to the need for an educated civil service. While the upper-class girls and women were invited to court and to attend balls and assemblies, the boys were sent off to government-run boarding schools to be trained as civil servants. The loosening of morals which accompanied this upheaval in society led to a vast number of illegitimate births, for whom Peter established 'hospitals'; he also found it necessary to decree that the killing of illegitimate children was a capital offence.

The schism between the Old Believers on the one hand, and Peter the Great and Archbishop Nikon on the other, finally led, in the marriage area, to the publication in 1762 of a document called 'The Sacrament of Marriage', which stated that the bestowal of grace in marriage had no particular connection with the ritual; that the real celebrant was the Lord Himself, with the priest only a witness; and that the church ceremony was only a custom confirming the validity and civil stability of the marriage. The dogma was not very different from the declarations of marriage of the Council of Trent, but the Catholic Church leant more heavily on the practical need, which it made an injunction, for the priest to be present and the marriage to take place in a church.

Catherine the Great continued the reforms instituted by Peter, and carried many of them further. Finding that very few women were literate, she ordered the daughters of the nobility to be sent away to boarding schools *(Stolnye Instituti)* with the result that there was one girl to every thirteen boys educated in a school; most however preferred to be educated at home by a governess, who would normally teach grammar, French, etiquette, music and novel reading. Perhaps they were simply being realistic in refusing advanced education: an eighteenth-century *domostroi*, written by one Tatishchev, still advises against love marriages, and leaves the wife under the unlimited *(neo-granichnyi)* power of her husband, with the family her only concern.

During the nineteenth century, particularly under Alexander I, the number of schools increased greatly, and many opened their doors to girls of less than aristocratic background. However, a strict stratification was practised, whereby the lower-class girls were only trained to be governesses or maids to the daughters of the aristocracy. It was claimed by Belinsky that they were never really encouraged to be people, but merely brides, with the result that they, like Tatiana, could not look at a man without seeing him as a future husband. Shashkova complains that they still sought the cultivation not of the girls' minds, but of 'a pure heart'. Prince Oldenburg began to rectify this in 1860 when he was put in charge of women's education, and founded Gymnasia for girls.

Indeed, whatever their faults, the one thing the nobility did do was encourage girls to read, and from the early nineteenth century a flock of women's magazines was devoured, many inspired by French feminist writings; there is a constant thread running through them of the notion of the equality of the sexes. The influence of George Sand was stronger in Moscow than it ever was in Paris, and especially susceptible to it were the *institutkas* whose education, as Elaine Elnett points out, 'had awakened in [them] instincts which were incompatible with the crude reality . . . The Russian George Sandist of the 40s and 50s was a type of woman who considers love as the aim of her whole existence and the only way out of harsh reality . . . The object of her choice often proved unworthy of her sacrifice, but anyhow he was a man of the new type.'[29] (Shashkova says disapprovingly that this fad was displaced by the notion of love based on human sacrifice. We should be aware of the twist George Sand's idealism has received on its way to Russia. While she lifted love on to an ideal plane, removing it as far as possible from earthly shackles, the Russian girls saw love primarily as a means of escape not from life itself but from an unsatisfactory form of existence to a new, freer one.)

The man of the new type, and indeed the New Woman, as presented by Chernyshevsky, will be studied later; for the moment we only need to note the extensive growth of education for girls during the latter part of the nineteenth century, leading to such a thirst for independence that many not only ran away from home to become *kursistki*, but entered into fictitious marriages which released them from parental control and were never intended to bind them to the nominal spouse.* It was a time of ferment for a small section of female society; but masses of women continued to abide by the traditional tenets of

* Extreme though this may seem, it was a measure designed to respond to the mildly outrageous situation in which a father or husband were the legal custodians of a woman's passport – a document necessary for her to move about *within* Russia.

church and state. For the Karenins, for example, divorce was perfectly possible – but unthinkable in terms of the scandal it would cause.

The difference between the small band of radicals (mainly associated with the Nihilist movement) and the main body of polite society can be gauged by bearing in mind the Karenins' situation while reading what Shelgunov, a well-known Nihilist, proclaimed in his memoirs : 'Never in Russia had there been so many wives and husbands living apart as in and after the 1860s. Unsuccessful families split up and then formed new illegal families with complete tolerance. The question of whether a woman was someone's legal wife became impossible and meaningless.' So dedicated were these free spirits to the creed of the liberated individual that Chernyshevsky, whose novel-cum-manifesto we shall look at in greater detail further on, positively incited his future wife to adultery even before he had got her to the altar, so that he could prove his truly unpossessive love. To his great satisfaction it all happened – unlike his more confused fellow-Nihilist Pisarev, who offered sexual freedom to his fiancée while challenging his rival to a duel. Shelgunov, on the other hand, maintained such a close friendship with his wife's lover that when the latter was exiled to Siberia, Shelgunov followed him – and then wrote letters to his wife, whom he continued to adore, begging her to forgive him for leaving her and causing her to suffer.

The 'love of the people of the sixties' has been thoroughly set forth in Bogdanovich's book of that name; and while it is fascinating to read of such idealism, its very unreality explains its lack of popular appeal. Far from wishing to introduce an era of general licentiousness, the Nihilists themselves were, if not sexually puritanical, at least fantastically high-minded; the pleasures they got from the new régime were more at the level of their higher feelings than of their lower instincts. They did not, for example, have any desire to undo the family system; they regarded nest-building as a natural and commendable instinct; moreover, they saw family life as necessarily based on mutual sexual attraction and conjugal love. What had to change was the nature of love; they were not satisfied with the half-way measure of seeking a new form of ancient emotions. It was axiomatic to them, says Bogdanovich, that man is capable of putting into practice what he clearly understands and believes; therefore no difficulty was attached to the hope of eradicating or basically changing any feeling judged to be irrational or damaging. The theory of 'rational egoism' proclaimed that 'in the family, as in society, there must be a basis of equality and freedom . . . But in the past the family was built on quite contrary foundations – the despotism of the husband, the enslavement of the wife and children, and the fettering of all feeling.'[30]

Chernyshevsky went so far as to write in his diary that women ought actually to be set above men for the moment, since this alone would redress the balance and create a situation of equality. Shelgunov also abdicates his husbandly prerogatives in favour of comradeship and equality, and enthusiastically offers to do only what his wife wants. (It seems however that these virtues were not enough to keep her; one wonders whether a little old-fashioned jealousy would not have kept her out of her lover's arms *and* caused her some primeval feminine gratification.)

In fact, to the Western mind, there is something odd, even suspect, about the way many Russians seem to take so easily to a situation which precludes what we would call 'normal' sexual jealousy. Billington believes that at least a contributing factor to this attenuation of sexuality was the deep influence on Russian philosophical thought of Jacob Boehme and his theory of androgyny.[31] In his original state of perfect union with God, thought Boehme, man had been spiritually perfect and without sexual differentiation; part of man's return to God would be the attainment of perfect androgyny, the union of male and female characteristics. Sophia – that mystic principle of true wisdom and lost femininity – is the common object of the strivings of both God and man. Hence, says Billington, the element of sublimated sexuality in the creative activity of the nineteenth century; the indifference of, for example, the writer Gogol and the artist Ivanov to women; the sexual impotence of Bakunin; the many venues for all male companionship provided by lodge, club and circle; the Platonic but emotional friendships between men which were scattered through the life and literature of the times.

Another theory brought to light by a modern psychologist suggests that 'a clue, not a cause of Russian behaviour'[32] is to be found in the habit of swaddling babies in such a way that they are in fact inhibited in various ways from the self-expression that Western babies enjoy. The inability to move their limbs and bodies which prevents the expression of emotion is so frustrating that they respond with a deep inner but undirected rage; this results in the development of pervasive but unfocused guilt feelings, and a lack of sharp distinction between other people in the environment. The authors of this interesting theory bend over backwards in their insistence that no such simple factor can alone explain Russian behaviour; but given it has some validity, it supports the view of a tendency in the Russian temperament to play down the highly individual and intensely personal relationship we associate with romantic love. A brief survey of the literature prior to and including the nineteenth-century novel would appear to bear this theory out.

It is well known that although an oral tradition of songs, rhymes, ballads and fairy-tales had existed since earliest times in Russia, book literature began only after Christianity had introduced a written lan-

guage, at the time of its coming in the tenth century. Since mona-
steries were the main source of cultural education, the literature
produced was strictly instructive and moralistic, though the co-existent
and unquenchable pagan traditions affected and were affected by the
ritual and story of the new religion. The secular material of the Kiev
period either came direct from Byzantium and was translated straight
into Russian, or arrived via Bulgaria and Serbia; it consisted of frivolous short stories, with a Christian moral tacked on, which resulted in
the Russian moralising parable, or heroic tales obliged by the Church
to omit any romantic element. The hero might fall in love, but after
a series of obstacles he must die, or be united with his love and live
happily ever after. Preferably and commonly, the emphasis was placed
on his warlike exploits. 'It is very indicative', writes Gudzy, 'that not
a single purely secular, let alone amorous, Byzantine romance . . . was
known in Old Rus.' The *Alexandria* embodies in Alexander the ideal
hero-figure; he remains constant to his wife Roxana, and she stabs
herself when he dies; the *Adventures of Digenis* tell of the abduction
by the Saracen chief Amin of a noble Greek maiden; but he embraces
Christianity, marries her, and they live happily ever after. Their son
Digenis has some trouble in selecting the correct wife, but having done
so their married life is an example to all. Gudzy comments : 'The piety
of Digenis is given considerably greater emphasis than the piety of
Alexander. He is not only a marvellous warrior, endowed with superior
physical qualities, but also a God-fearing Christian, relying upon God
in all matters, and never undertaking anything without prayer *and his
mother's blessing*.'[33] (my italics).

The mother of a family did indeed in fourteenth-century Russia
enjoy unusual reverence and affection, while her call to fidelity was
sustained by the image of her beloved Holy Rus always faithful to
her husband Tsar. The tale of *Peter and Fevronia* is particularly significant; not only do they embody in their married life an ideal love
which never lessens in spite of all obstacles, but they manage to die
simultaneously. When their bodies are put in separate coffins, they
turn up next morning in the same one. But over and above this exquisite tale of love and fidelity, Gudzy sees a new trait : Fevronia and
not Peter is the exponent of the active principle of love; it is she who
awakens an answering spiritual awareness in the somewhat pedestrian
Peter; 'she is the orderer of her own fate, and of that of the man she
loves, while he is her obedient slave, loving her for her superiority to
himself and subject to him in all things.' It was an immensely popular
tale, which seems to give much support to the persuasive hypothesis
that Russians truly want an ideal before their eyes of a faithful and
morally superior woman.

It appeared in fact for some time that the natural taste of the reading and listening public either coincided with, or was naturally docile to, the strictly moralising character demanded of literature by the Church. 'The story could not be liberated from its moral task', writes Miliukov, 'and the ascetic Byzantine influence was preserved among the outstanding members of Russian society until the end of the seventeenth century.'[34]

However, the parsimony finally bored its audience; looking round for more entertaining reading-matter, they could find nothing in their own native literature similar to the secular novel or story of the West, and so had to look to the import trade. The role of intermediary was played largely by Poland, and so successfully that the style of books read for entertainment changed radically during the last part of the seventeenth century. Tale after tale appeared without benefit of maxim or moral, and while daring deeds may have first held the major interest, the reader soon became fascinated by the beautiful princess as well. 'Thus', writes Miliukov of this dramatic moment, 'the erotic element appeared in Russian narrative fiction.' Producing, it must be added, realism in literature, idealism in life, and *new* feelings for the Russian reader.

Another source of this novel and delightfully disturbing trend was again by way of Russian translations of Serbian tales, many of which related back to the chivalric tradition. Tristan and Lancelot appear, as does Bevis in the guise of Bova; but as with the Byzantine religion, nothing takes root in the Russian earth without being vitally affected by it. I am indebted to Gudzy yet again for a concise account of the characteristics of seventeenth-century Western-derived Russian literature : firstly, it is avowedly secular, with the amorous intrigue its stock in trade; secondly, to the lovers love means not only joy, but suffering as well; love and success in love become a *raison d'être;* BUT the lovers always overcome all obstacles, and are finally united, never to part; constancy in love is a distinguishing trait; and affairs are always crowned by legal marriage, followed by a long, happy-wedded married life. Perhaps the first, rare, depiction of forbidden love appears in the seventeenth-century story of Savva Grudsyn, who commits adultery with the wife of Bazhen; but after many adventures he repents, and becomes a monk.*

Under Peter the Great, there was a widening gap between the really educated and the merely literate; the former pursued every Western

---

* Dmitrij Čiževskij points out in his *History of Russian Literature* that in neither the tales of lawful love, such as *Peter and Magilena,* or the unlawful *Savva Grudsyn,* can the language do justice to its theme. Peter can only 'bow himself before love', and 'hope for a lawful matrimony', while Magilena's girlish dreams are expressed as 'thinking about matrimonial affairs'. In *Savva,* the only phrase the author can think of for adultery is 'to roll in the dirt of lechery like a swine'. This, says Čiževskij, is repeated several times (pp.333–4).

literary trend, and thereby acquired a taste for vicarious emotion which was foreign both to the previous generation and to the contemporary common man. Until the 1820s the reading choice of the semi-educated person was at first between didactic books, folklore, and tales of adventure with a dash of chivalry, later replaced by stories distinguished for their sentimental appeal. The first piece of realistic writing was Pushkin's *Evgenii Onegin*,* in which, in Mirsky's words, 'Superfluous Onegin and the lovely Tatiana became the authentic Adam and Eve of the Mankind that inhabits Russian fiction.' And he is far from alone in his conviction. It would be useful, as it was with George Sand's *Indiana* to look more closely at *Evgenii Onegin* in anticipation of the later nineteenth-century literary novels.

The work is in fact helpful to us from three angles; it contains a strongly personal presentation of the traditional Russian ideal woman; it gives a realistic portrayal of various contemporary attitudes to marriage; and it offers a view of the Romantic hero which is individualistic, but not uncharacteristic of the time and society it was written for. Onegin contains a good deal of personal Pushkin, specifically the Pushkin who existed before he moved towards a more conservative classicism – but Pushkin himself summed up many of the attitudes and aspirations of the young men of his time.

Tatiana appears in two guises. At first she is an open-hearted, simple, romantic girl, not too proud to proffer her untried love. Her warmth and spontaneity are contrasted favourably with the tedious circumspection of the young society girls of the *grand monde*; their selections are made coldly and dispassionately, whereas Tatiana yields earnestly to love 'like a sweet child'. Like Emma Bovary, Tatiana is influenced by her reading; however, she chooses as her heroines Clarissa, Julie and Delphine, who, in spite of the significance Fiedler reads into their stories, do in fact preserve their integrity and sometimes that of their lovers. Tatiana dreams her girlish dreams, but there is a positive, life-affirming quality about them which makes them seem, in contrast to Emma's death-inviting fantasies, almost anti-romantic. Tatiana would enthusiastically opt for a fate less than death if only Onegin would accept her offer. Nor does his rejection send her into a permanent decline, though without question she suffers long and deeply.

After an interval of time we meet her in her second guise – that of the faithful wife. Tatiana has accepted a loveless marriage with the fat general produced by her parents; now, when Onegin finally comes to value and love her, she refuses to have anything to do with him, even though she admits she loves him still. What then are the reasons for

* Although *Evgenii Onegin* may of course be considered pure poetry, its author defined it as 'a novel in verse'.

this stalwart fidelity in defiance of mutual love? Tatiana certainly does not invoke any sense of religious obligation, nor does she act out of a spirit of revenge. Nothing could be sadder nor more sincere than her simple statement : she loves Onegin, but having been given to someone else, to him she will be faithful all her life. There is in fact no 'explanation'; Tatiana simply conforms to 'the dear ideal' of a tradition in which illicit love is practically unknown, and wives are always faithful. In doing so she not only complies with a widespread belief, but strengthens it to an inestimable degree. For a long time after her, no one dared break the mould.

The qualities briefly distilled in Tatiana conform completely to the ideal heroine of the Russian tradition already glimpsed; the information about attitudes to marriage yielded by the book falls into two categories : what Pushkin observes and describes dispassionately, and the problems he feels and tries to sort out by projecting them on to his characters. In the first category comes the arranged marriage, which may be fixed by a matchmaker, as was the old nurse's marriage ('we never heard of love', she cries) or by the parents, as in the case of Tatiana's own marriage and her mother's, or which may be a matter of mutual attraction abetted and approved by the families involved, as in the case of Olga and Lensky. Whatever the process required to bring it about, the arranged marriage has, according to *Evgenii Onegin*, these characteristics : a rather separate but amicable co-existence – Tatiana's father tends to keep to his room while his wife is busy about the estate; equality of importance between husband and wife – she does everything from pickling mushrooms to keeping the accounts without consulting him; and a degree of content achieved through familiarity and domestic activity. Pushkin writes – whether with approval or bitterness, it is almost impossible to tell – that 'habit is given to us from above, as a substitute for happiness'.

This, Pushkin implies, is more than adequate for the average man and woman – but what about the special people, the poets and romantics, the idealists? Pushkin's very ambivalent personal views are reflected in Lensky's eagerness for marriage, and the commentary upon it : it is another expression of the question raised earlier – is marital bliss worth the loss of independence it entails, can its joys efface the prospects of a monotonous and dreary routine? Lensky is merry as he anticipates his wedding day; in his naïve enthusiasm there is no room for thoughts of the tedium or boredom that Pushkin, in the role of worldly-wise commentator, foresees. Unfortunately, Lensky's death saves Pushkin from answering the unanswerable.

Onegin, in the person of the Byronic-hero figure, stalks the periphery of the marriage circle, but though he creates a temporary skewing of it he is finally ousted. He can neither join it by responding to Tatiana when she loves him, nor entice her away from it when he tardily falls in love with her. As with Emma Bovary, romanticism leads to failure and unhappiness; but with Emma the route is via love outside marriage, whereas with Onegin it is the failure to embrace love at all. Pushkin has no serious criticism of wild-oat-sowing, but the inference is strong that what happened in his own life is actually a moral imperative. A time comes when one *should* settle down; it is wrong to let the natural course of things be interfered with by the romantic cult of *ennui* and withdrawal from the world. With that ever-present mixture of wry cynicism and philosophic optimism he heads one of his chapters with Necker's aphorism, 'La morale est dans la nature des choses.' Pushkin himself not only accepted its truth, but came to draw support from it. And the message is clear – we should all do likewise.

This compromise with the prosaic appears to be a betrayal of all that romanticism stands for, and it is true that the romantic youth whom Pushkin had been was gradually transformed into a much sterner man. But Onegin is the projection of a Pushkin who refused to move towards the centre; and Pushkin allows us to see in him the glimmer of a flaming idealism, buried though it may be beneath a bushel of bored cynicism. Although when we first meet him Onegin is passing through a phase of weary indifference, we know that he has had in the past many tempestuous yearnings; he is less disdainful of routine than downright terrified of it. He cherishes in fact such an exalted notion of love that he dreads to reduce it to everydayness; glorious moments are by their very nature ephemeral, so 'whom to love? Love your own self, my worthy, honoured reader.' The cynicism betrays not contempt but fear – fear of commitment which in turn springs from fear of disappointment.* Such a paralysing fear indicates an idealism which Pushkin has projected on to Tatiana as well as on to Onegin. He truly loves the fruit of his creation; he tells us frankly, 'I do so love my dear Tatiana . . .' The real difficulty was not the acceptance of the tedium of marriage but the inability to find a suitable husband for Tatiana – the ideal strong woman of Russian tradition. Instead he gives us the first in what will be a long line of unfulfilled lovers, of *adultères manqués*, of weak men unable to respond to the challenge of romantic love. Onegin stands at the meeting-point of two traditions: the old one in which there are no infidelities, and love is always subsumed in marriage; and the new in which love fails to find fulfilment at all.

Neither of these situations leaves much room for adultery, as the post-Pushkin novels testify.

---

* There is a striking parallel with Chekhov's inability to commit himself to marriage with his much-appreciated Olga, at least until the last four years of his life.

Conclusion

This section has been devoted to a bird's eye survey of the social and literary background to marriage and adultery in four societies, up to the middle of the nineteenth century. As, from now on, we shall be taking the novels of the latter half of the century as our source of information, it would be premature at this point to force any conclusions or draw any morals. Yet a pattern is already emerging of universal tendencies and national differences whose broad outlines may serve at least as orientations in the closer perusal of the novels. So, drawn on the one hand to accept the overwhelming evidence of certain indications, and reluctant on the other to predetermine the literary issues, we sum up this section in an oblique and speculative fashion – which nevertheless confirms the findings already made.

The first comment relates to the various popular appellations of Mary, the mother of Jesus Christ. The Russians call her 'Bogoroditsa', meaning Mother of God – a title proclaiming an assimilation which took place when the cult of the *rozhanitsi* (the female spirits who presided over births) was fused with that of the Greek Theotokos (mother of God), with all the emphasis laid on the last syllable in the word, the part meaning parent or birth-giver. Thus her essential quality is, for the Russian mind, her maternity. The French however most commonly refer to 'La Sainte Vierge', obviously putting virginal purity above maternal solicitude. And English Catholics pray to a Mary called 'Our Lady' – an ambiguous title which avoids strict categorisation under either of the other two nomenclatures, and is not without overtones of the lady of the manor, the active but gracious wife.

Moving from semantics to hagiography and iconography, we find that although many of the virgin saints of the Greek Church are included in the Russian calendar, popular devotion leaves them virtually ignored. The Russian Church has itself canonised twelve female saints, of whom only one is a virgin, while the favourite, St Paraskeva, to whom barren wives prayed for fertility, was the sole one to be represented on icons. By contrast, only one married woman has, in popular knowledge, been canonised by the Roman Catholic church – St Barbara – while the most popular female saints are noted for their single-minded virginity, whether they be a St Joan or a Little Flower.

Lastly, Fedotov points out that two basic iconographic models were imported from Greece to early Russia: one portrays the Queen of Heaven with both mother and son looking outwards from the picture, while the other has the mother gazing down over the child, so emphasising her role as mother of the Christ-child. The former image was more common in Greece, but the Russians gave their preference to the latter, thus displaying yet again the depth of their devotion to maternal tenderness. Moreover beauty is not her main feature. In fact, in the absence of popular female saints, beauty of form is ascribed in the Russian Church to the enchanting but desexed angels, particularly Saints Michael and Gabriel.

The opposite is the case in the French Catholic Church, where Mary is usually girlishly pretty in her blue or white robes, and is very frequently seen without her son.

The Anglican Church has not canonised anyone since the Reformation, and its parish churches are mostly bare of religious imagery. But perhaps it is not too far-fetched to think that the absence of icons and statuary is at least partially compensated by the brasses, many of which depict married couples. They may be said to signify the esteem in which the English hold the institution of marriage, in contrast to the French obsession with virginity and the Russian fervour for motherhood.

In the light of these pointers, and of the social and literary traditions from which they spring, we turn to the novels themselves, and specifically to the characters in them who became involved in adultery.

2 The Breaking of the Order

The reasons why the literary characters of the latter half of the nine-teenth century entered into adulterous relationships are variable – presumably to at least the same degree as those restraining the remainder from doing likewise – while the components of the infamous triangle – husband, wife and lover – remain ever the same, and shall be dealt with in that order.

Practically all of the authors who deal primarily with an erring husband situate their villains in the upper echelons of society. The social positioning is not fortuitous. An obvious occupational hazard for the adulterous husband was the need to contribute financially to the support of the mistress, while continuing to maintain a home and family. A liaison with a married woman might be economically more advantageous, but was tactically more risky. However, the variety of examples provided by the novels is wide enough to indicate that monetary motivations were marginal to the main issue. The gamut ranges from Zola's wealthy Count Muffat, who spends lavishly in order to satisfy the extravagant demands of his kept courtesan, to Hardy's middle-class doctor, Fitzpiers, who contributes nothing but his charm.

The length of the affair is also a matter of considerable variation. I have already defined an adulterous relationship in a way which ex-cludes what is sometimes known as 'the one-night stand', but there are at least two novels *(Richard Feveral* and *Une Page d'Amour)* in which an isolated act of intercourse betokens a personal involvement of suffi-cient duration to give the couple adulterous status. There are many more examples of affairs which last emotionally and physically for a period of years.

However, two points are self-evident : firstly, that while insufficiency of time or money may place negative strictures on the adulterous hus-band, inclination is his most positive incitement; and secondly, that the quality of his marriage is intimately bound up with the degree of his inclination.

c

Contrary, perhaps, to expectation it is not the case that any of the husbands are driven to adultery by a nagging wife or an intolerable domestic situation.* I cannot account for this, unless it be that the nagging wife belongs primarily to comedy – and few, if any, of the novels are comic. Their essentially sober countenance appears to be a condition of their existence.

Zola's Muffat is perhaps the most pitiable of the husbands for he, more than the others, is depicted as a victim of the social system into which he was born – a system which gave him a strict religious up-bringing and ensured that he was a virgin tortured by inhibitions and scruples when married off to a girl of seventeen in a typical *mariage de convenance*. Zola does not elaborate upon the intimacies of the union, though we know the Countess Muffat certainly learnt to find discreet pleasure elsewhere; we receive however the distinct impression that its tenor continues cold, polite and superficially undisturbed, until Muffat discovers for the first time, with Nana, the force of sexual desire and the pleasure of its satisfaction. Zola insists upon the burning pathos of his situation : 'The ideas and beliefs of forty years were flooded with new life . . . he would have given up everything, sold all he had, to have her for one hour that night. It was his youth awakened at last, the greedy puberty of adolescence burning suddenly within the cold dignity of the mature Catholic.' Zola's aim is surely to persuade us that this is not mere lust, but the inevitable undamming of artificially constricted emotional and physical floods, just as Feuillet's Mme Camors rebuffs her lively husband's attentions with her cold religiosity – 'she was not simply an *honnête femme*', that is her dutifulness sprang not just from habit but from zeal; she was not circumspect, she was truly chaste; she was not merely church-going, but genuinely pious. While quite pleased to enjoy her company as an 'amie charmante', Camors nevertheless looks for, and discovers, more voluptuous charms in a liaison with a lively lady married to an old general. Camors finds his double existence most satisfactory – even to the added prestige and the realisation that the identity of his mistress is publicly suspected but not proven.

Again, the problem of the beautiful-souled but sexually passive wife is the cause of the return of Barbey's Comte de Marigny to his super-passionate, exotic, and slightly dusky ex-mistress, Vellini, after a brief period of marriage to the morally pure and spiritually uplifting Hermangarde. Hermangarde's image is engraved upon her husband's soul,

* Theodore Dreiser foreshadows the literature of the next century by posing a new reason for seeking an extra-marital relationship : his sister Carrie (the novel of the same name appeared in 1900) takes up with a married man who is driven to her arms by a shrewish and grasping wife; but this syndrome is not a feature of the nineteenth-century novels.

insists Barbey, but the allure of Vellini is irresistible; she alone can drive him to transports of desire, and satiate him with the 'intoxication of an accursed delight'. And, in *Ce qui ne meurt pas*, also by d'Aurevilly, marriage to an *ingénue* girl-wife does not prevent the husband's returning to the more experienced arms of his bride's mother. In neither case are the marriages arranged, as in the first two novels; but always the virtues of a cold but dutiful wife pale beside those of a sexually responsive mistress.

The desire for erotic excitement on the part of the French husband seems thus to be amongst the *données* of the situation and is matched only by the *froideur, naïveté* and indifference of the wife. Though the explanations and grounds may vary, she is, to be crude, just a great deal less sexy than the mistress. The husband does not wish to leave either her or the family home, but finds it pleasant/alluring/necessary to spice a deadening domestic situation with additional relationships. These in each case attach to one other woman only; but she must be a woman capable of supplying the sexual passion absent from the marriage bed.

The English on the other hand are not drawn to the triangular life; while there are various examples of the long-term *de facto* marriage, the maintenance of a wife and a mistress simultaneously is far less frequent in the novel no matter how factually common the occurrence in the upper echelons of English society. Often, too, the author is not really concerned with the adulterous liaison *per se*, but uses it as a means of making a separate point. For example, Richard Feveral, in Meredith's novel of the same name, is allowed to be seduced by the professional Bella as a sign of the tragic results of parental interference with the course of true love. Richard has loved and married Lucy against his father's wishes – an opposition based purely on the grounds of her social status. The young couple are forcibly separated, and it is during this period that Richard falls prey to Bella, only to be so consumed with guilt that his self-punitive measures finally destroy the marriage.

Richard Feveral however appeared in 1859, and is considerably different from Meredith's later novels, most of which become increasingly preoccupied with the idea of the 'real' as opposed to the 'unreal' marriage. Thus Victor Radnor, in *One of Our Conquerors*, is technically an adulterous husband, since for the entire duration of the book he is living with his *de facto* wife Nataly, having simply abandoned an earlier, loveless marriage, entered into for the sake of money, and broken off for the sake of love. But Meredith ignores the question of whether Victor should or should not have taken the step he took; the feelings of the deserted wife are simply not raised. The novel is better seen as the portrayal of a *de facto* marriage than a study of adultery. By contrast a minor character in *Diana of the Crossways*, Sir Lukin, reveals far more of Meredith's interpretation of infidelity when he makes a pass at Diana, even though his lunge is instantly rebuffed. Meredith disapproves more of this momentary and abortive betrayal of a wife with her best friend than of Victor's whole life-style, because Sir Lukin's marriage is supposed to be, and normally is, a 'real' marriage, that is, a love-match which has endured. He has Diana so shocked by the slip that her faith in her own ability to live alone in the world is undermined; she rushes headlong into the hasty and unhappy marriage which is the pivot of her troubles.

A not dissimilar, but infinitely more agonised, concern for true and false relationships preoccupies Thomas Hardy though, as with Meredith, the preoccupation with this theme intensifies with his literary development. On the whole the mutual involvement of men and women in the majority of his works makes it unfair to include them in a section devoted to adulterous males. However, *The Woodlanders* certainly centres around Fitzpiers's affair with Mrs Charmond, and the novel can be seen as a relatively simple exploration of the old way of life and the new, with marital infidelity the watershed between the two. For the simple country folk, marriage is a relationship of equality, protectiveness, and 'dear, familiar friendship', grounded in sympathetic interdependence and enduring and staunch affection. Such is the bond between Grace's parents; so successful is it, and so simple are they, that the mere thought of infidelity in their own or anyone else's marriage literally never occurs to them.

Fitzpiers breaks into this tranquil existence with his clever godlessness and roving eye; he plucks Grace as though she were a new peach, and is soon unfaithful for reasons similar to those already presented by the French novels: Grace is too good, too sweet, too anxious to please; her charm diminishes, for Fitzpiers, with the conquering, and his ambitious, vain nature is easily flattered by the unscrupulous and experienced Mrs Charmond. Restlessness and vanity are the internal motivations for his adultery; but Hardy also implies that the clash of the old ways with the new, the simple with the sophisticated, the religious with the godless, is prophetic. Grace will never know the kind of marriage her parents lived, because she herself, through being sent away to school, has become a hybrid between the two modes; and in throwing in her lot with Fitzpiers she has opted for a situation in which adultery is no longer the abhorrence it had been to the generations of her forefathers.

Hardy makes it perfectly clear that Grace, though honourable and upright, is neither spiritless nor unformed, and in this he is more complimentary to her sex than any French author allows himself to be; yet even the latter are beaten at their own game when it comes to the deceived wife in John William de Forest's *Miss Ravenel's Conversion*. Written during America's period of high gentility, this novel is bold in that it dares introduce a physically unfaithful husband, but rigidly conventional in its characterisation. Not only is the virginal bride exceptionally fair-haired and blue-eyed – she is actually called Lillie. Moreover, she is pulled only very reluctantly over 'the lintel of puberty', for she brings her incredibly naïve, father-orientated, doll-loving habits with her to the marriage, and thereafter is constantly doting, adoring and blushing. So delicate is she that she can only tell her husband about their forthcoming parenthood in the dark, and the effect of her pregnancy is to make her not less, but more 'childishly' dependent (the author's word) on him than before. (The nine months however does bring about some change, for – again in the author's words – when she finally gives birth, Lillie attains with miraculous rapidity 'the apotheosis of womanhood'.)

Lillie's husband is several years older than she when he marries her, and has already acquired the habits of hard-drinking and loose living. He is at first uplifted by marriage with the pure Lillie, and is positively sanctified by her impending motherhood. However, he has to take a business trip to Washington, and *en route* falls into the clutches of Lillie's cousin, a vain, amiable, corrupt, and predictably dark-haired Frenchwoman. Carter succumbs to her, though reluctantly at first; we receive the impression that he is a weak man, vacillating between the calls of his higher and lower nature. He would like to have the strength to choose the former, but is unable to withstand the sexual allure of the woman who has now become his mistress. Carter is not quite the pure American boy, but he is more sinned against than sinning.

The one woman author who dares take up the theme of would-be adultery reiterates the message of inner conflict. Although Edith Wharton did not write *The Age of Innocence* till 1920, she sets her story in the New York of 1870; looking with hindsight at the manners, marriage and morality of that time, she endorses the conventional picture of the gulf between the good and the bad woman, and the attraction each exerts over the hapless male. She adopts the conventional symbols : May, the virtuous wife is tall and pale, with fair braids; Ellen, her cousin, has brown hair, and has been Europeanised by a lengthy stay on the Continent and marriage with a foreign husband. Newland, May's husband, does not actually exchange more than a kiss with Ellen, but the fires of passion smoulder within them. Edith Wharton, still a product of the twentieth century no matter when she sets her book, dares show a passionless marriage as dignified, but 'lacking in something'; although Newland does not quite fall, we understand that he would very much like to, and that his reasons are identical to those of Carter, Fitzpiers, Marigny, Camors and Muffat – all swinging from debauchery to moral uplift, and all convinced that virtue and *volupté* are never to be found in the one woman.

Henry James, writing as late as 1904, does not break away from the convention in his portrayal of Prince Amerigo's defection in *The Golden Bowl*. This is all the more surprising in view of James's subtle and complex treatment of the outcome and effects of adultery; nevertheless, his Maggie is initially a naïve and adoring *ingénue*, who refuses to give up a close and intimate relationship with her father even when it works to the detriment of her marriage. However, his wife's tendency to revert to childishness is far from being the Prince's only motivation for an adulterous relationship with Maggie's friend, Charlotte Stant; apart from the difficulty of rebuffing a beautiful former mistress who still lusts after him, Amerigo's susceptibility to his own particular form of vanity also contributes to their mutual involvement. Cherishing a conception of himself as a *galantuomo*, he cannot bear the ignominy of being constantly with Charlotte, after her marriage to Maggie's father, without fulfilling his own expectations of his role; his aesthetic self-image is offended by the moral naïvety of remaining faithful to his wife, when a more alluring and lascivious creature is throwing herself at his head. But the extra subtleties of the Jamesian situation do not deny the familiarity of the *données*: Maggie's inability to be a full and integrated woman, a totally satisfying wife to her husband, is the main cause of his turning to Charlotte.

It seems in fact that, with the exception of Meredith's Richard and Victor, the adulterous husband in Western literature can be seen to be running to a recognisable form; but in Russian literature he seems hardly to run at all. And while his relative scarcity in the English and American novel is related more to those societies' images of themselves than to the actuality, the Russian attitude to the adulterous husband appears to be one not of pretence but of indifference, the question of infidelity being used most frequently to highlight some other, more important, issue.

It was natural, for example, for the Feminist question to raise peripherally the matter of the adulterous male, but as in the case of Pisemsky's novel *In the Whirlpool* the emancipated mistress was of far more interest to the writer than was the faithless husband. Yet even Prince Grigorev shows a new aspect of the attraction of adultery. The reasons for his infidelity remind us superficially of the French situation : having made a suitable alliance with a girl of his own elevated social status, he is not dismayed to find that he has no love for her, but is considerably irritated by the fact that she shares none of his ideas. He provides himself therefore with a self-educated, working-class mistress, of thoroughly *avant-garde* ideas, with whom he reads and discusses

Darwin. The strength of their attachment lies not just in her vivacity and passion, but also in her independent opinions and the intellectual stimulation she offers, for she believes a real man will love her independently of whether he is married to her or not, and will even bring up their children. And while she knows these views make her unpopular with other women, whom she of course threatens, she feels no compunction for a wife who cannot retain her husband's affections.

Grigorev's situation is somewhat the antithesis however of that of the gentleman who may well be considered the outstanding adulterous husband in Russian literature : Stiva Oblonsky can certainly not be charged with seeking out blue-stocking mistresses. Indeed, he, with his unfailing winsomeness, puts more simply, as well as more persuasively than any other errant spouse, the basic attraction of the other woman : even after a good dinner, 'rolls sometimes smell so good you can't resist them'. However, it is important to note that Stiva has been unfaithful only in a passing way; his brief affair with the governess (always fair game for the master of an aristocratic household) is in no way comparable with the consuming passion of a Marigny, or the prolonged liaison of M. de Camors. Stiva's peccadillo is important to the structure of the novel because it sets off the train of events which brings his sister Anna to Moscow, and because it will, when seen in relation to Anna's affair, throw light upon Tolstoy's vision of marriage and sexuality. But it would be misguided to attach too much weight to the episode in itself or to its contribution to the psychology of the adulterous husband. Stiva's motivations are contained within his own character : his shallowness, his dislike of dull responsibilities, his zest for enjoyment and the good things of life, his accommodating though not altogether muffled conscience, and, above all, his ability to lead an existence independent of his simple, 'uninteresting', and faded wife, Dolly. His affairs are, like his nature, shallow and simple. Their very frequency removes their power to seriously affect *his* desire to maintain his family life, though, naturally, their effect on Dolly is much more damaging. Yet she knows he will never leave her – nor even want to. Stiva is incapable of true passion. Although his taste for rolls takes him to the same shop as the other adulterous husbands, he is isolated from them by his lack of intensity. Though one prefers rolls and the other Darwin, he and Prince Grigorev both point to the relatively weak sway of romantic love over the Russian temperament.

Two major points which have emerged from the foregoing examination of the reasons for the infidelity of the nineteenth-century husband are firstly the profundity of motivation common to them all, and secondly the fact that there are some apparent national differences. The most interesting overall inference is that the male operates as a divided person : the aspirations to which he wants to assent are always higher, but weaker, than his physical desires. His basic inner conflict is then acutely aggravated by the fact that the complete woman – that is, one able to cater to both levels of his needs – does not exist. In his eyes or those of his author, womanhood must be divided into two halves, each separately able to satisfy the two halves of *his* divided self. He marries the representative of pure womanhood, but inevitably finds her to be too naïve, too innocent and too sexually inhibited. He therefore seeks external sexual excitement amidst the ranks of the other women, who are experienced, worldly and unrestrained.

The simplicity of the solution is however only apparent. More damaging than the mere fact of the infidelity is the complex effect on both spouses of the culpability engendered in the erring husband. Whatever its source – that is, whether the sort of Order he feels he has broken is religious, social or personal – guilt eats at the heart of the adulterous husband and persuades him that the gulf between his imperfect self and his too-virtuous wife is overwhelming. His self-image suffers, he needs to feel better. His mistress not only provides physical consolation, but, more importantly, restores his self-esteem – for when compared with *her* he personally feels almost virtuous. The sense of inferiority he suffers in the presence of his wife is reversed; the elation of moral superiority floods through him. And the stocks of his mistress go up by leaps and bounds, while those of the wife trail in the dust.

But the situation is not solved. A perverse idealism makes him unwilling to deny that part of his nature which in the first place sought to ally him with a virtuous woman. He does not wish to remain in that halfway position of being superior only to a creature he despises. So he ends up as we have seen, swinging frantically between the two, his divided self cracking further apart, his sense of destructive internal conflict increasing daily. Small comfort now are his aristocratic birth, his money, and his leisure.

The most acute sufferers are found in the French novel, where the arranged marriage also predominates. While the type is also present in the other literatures, it is already evident that the preoccupations of the English novel were leading towards an examination of the writers' beliefs that the adultery of the husband was less significant than the 'genuineness' of the relationship involved. The Russian novel, which provides even fewer examples of the erring husband than the English, tends to treat adultery as part of a wider context of related social issues, and does not readily isolate it.

Altogether the adulterous husband receives a good deal less literary attention than the erring wife. This is consonant with the long tradition that the transgression itself is of greater gravity when *she* 'falls' than when her husband merely 'strays'.

The arranged, the mistaken, the loveless marriage are always the guilty root-causes of adultery on the part of the wife. Sometimes the marriage has all three components, sometimes only one; certainly national attitudes are revealed in the emphasis allotted to each variant. But above all the nineteenth-century author seeks to persuade his readers that women and men are in basically different situations when adultery tempts : men are torn between two contrasting aspects of love, but the conflict faced by women is the one between love and duty, freedom and obligation.

This is not to say that there are no compounding reasons, nor even some which may be more important; but the lovelessness of the marriage is always a contributing factor. For example, no one would want to claim that Emma Bovary's marriage situation was the sole cause of her infidelity; one cannot even say that her marriage was an arranged one in the harshest sense of the word, when her father took good care to enquire how she felt towards Charles. Nevertheless, it was not a real and informed choice on her part, since Charles was the first and only comer. She accepted him because he alone could provide her with the realisation of her dream of a midnight wedding with torches; he was simply the open door to an existence still to prove itself more dreary than her father's farm.

Similarly, a formal contract of marriage is arranged for a half-interested young couple in Huysmans' *En Ménage*; André initiates the formalities when he gets tired of his bachelor situation, characterised by cold meals, missing buttons and frayed cuffs. He negotiates with a friend of the family to marry a suitable girl, on the look-out for a husband. Once introduced, Berthe declares him to be suitable since, although he is an artist, he still has an income. For the cold Berthe however disillusion follows : she finds the transports now permitted by the Church repugnant and dirty. She begins to take pleasure only in the company of other young married women, who egg her on to take a lover, and so, out of disappointment, resentment and an unquenched desire to know if there is really such a thing as love, Berthe succumbs. André, equally dissatisfied, and angry because Berthe will not let him see his old male companions, is almost glad of the excuse to send her packing.

Even more in the sophisticated world of Maupassant, that of the *haute bourgeoisie* bordering on the high political and official circles, is marriage seen as an arrangement that has nothing to do with love. *Bel-Ami* provides several examples : Mme de Marelle, for instance, tells us little about her marriage, but clearly it is an arrangement which allows her almost complete freedom provided she is discreet. Simply because she likes them, she indulges in so many extra-marital relationships that she is practically a professional, though high-class, mistress, only protected from accusations of prostitution by her husband's name. The Walter couple are another variant : M. Walter is a Jewish parvenu, the marriage an exchange of respectability for money. At most it involves a modicum of punctilious affection, but since M. Walter is preoccupied entirely with finance, and since Mme Walter is basically a silly, emotional woman, whose capacity for sexual passion has never been engaged, she falls an easy victim to the first dedicated *arriviste* willing to sacrifice taste to career. The third example is Bel-Ami's own Madeleine, whose motivation is quite simply ambition – she marries Bel-Ami when his journalistic success can be of use to her. In Maupassant's world the true *raison d'être* of a venal and corrupt society is found to lie in luxury, comfort and excess. The theme reappears throughout his novels.

In *Mont-Oriol* the girl is reluctant but uncomprehendingly docile, consenting to marry a fat rich-boy, not ugly but not attractive either, just as she might have agreed to spend the summer at a disagreeable resort. Ironically, she is thrown together at a health spa with the intelligent, impetuous, and equally rich Paul (at his first meeting with Christiane he reeks of the Russian perfume worn by an actress he has recently carried off). Taken seriously by a man for the first time in her life ('her father . . . had always treated her like a child . . . her brother made her laugh but not think . . . her husband believed you could only discuss with your wife what pertained to your life together . . . ')[1] Christiane is easily seduced, to their mutual pleasure. And an almost identical situation overtakes the heroine of *Fort Comme la Mort*, also by Maupassant, whose heroine immediately accepts the advantages of the projected match, like a well brought up child. Lacking any feeling for her husband, she is highly susceptible to the advances of the handsome, sensitive and socially *arrivé* artist who begs to paint her portrait, and succumbs to his caresses without demur.

It must also be noted that the feeling of universal resentment against the arranged marriage and its inevitable consequences – conjugal frustration and extra-marital satisfaction – is not confined to the upper classes. Apart from his picture of the adulterous aristocratic husband in *Nana*, Zola deals with adultery in the lower orders of the bourgeoisie in at least three novels – *La Bête Humaine*, *Thérèse Raquin* and *Pot-Bouille*. In these, marriages are still motivated by considerations of dowry and material advantage, and still cause passivity, lack of response and hostility towards the husband.

However, although adultery is a frequent outcome, Zola is curiously less interested in this than in the other crimes to which the characters turn – as if he simply assumed that in these lower ranks adultery was so routine that it was not worthy of detailed examination. Almost Zola implies that adultery only becomes interesting when it is accompanied by something else; in the lower classes this factor will not be anything in the order of the remorse, shame and conflict highlighting the moral torment of a Count Muffat, but can only be another action at the same mean level as the original sordid affair. It is possible of course that Zola may simply have intended to study *crime*, and found adultery to be an effective catalyst in its perpetration. But in either case the assumptions he makes support the hypothesis that the arranged marriage is the principal cause of marital infidelity. In *La Bête Humaine*, for example, the middle-aged Roubaud falls in love with Séverine to the point where, adoring her from afar, he feels he would marry her without a sou. Nevertheless, the formalities are not ignored, and he receives both dowry-money and patronage from Séverine's guardian. Séverine remains unconsulted, and is quite distinctly *given* in marriage. The resulting relationship is half-familiar to us : the adoration on his part is unusual, but the filial affection and compliantly docile sexual response of Séverine place her in a direct line with Hermangarde, Grace and Lillie. This time, however, it is not the husband who tires of the child-bride, but the latter who falls in love with a young man. Zola insists upon the element of sexual awakening caused by this *coup de foudre* : 'In spite of everything she had remained virginal; now she had given herself for the first time, to a boy whom she loved.'[2]

And similarly does Thérèse Raquin, ground down in a loveless arranged marriage with a dreary, puny, and dull little man, fall in love when passion strikes with its customary invincibility. Untouched by moral qualms she makes no effort to withstand its onslaught.

Finally, ire and indignation over the gulf between morality in preaching and in practice led Zola to write *Pot-Bouille*, in which he paints a picture of universal promiscuity amongst the bourgeoisie. On the 'trottoirs autorisés des salons bourgeois', marriages are arranged by mothers who have taught their daughters 'tout un cours de prostitution décente et permise'. The young men, rendered randy, fall into the prepared trap, and the negotiations close around their heads. The ensuing marriage is distinguished by mutual irritation and indifference. From this point, Zola looks at five women, all of whom commit adultery for reasons which are variants of the common desire to escape the grinding misery of loveless unions and dreary lives. Valérie's physical ill-health leads to a nervous condition which her marriage exacerbates; her shredded nerves lead her to look for consolation with the first comer. Berthe, victim of her parents' efforts to marry her off, finds the promise of rich clothes and fine jewellery to be quite empty, and seeks a more affluent existence through a lover. Marie Pichon is the only female to live up to Zola's own assertion that 'novels are always the source of infidelity in wives'. In the case of Marie, her reading nourishes her desire for a young man with either delicacy or good looks, in contrast

to her brutish husband and her general feeling of disgust for her circumstances; Zola makes it clear that it is scarcely idealism which motivates
Marie, but rather stupidity, naïvety and ignorance. Mme Suzeur, who
has been brought up in a convent, is in a tremor of conflict between
her moral scruples and her desire for love; she solves it by doing 'tout
sauf le coit'; and when Rose rather obscurely commits adultery 'par
maladie de matrice chez la femme' – it is understood that she hopes
to find relief. Thus a picture emerges in which adultery is sought and
taken for granted as the only soporific available in a media-less society,
though in each individual case it is sparked off by a particular misery –
avarice, stupidity, nerves, illness or boredom.

One would expect that in England, where there is good reason to
believe that the coercing of daughters into matrimonial alliances
was far less acceptable than in France, the evil effects of the
arranged marriage would be absent from the literature. Certainly they
are less common. However, abhorrence of the *loveless match* rouses
Thackeray to such ire that he devotes an entire novel to its condemnation.

While the more famous Becky Sharpe is entirely responsible for her
successes and failures in and out of marriage, the less well-known novel,
The Newcomes, is the vehicle for a savage attack upon the marriage-
markets of Victorian upper-class society. English girls were not actually
forced into marriages with unknown suitors, but they were nevertheless
brought up to understand that wealth and rank – desirable if not
essential attributes in any potential husband – could be acquired in
exchange for the delights hinted at by an elegant pair of shoulders
or a pretty ankle. The fact that such transactions were implemented
by parents and friends, and sanctioned by church weddings, so angered
Thackeray that he exposes no less than six pairs of relationships all
showing the blighting of true love by the marriage of interest. Re-
stricted as he was in what he might or might not write about, he nevertheless allows one of these marriages to terminate in the adulterous
flight of the persecuted wife with another man. Inevitably he avoids
not only sordid detail, but also any serious study of the triangular
situation; however, we are given to understand that Clare's flight arises
from the physical brutality of her husband. This case of conjugal
violence is, interestingly, a rare if not unique motivation for adultery
in the novel, and it might appear as singularly important. But in fact
it seems more the case that in employing this tactic Thackeray was
actually dodging the real issues. Absolutely ungentlemanly behaviour
he could afford simply to dismiss, letting the point make itself; the
muddier but more turgid waters of *discreet* marital infidelity was a
stream he was more chary of wetting his feet in, simply because he
might be expected to delve deeper. Unfortunately his case against the

marriage of interest, and its failure to conform to the sentimental Victorian model of the successful love-match, lacks conviction in areas other than its relationship to adultery : his perfect wife, Laura Pendennis, is, unlike some of Trollope's genuinely admirable women, a perfectly insufferable prig.

If the arranged marriage is not in itself a vital feature of either the English novel or of the American, it certainly plays a role in the Russian, though a distinct sense of uneasiness accompanies it. Both sides of the question are aired with striking frequency : Tatiana is in fact married off, as was her mother; but there are other characters in *Evgenii Onegin* who marry 'honourably for love'. The breakdown of Fedia's marriage in *A Nest of the Gentry* is ascribed to its being a love match, that of the Grigorev's in *In the Whirlpool* to theirs being arranged. In fact the dilemma of the arranged versus the love marriage seems to be a constant preoccupation, with the middle ground of worry and confusion exemplified by Princess Shcherbatsky, who cannot decide whether to marry off her daughters in the French manner, or allow them the freedom of choice customary in England. Personally she leans towards the former, being secretly convinced that to let a girl select her own marriage partner is tantamount to letting a child play with a knife.

The feeling that arranged marriages were unworthy grew stronger with the growth of feminism and the concern for individual personal freedom : a particular harrowing instance of the arranged marriage is depicted in Markevich's *The Forgotten Question*. Not only is Liubov Petrovna married against her will at an early age, but her husband, whom she never loved, has after sixteen years of marriage had a stroke. The paralysis is so bad he cannot even speak but his devotion is revealed in the pitiful eyes he keeps constantly fixed upon her. We learn that even though the husband had once been healthy and handsome, Liubov Petrovna's love had been irrevocably given to a poor student, unacceptable to her parents. In spite of her husband's jealous temperament, Liubov Petrovna makes a practice from the first of consoling herself by a gay and flirtatious life. However, she keeps within the bounds of propriety until, sixteen years later, she listens to the persuasive arguments of the sophisticated Baron Felsen. Beginning by attacking the impossibility of a marriage where there is no perfect harmony, he goes on to propose a theory that society women not only lack the bourgeois virtues of the faithful wife and good mother, but are right in doing so, for while these qualities are estimable, they are limited. If the world had relied entirely on such dull aspirations, there would be no Helen, no Paris, no Homer – in short, no culture. He further argues that since every man's happiest hours are those spent with a woman, whether lawfully or not, then a woman *must* give happiness – it is her bounden duty to do so. He concedes that the woman should receive some happiness in return for what she gives; however, she is so idealistic that the man is often unable to fulfil the ideal – hence he cannot be held to account for the unhappiness of the abandoned female. The Baron rounds off his campaign by an alarming picture of women who perish or fade before their time, frozen by the icy atmosphere in which they are forced to live, or beaten down by the selfish demands of the very husband they should love with freely given emotion.

Liubov Petrovna's scruples melt before such an accomplished verbal onslaught, and she speedily finds arguments to justify her fall : she is thirty years old and has not yet known happiness; it cannot be a sin to love; it cannot be a duty to stay with a husband whom you hate. When reproached on the grounds of the promises made during the wedding ceremony she simply asks who made the vows – she, or those who forced the marriage upon her. The dilemma has been put more explicitly than most novels were prepared to, and may be said to have something in common with the English concern for 'true relationships', although the truth of both married and extra-marital relationships is frequently explored by Markevich's compatriot, Anton Chekhov.

In *The Lady with a Dog*, for example, the lady's indifference to her husband is revealed both in her unconcerned length of stay away from him (a matter of some weeks) and in the fact that when asked, she cannot even say what his job is. The liaison is seen to bring something meaningful into the drab lives of both her and her lover, just as the pre-adulterous pursuit by a neighbour makes Sophia Petrovna in *Misfortune* see how baseless is her assumption that she loves her husband. She suddenly realises that all her protestations are only half-true. And the realisation that she secretly likes it when the neighbour embraces her knees accompanies the admission, to herself, that she is in fact indifferent to her husband, that their marriage is a mere conventional form, and that there is a vast gap between her true feelings and those she imagines herself to have – the ones society says she should have. Marriage has lulled her into indifference and acceptance; the opportunity for infidelity presents itself as the chance to experience positive emotion for the first time.

Even the fall of Anna Karenina is directly attributable to her love-starved existence with a husband allotted her (in a way quite contrary to Kitty's free acceptance of Levin) for reasons of social suitability and financial security. Everything about Karenin – the lifeless artificiality of his existence, the coolness of his nature, the repressiveness of his beliefs, the stiffness of his manner, and his sticking-out ears and cracking joints – denotes utter incompatibility with a woman outstanding for her warmth, responsiveness, vivacity and ability to love. Yet it is not until the first hint of Anna's interest in Vronsky that Karenin looks at his wife for the first time. As if she were a bird in a cage, he had shut the door on her on the day of their marriage and never since bothered to glance between the bars at his captive. In the words so pregnantly spoken by Vronsky himself, 'How often do marriages of convenience crumble into dust precisely because that very passion which was inadmissible suddenly asserts itself.'[3] The blind force of insidious parental pressure is at work also in Pierre Bezukhov's first marriage to the Princess Hélène. 'As if absentmindedly, yet also with total certainty that it all had to be, Prince Vasili did everything to make Pierre marry his daughter . . . Something always drew him towards people who were stronger or richer than he, and he was endowed with the rare skill of being able to catch exactly the right moment for making use of people.'[4] The incongruity of a union between the worldly, corrupt Hélène and the bumbling, earnest Pierre is ignored for the sake of the 'suitability' of the match – a criterion which I think has been amply proven to be a persistent and widespread source of wifely infidelity, though the force of the pressure may range from gentle persuasion to forceful inducement, and may be exerted by circumstances as well as by parents.

From the evidence so far presented, it might be supposed that the frigidity of the arranged marriage was the sole and sufficient cause of wifely infidelity. But since we have already seen that in England the parentally arranged marriage was not at all the norm, and that in Russia it was present but not universally approved, it is obvious that indifference, sexual frustration and boredom may appear like weeds even in the garden of domestic bliss.

Perhaps it is because all the authors are male that none of them deals with sexual frustration on the part of a wife motivated in her choice of marriage partner not by love alone, but also by faith and hope in a rewarding sexual partnership. It is certainly the case that this theme is never broached overtly, though along with Huysmans and his Berthe, Meredith comes close to it in his perfect, though *en passant*, vignette of a Mrs Blathenoy, 'young in years and experience, ten months wedded, disappointedly awakened, enlivened by the hour, kindled by a novel figure of a man, fretful for a dash of imprudence . . .'*

While no other writer expresses quite so succinctly the unhappy situation of the frustrated wife, a comparable frustration takes a stronger, subtler, and more insidious form in James's Charlotte Stant, who has

---

* G. Meredith, *One of Our Conquerors* (London, 1914) p. 205. Meredith is unusual amongst Victorian writers in referring almost directly to sexual desire as a ubiquitous and motivating force in society. A concession to delicacy lies in his use of the euphemism 'electricty': Dartrey feels sparks shooting from Mrs Blathenoy's arm into his own.

married the father of her friend Maggie for the sake of financial security.

James shows that the relationship between Charlotte and the Prince is primarily a physical one, but implies that they use their common impulse to be together as an actual justification – or rather a rationalisation : 'If such unarranged but unerring encounters gave the measure of the degree in which people were, in the common phrase, meant for each other, no union in the world had ever been more sweetened with rightness.' But he further insists that Charlotte herself is the prime mover : 'What in fact most often happened was that her rightness went, as who should say, even further than his own; they were conscious of the same necessity at the same moment; only it was she, as a general thing, who most clearly saw her way to it.'[5] Once we have Charlotte's measure, we can entertain no illusions about her; James's portrait of her is not harsh, but it is judgemental.

Marie de Vionnet, on the other hand, is seen only through the ingenious eyes of Strether, whom we accompany on his painful search for a truth which, when it finally comes out, is almost too much for him to take. Strether starts off with the assumption that Chad has got himself entangled with a bad French woman, and accepts his mission to prise Chad away from her with not an ounce of sympathy for the woman, Marie. But having met her, and been utterly disarmed by her charm, he is glad to believe anything that people put into his mind to re-credit her. First he swallows the notion that Chad is really in love with Mme de Vionnet's daughter. When this belief is proved false he assures himself that whatever Marie does is excused by the fact that she was the unwilling victim of an arranged marriage, and her husband a brute who has long since deserted her. When forced to acknowledge that there really is some kind of liaison between Marie and Chad after all, he is still determined to see it as a 'high, fine friendship' capable of exerting a wonderful influence. Cotton-woolled inside a cocoon of self-delusion, Strether staunchly refuses to look at anything but the beautiful effect of Marie and Chad; and so his shock is all the greater when, in a chance encounter in the country, the bald truth about their relationship is at a stroke revealed. Mme de Vionnet *is* having a perfectly ordinary affair with Chad, and always was; her interest is simply sexual, though it is tinged with that slight unnaturalness and deep insecurity that accompanies a liaison between an older woman and a younger man. The 'deep, deep truth of the intimacy revealed' jolts him into admitting that all the time he had really been trying to 'suppose nothing'. The combination of the hypocrisy and the sexuality is stark, and the shock is great; what it means for the reader as much as for Strether is that without doubt there are women who deliberately, freely and lucidly engage in adultery without any illusions about their own motives, no matter how much they succeed in deceiving others. It was Strether who needed and made excuses for Marie, not she for herself.

On the whole, James himself does not make it part of his concern to probe the reasons which lead women into adultery; rather, he uses the adulterous situation already arrived at as a kind of laboratory glass-case through which he peers at the behaviour taking place underneath. Thus for lack of explicit comment from the author we are forced to assume lust or restlessness, or marginal improvement in their personal situations, to be the motivations of the adults in *What Maisie Knew*, all four of whom deceive both their legal spouses and their lovers. To the original set of parents, Beale and Ida Farrange, marriage is 'the unbroken opportunity to quarrel' – as indeed their divorced state also is – and it is not unnatural that when opportunity knocks, as it regularly does, they should seek more congenial partners. Through Maisie's unconsciously sagacious eyes, though, James offers a clue he refuses to state overtly to Ida's personality : when by chance the child meets the mother with one of her numerous lovers, she feels an uprush of strange deep pity, and pleads passionately for a declaration of love for her mother from the new gentleman. Embarrassed and amused, he gives it; Maisie, in dead earnest still, then asks him to provide the stability she senses her mother desperately needs. 'You do love her? . . . Then don't do it just for a little while . . . like all the others.'[6]

She is equally moved at meeting her father with one of his girlfriends, and extends to him a pity unshared by the reader, to whom Farrange appears a selfish and carnal brute. Maisie seems to feel that there is some deep, unspecified need in him which is not being answered by his mistresses. 'To give him something, to give here on the spot, was all her own desire.'[7] But not even James is willing to play the psychologist to the extent of analysing Beal's lust in terms of emotional deprivation; all he reveals is what the eyes of a sensitive child can glimpse. In spite even of *The Golden Bowl*, James, like the majority of the English and Russian writers, is content to accept that adultery exists, and that only its course and outcome – never its motivations – are worthy of investigation.

How striking is the contrast with Flaubert, whose account of Emma's sexual development is like a carefully prepared brief, each page of which contains a record of some aspect of incipient romantic love. The stifling arranged marriage,* the heat of lust – both were contributing factors in Emma's affairs, and are not to be ignored; but without the thrall of passion Emma would be buried in the dust of oblivion in her

---

* Flaubert was deeply impressed by the fact that his parents' marriage was a love match, in which the wife loved her husband, after thirty-five years of married life, as passionately as on the first day. (See E. Starkie, *Flaubert: The Making of the Master*.)

stagnating provincial village. Victim to it, she emerges as the anti-heroine of a revitalised cult of romantic love interpreted by Flaubert as the most damaging disease in contemporary French society.

The formation which will culminate in Emma's adultery begins early. Her inherent temperament is fed by the reading-matter she finds at school; it ranges through all the categories of 'Romantic' literature : the exotic *(Paul et Virginie)*, the unworldly (giving rise to her religious phase), the stormy and historic (Sir Walter Scott) and the sentimental and melancholic (the *méandres lamartiniens*). She sees matrimony in terms of a candlelit midnight wedding (though in the event the time and trappings are directed otherwise by her father); but marriage itself utterly disappoints her craving to experience the *félicité, passion* and *ivresse* she has read about in her books. She begins to dream of a happiness that can only exist in faraway places – chalets in Switzerland, cottages in Scotland. She goes into the garden at night and recites by moonlight all she can remember of the passionate love poems she has learnt by heart, or sings melancholy adagios in the hope of rousing herself to a more passionate appreciation of Charles. But all in vain. She finds herself as calm before as after, Charles as pedestrian as ever. After some time she acknowledges her discontent; the first words she utters in the book are, 'Pourquoi, mon Dieu, suis-je mariée?'[8]

The new avenue of wilful escape from everyday reality begins with her dreams of town life – the bustle of the streets, the murmur of the theatre, and above all the balls where the heart throbs and the senses faint. This is incipient passion *à la* de Rougemont indeed – no material lover is needed, only the opportunity to be in love with love, to swoon to real life, to half-die. Like a stone thrown into a pond, Emma's monotonous existence is disrupted by the invitation to a real ball; and there she finds the waltz as overpowering as she had imagined – as whirling and twirling, in fact, as the giddy ride in the cab with Léon at the height of their mutual passion. Slowly her fantasies come to crystallise in a particular town. Paris is in her mind the symbol of all exotica – and also perhaps, of erotica. She buys a map, and in her imagination strolls the boulevards, climbs every flight of steps, shops in expensive stores. Her Paris is peopled with unreal characters, full of 'idealistic aspirations' and 'delirious fantasies'; she approaches the de Rougemont ideal almost explicitly in her creation of a world between heaven and earth, somewhere in the clouds, somewhere sublime. As for the rest of the world, it was nowhere, lost, non-existent. Moreover, the closer she is to things the more she turns away from them. 'Everything around her – the dreary countryside, the stupid townspeople, the mediocrity of her life – all seemed accidental, a kind of special trap she was caught in, whilst beyond it stretched, as far as the eye could see, a huge land of pleasure and passion.'[9] Confounding the sensualities of luxury with those of the heart she makes unreality a condition of love. From this point begins the expansion of selfishness, the growth of self-love seen by de Rougemont as an aspect of the passion-love that ultimately seeks only the luxury of its own death, holding in contempt the happiness of the other. It is accompanied by neglect of all material details of daily life – her music, her drawing, her sewing, her household chores – even the preparations for her future child. She is in a highly nervous state, over-ready to fall in love, but – and this is where Flaubert and de Rougemont are at one in their interpretation of romantic love – it is not physical love that she craves. The non-consummation of her first affair with Léon makes de Rougemont's point : Emma is at this time the prey of romantic passion. Not until her affair with Rodolphe does she fall into the grip of carnal desire.

The Rodolphe affair is in fact a kind of physical parody of the idealised relationship Emma has so far maintained with Léon. Rodolphe exists on a lower plane than Emma and Léon – literally, Flaubert puts it, an animal existence. His intelligence is nonetheless perspicacious, and he sees immediately just where Emma is emotionally, except that with his totally animal nature he cannot imagine the echelons on which her imaginery activity operates. All he says about her is true, but it is incomplete : she has a stupid husband with dirty finger nails, of whom she has become tired; while he is always out on visits, she stays at home darning the socks; she is utterly bored, would like to live in town and dance the polka every night; she is so yawning for love she will fall for the first gallant address . . . and she will be hard to get rid of . . . His estimate is remarkably accurate, and his game commensurately successful, for he launches his attack in an area Emma hardly knows exists – that of physical desire. His declaration of love at the fair is a brilliant success, even though he is only half aware that in wooing her with the *arguments* of passionate love, while there is nothing more in his intent than rapid physical seduction, he has hit upon the one tactic sure to topple her – fate has destined not their bodies but their souls for each other.

Emma is lulled into believing that here is another romantic situation : but Rodolphe cunningly manœuvres to let her cool her heels for six weeks, thus inducing her hitherto quiescent physical desires to betray her. By the time Rodolphe turns up to take her for a lonely ride in the forest, where the sudden emergence of the cloud-hidden sun seems like God's seal of approval,* and treats her alternately to a masterful courtship such as she has never known with Charles and a respectful solicitude which makes her fear she will lose him, she is thoroughly undone. Her seduction is accomplished with consummate ease. The

* The unfailing belief that either God or a deceased mother approve from 'on high' is a recurrent characteristic of the adulterous wife.

early days of their affair moreover provide her with her biggest role to date – that of the woman-with-a-lover. The 'légion lyrique de ces femmes adultères se mit à chanter dans sa mémoire avec des voix de soeurs qui la charmaient'.[10] Thus, paradoxically, Emma's romantic formation, which actually protected her against physical consummation with Léon, is in the end her undoing with Rodolphe. Her marriage, her boredom, her newly awakened sexual desires, her romantic dreams – all contribute to her fall. How clever was Rodolphe, as Flaubert warns us from the very first!

There are pale reflections of Emma in one or two other novels, notably the heavily derivative Kate of George Moore's *A Mummer's Tale*. But Emma was not in fact a prototype; in spite of the banal familiarity of the adolescent girl with her head stuffed full of romantic nonsense, of the wife standing at her door yearning for a knight on a white horse, the fact remains that no other serious novelist of the nineteenth century made a detailed study of the phenomenon of the romantic wife – though films like *The Last Picture Show* have taken up the theme in this era.

Hardy alone stands beside Flaubert, not because he produces any Emma-like heroine, but because he too interprets adultery in terms not of physical lust, but of the desire for desire, that love of love which characterises the passion-love described by de Rougemont.

This dimension of Hardy's philosophy has been convincingly argued by J. Hillis Miller in his work studying the forces of 'distance and desire' as dual and opposing compulsions in the human psyche. Taking as a key sentence the statement found in Hardy's notebook, 'Love lives on propinquity but dies of contact', Miller claims that for Hardy the God of the Bible was superseded by a force which he called the Immanent Will, and defined as the secret energy moving both nature and history and causing in its effects more pain than joy. The only safety from pain lies in passivity, in not causing greater ripples in the Immanent Will than necessary. Hardy, knowing this, was nonetheless fascinated by what happens when man does meddle in the forces that shape our lives, when he chooses to get involved. In particular, he is drawn to examine the theme of fascination of one person for another, because it is the only alternative to the two beliefs he has already rejected – the first, that there is a God manipulating the lives of men for good ends; the second, that man is capable of being his own source of order and determination. Hardy therefore explores the idea that love means finding some one other person, neither God nor self, who appears to radiate love and energy around him, who seems to establish a measure of the worth of all things. In this he may be said to be trying to work out an answer to his personal nihilism, though it is a nihilism which has very little in common with either the French or Russian forms. From it springs the essential hopelessness of the situations he creates : fascination for another is born only after boredom with the first partner has set in. The protagonists have always committed themselves previously in love or marriage and have tired of the old mate. If it was a married situation, then it is usually a hastily arranged and ill-assorted one; on both counts a potentially adulterous situation is the given starting point. Thus, from the five Hardy novels which bear on adultery, a kind of table can be worked out :

1. Grace marries Fitzpiers, loves Giles
2. Jude marries Arabella, loves Sue
3. Sue marries Phillotson, loves Jude
4. Eustacia marries Clym, loves Damon
5. Damon marries Tamson, loves Eustacia
6. Henchard marries Susan, loves Lucetta
7. Tess lives with Alec, loves Angel

In point of fact (as we shall discuss later), Hardy reaches the threshold of adultery, but rarely goes further. Eustacia and Damon only hover around its edges, and although Tess, out of need for protection, goes to live with Alec, it is doubtful whether on either psychological or technical grounds one can consider her married to a husband who deserted her before consummating the marriage.

Jude the Obscure comes closer to the issue; Jude is tricked into marriage with the unappealing Arabella, and even before he marries her is well aware of what a disastrous match it must be. After the event, schooled by a combination of conventional morality and religious beliefs, Jude will not go beyond the limits of cousinly friendship in his relationship with Sue, who impulsively marries the devoted but limited Phillotson. Less blatantly ill-matched than the Jude–Arabella union, Sue and Phillotson have nevertheless built their marriage on shaky ground : Sue's motives are prompted by anything but ardent love. She marries Phillotson partly because she has lost her job and needs respectability, partly to prevent herself wanting the divorced Jude to marry her when she fears she would hurt him in marriage, partly to punish herself for wanting Jude at all, and partly for what she terms 'the love of being loved'. The union fails, and Sue finds herself unable to resist turning to Jude, with whom she finally goes to live. Hardy intends the reader to see Sue and Jude as destined for each other by some compulsion which overrides the normal concepts of adulterous/ false, legal/true, unions; it is in deference to this concept of relationships that Sue leaves her husband to live with her lover. About legal marriage she says, 'I think I should begin to be afraid of you, Jude, the moment you had contracted to cherish me under a government stamp, and I was licenced to be loved on the premises – Ugh, how horrible and sordid.'[11]

And how tortuous. Of course the reader feels Sue and Jude are made for each other; and of course Hardy creates barrier after barrier to their union. The 'true' relationship is prevented, the legal one falsified. Infinitely more complicated than either passionate love's love of desire, or Meredith's straightforwardly 'true' illegal unions, Hardy's picture of self-punishing and self-frustrating love makes plain adultery seem like mere parents' play.

The preoccupation of the English novelists, as we have already glimpsed, lay not in fact with passion, or rather not with passion *per se*, but with the authenticity of the interpersonal relationship, of which sexual attraction may be only a part, and whose legality is not the most important aspect. Meredith depicts two runaway wives: the first appears extremely briefly at the beginning of *The Ordeal of Richard Feveral* as Richard's mother, who runs from Sir Austin's cold egoism to a poet's warmth, and receives sympathetic treatment from the author (Sir Austin's inability to forgive her is cuttingly portrayed as irritation at her ingratitude in rejecting what he had condescendingly offered her). The other is Lord Ormont's Aminta, who is the heroine and major subject of the novel of that name. Aminta is unsatisfactorily married in the first place, in that her union with Lord Ormont was effected hastily, in an embassy in Madrid, and that her husband will not acknowledge her publicly when they return to England. When he delivers the final blow of refusing her entrance to his ancestral seat, Aminta runs away with her ex-schoolboy lover who has reappeared as Lord Ormont's secretary. The new twist, however, is that Aminta is seeking not just sexual satisfaction, nor even balm to a wounded pride, but rather opportunity to be of service to the world – she and Matey plan to set up a co-educational school in Switzerland. Their ideals and self-righteousness are summed up in a slightly parsimonious plea for understanding and vindication :

> I shall not consider we are malefactors. We have the world against us. It will not keep us from trying to serve it. And there are hints of humane opinions; it's not all a huge rolling block of a Juggernaut. Our case could be pleaded before it . . . We commit this indiscretion. With a world against us our love and our labour are on trial; we must have great hearts, and if the world is hostile towards us we are not to blame it. In the nature of things it could not be otherwise. My own soul, we have to see that we do – though not publicly, not insolently, offend good citizenship. But we believe – I with my whole faith, and I may say it of you – that we are not offending the Divine Law.[12]

Thus adultery is in the eyes of the perpetrators, at least, vindicated; Aminta has already declared that in her unnatural relationship with

Lord Ormont she was no wife, but a slave. Now she uses an illegal union to give her the opportunity she needs to justify her existence to the world.

She has remarkable similarities with some of the Russian New Women, in particular Chernyshevsky's Vera, who in *What's to be done?* shows what to do, the Nihilist way.

The Nililist philosophy of marriage had already been expounded by Belinsky:

> A time is coming . . . when there will be no senseless forms and ceremonies, when no terms or conditions will be imposed upon feeling, when there will be no duty and obligation, no husbands and wives, but lovers of both sexes; when the loved one will come to her lover and say, 'I love another', and he will answer, 'I cannot be happy without you; I shall suffer for my whole life, but go to him whom you love . . .'[13]

(The somewhat morally earnest trend was satirised frequently: notably in Tolstoy's unpublished plays *The Nihilist* and *A Rotten Family* but also, if briefly, in the person of Lebeziatnikov, in *Crime and Punishment,* who declares impassionedly that if his wife took a lover, he would say to her 'My dear, until now I only loved you – now I respect you!')

Although Chernyshevsky subscribed to the new belief in true unions, the rights and wrongs of marriage and adultery were only a very small part of the greater question of the freedom of the individual. In his review of Turgenev's *Asya* he shows his impatience with sexual concerns ('Away with erotic problems. The modern reader has no interest in them') and elsewhere was heard to comment that the woman question was all very well when there was nothing more important to be discussed. Nevertheless, *What's to be Done?* was the holy writ of the Nihilist view of sexual relationships, its aim being to advocate free unions and female emancipation. However, the freedom they advocate is far from licence, and the emancipation they advocate entails enormous devotion to work. The New Man and the New Woman subscribe to a philosophy of rational egoism, admiring and propagating such qualities as cold-blooded practicality, regularised and calculating activity, recognition of individual freedom, the subordination of emotion to reason, the clarification of feelings by meditation, and the rejection of traditional social and religious conventions and beliefs. They also believe that the woman must devote herself to serious non-profitmaking work: Vera runs a kind of dressmaking co-operative.

The opening of the story shows her still living with her greedy and ambitious parents and proving that she is the true New Woman by refusing to be married off to the rich and repulsive suitor they produce

for her. She and Lopukhov, the tutor of her younger brother, find they
are kindred spirits, and prevail upon Vera's parents to allow them to
marry. From the beginning the relationship is startlingly unphysical:
their first kiss occurs when they think they had better have a practice
to avoid embarrassment during the wedding ceremony. Love is declared to be an admissible, even desirable, emotion, but it must be
good-humoured and undisturbing; it should not lead to disorder like
loss of appetite – the New People only fade away when love goes
wrong: when they marry, normal intimacy is replaced by courtesy,
eroticism by comradeship and work in common. Vera and Lopukhov's
marriage appears to remain unconsummated, since they do not share
a bedroom and only visit each other's room when fully dressed. Nevertheless, they pass three years of productive, contented, and tranquil
existence. Why then does the New Woman suddenly fall in love with
her husband's best friend? Vera understands via a dream (shades of
Tatiana) that she loved not Lopukhov, but the deliverance he brought
her. She writes him a note in which the rational determination to keep
on loving her husband struggles with the *coup de foudre* she has been
smitten by in her love for Kirsanov. Real love appears to be irresistible
and as unpredictable for the New People as for the old. Loudly utter-
ing such phrases as 'I cannot live without you' and 'I would happily
die for you', the New Woman turns out to be putty in the hands of
old-fashioned love, and very torn about giving way to it. But give she
must; the rationality of changing one's partner when the situation
requires it is the vital message of what *was* to be done.

In general the findings about the motivations of the unfaithful wife
are rather unsatisfactory, for although the arranged marriage appears
to contribute considerably to an unsatisfactory conjugal life, two
essential qualifications must be made in regard to this surmise.

   The first is that the male authors are patently more willing to blame
convention, circumstances or parents for an unhappy marriage than to
probe any sexual inadequacy on the part of the husband: a few may
touch upon the subject, but even they do so only in an oblique and
quite non-analytic way.

   The second point is their lack of imagination in trying to consider
the real causes of dissatisfaction in marriage which can scarcely be
considered to be of the sort where the parents hold a gun at the daughter's head. (No choices are made between marriage and the convent
nor even between marriage and a régime of bread-and-water.) All
three societies are simply portrayed as united in their tolerance of
marriages entered into for the sake of financial gain, protection, ambition – or, in that cold but universally understood word, security. But
from there on the novelists fail to pursue the everyday circumstances of

the marriage. Flaubert excepted, there is little analysis of the causes of dissatisfaction we can easily guess at ourselves; the boredom arising in a house where the sewing, cooking and child-care are all the domain of the servants; the impossibility of developing either intimate or stimulating conversation between husband and wife when the same servants are always about; the lack of resources available to the wife with conventional, but in fact very inadequate, education; the limited range and nature of the activities available to her outside the home ... it makes the modern reader wonder exactly when the phrase 'driven up the wall' originated.

Some grasp of the situation must have been interiorly nurtured by the English and Russian authors, whose New Women are allowed to be ardent and active protagonists for their emancipation into the world at large; thus the theme of 'authentic' versus false relationships emerges as a justification for the action of the errant wife, and as a pointer to the future. And perhaps the veiled hints of sexual frustration may be the first crack in the door that was to continue to widen until Kinsey could shove it open with his shoulder.

But the fact remains that the loveless marriage-arrangement (perhaps a more applicable term than the arranged marriage) is seen by the writers to be the *grand coupable* of the nineteenth century; and in this we must see a difference with our own age, where it would surely be true to say that discovery of incompatibility *following* the *love-match* most commonly entails the success of the lover.

And so to the lover we now turn – to those monsters who beguile and seduce the unhappy spouses, and to those victims who are enveigled in their snares.

As with the adulterous wife, few writers pursue to any depth the motivation of the lover; and inevitably, the writers who tell us least about why the third party chooses or accepts to become involved in already established marital partnerships are those who simply subscribe to common assumptions. For example, in *The Woodlanders*, Hardy probes with painful care the outcome of a marriage between a 'good' girl and a born philanderer, but he still, in passing, takes it for granted that among the village girls there will be those who need no persuasion to roll in the hay. And in spite of the enormous difference in tone and style between Suke Damson, the local slut, and the elegant Mrs Charmond, the latter's reasons for seducing Fitzpiers are no more analysed than Suke's. Mrs Charmond copulates on silk couches instead of scratchy bracken, but the desire for flattery and physical pleasure is assumed to be common to their equally bored lives – even though their tedium is caused in Suke's case by work and in Mrs Charmond's by idleness. In neither case does Hardy attempt to postulate any more profound motivation.

De Forest gives a fuller account of Mrs Larue, confident in his belief that the race of women is neatly divisible into the two classes of the Virtuous Blonde and the Wicked Brunette. Mrs Larue is 'as corrupt as possible without self-reproach, and as amiable as possible without self-restraint'. Interestingly, de Forest makes it clear that she is motivated not by passion but by vanity, stressing that she is cool and sure in her coquetries, caring little for that 'divin sens du génésique'. The threat of the violently passionate female was so terrifying, it seems, that she made a genteel author chary of handling her even in the role of the mistress. Part of this concern relates to the technical problem of how to dispose of the Bad Female once her damage has been done. It would be culpably imprudent to let her loose in society only to do more harm. She must be seen to be dealt with. So, de Forest chooses to let her go free, but makes sure she never had any real claws. Edith Wharton's Ellen, on the other hand, is packed off back to Europe, where it is assumed she poses less of a threat – perhaps because French society is tougher in its recorded dealings with profligate women. One has only to think of Choderlos de Laclos' methods. Unfortunately smallpox was not a raging disease in de Forest's America, nor was the convent a usual place of consignment.

Assumptions of a different sort lie behind Turgenev's picture of the lover. He is typically a male (Litvinov in *Smoke*, Sanin in *Torrents of Spring*) and is distinguished not by his potential danger, but by his weakness. The strong woman/weak man tradition is expressed in terms of the sexual attraction exerted by the former over the latter, regardless of marriage ties. But the lover is always unable to accept the challenge; his *lack* of passion fails to catalyse the triangle into a fulfilling rearrangement – and the whole thing falls apart. The Russians were indeed hampered in their emulation of Western romantic love by the unavailability of suitable protagonists.

The motivations of the lover begin to emerge more sharply with Maupassant. Bel-Ami, like his predecessor Eugène de Rastignac, uses the wives of influential men to gain entrée into the highest circles, and to acquire positions leading to professional advancement. Maupassant uses adultery as the venal symbol of a society 'repue, gorgée de plaisirs' during a period of economic stability and false security. At the same time he weeps bitter tears for the nihilistic despair he sees around him. Between the unbounded hopes of man and the narrowness of his pleasures and joys there is no correlation; happiness is impossible, except of the most immediate and selfish kind. What does it all matter, who is there to care? Women use, and are used : Bel-Ami marries the wife of the friend he had cuckolded till his death. only to be deceived himself.

The only comparable account of cupboard – or rather staircase –

love is the heavily derivative George Moore, whose hero Lewis Seymour is modelled on Bel-Ami and is seen to scale the heights of the British Academy via the shoulders of a married woman with a Good Heart and an absconding husband. But the bite is absent; Moore complained in a letter to Zola, 'I was obliged to attenuate dreadfully, but what could I do?' Perhaps he was of some service to those members of the English public to whom Maupassant was inaccessible; but to the reader of *Bel-Ami* Moore's usefulness is limited to what his timorousness reveals of the censorship operating in Victorian England.

There are other more subtle ways of using adultery for the acquisition of a required good. Already rich and assured of his position in American society, Chad Newsome has no need to use women in the ordinary way of ambitious self-advancement; but he does trade love for whatever it is Strether is convinced he has acquired through his intimate contact with French society – some rare and indefinable veneer of culture, polish, experience and worldly wisdom now forever grafted on to the raw American youth. Although twenty years separate *Bel-Ami* from *The Ambassadors,* and one hardly recognises the Paris of Maupassant in the silken toils which charmingly wind themselves around Strether, in point of fact the difference is not so great. Both pictures offer a Paris of distinction and elegance, of venality and amorality, and both paint the lover as someone who offers a semblance of love in exchange for something he lacks, whether it be social position or acquired sophistication. For all the wonderful things the relationship with his French mistress is supposed to have done for him in Strether's eyes, Chad emerges as less than great – as, indeed, a user.

Maupassant is much less savage towards his other lovers; both Oliver in *Fort comme la Mort* and Paul in *Mont-Oriol* find their level somewhere between mere carnality and the heights of everlasting love; nor are either of them motivated by money or ambition. Maupassant appears not to question the assumption that if a man is thrown together by circumstances with a charming and unhappily married woman, he will naturally try, in her interests as much as his, to offer some consolation for her sad situation. Nor will he regard himself as acting immorally.

And this is in fact the initial viewpoint of Anna's lover Vronsky; before his love has grown into the overwhelming passion it reaches at its peak, Vronsky's behaviour is dictated by his view of society:

In his Petersburg world the people fell into quite different categories. The lesser breed were vulgar, stupid, and above all ridiculous people, who believed that every husband should live with the woman he was married to, that girls should be virtuous, women chaste, and men manly, self-controlled, and strong . . . But the other sort, the real people, to which they all belonged, had to be above all broadminded, bold, gay, and willing to succumb without a blush to every passion, and to laugh at all else.[14]

He first thinks of Anna as a delightful object of dalliance; by the time he has realised that neither her character nor her circumstances will concede an easy conquest, he himself has succumbed to that ambiguous mixture of desire of possession and delight in the presence of the other called falling in love. But despite his carelessly selfish approach to women, it is not the case that Vronsky is a seducer of the Rodolphe type. The essential quality of the Don Juan is his restless desire to see, conquer, and pass on to the next challenge; Rodolphe was already wondering how to get rid of Emma before he had even begun to plan his seduction campaign.*

Vronsky stands apart from Rodolphe precisely because of his ability to get off the merry-go-round he was on before he met Anna; we know that his meeting with her will arrest him, just as he soon accepts that his love for her will keep him chained, destroying his interest in all other women. Léon accepts a similar devotion to Emma; motivated by sheer adoring love, at least initially, his hopes are centred uniquely in the one woman. In these cases the actual adultery is the final devoutly-to-be-wished-for culmination of a long-standing passion, to which the married state of the object of love has been a hindrance but is now thrown overboard. The most starkly poignant expression of this frustrated emotion – perhaps in the whole of English literature – is evinced by a quite minor character in *Tess of the d'Urbervilles*. When Angel Clare has abandoned Tess on their wedding night he plans to go off to South America and, quailing at the thought of the solitary journey, he invites one of Tess's work companions to go with him. He reminds her that if she accompanies him it will be without benefit of legal married status; he is unaware that the object of his careless choice. Izz, has long loved him, believing her passion to be hopeless. Izz's answer has a dimention of fatality that makes her unforgettable : 'I don't mind that; no woman does when it comes to agony point and there's no other way.'

In stark opposition to the Bel-Amis and Chad Newsomes, Izz represents the other extreme of the gamut of motivations urging the lover to seek a partner already tied to someone else – a gamut which

---

* Fiedler has it that the Don Juan figure is transformed beyond recognition in the transition from the eighteenth to the nineteenth century, blurring into the exiled, sensitive soul, or debased by the trammels of the bourgeois inheritance; certainly these two new variants can be detected in Vronsky and Rodolphe, if one is looking for them.

extends from self-interest to self-forgetfulness. Beyond the fact of this complexity the author tells us little.

However, frequently no less poignant than Izz's case, and of equal importance are the reasons why certain characters choose not to break the Order; the *adultère manqué* is as revealing of the society in which it occurs as adultery triumphant.

There is only one outstanding example of an ardent lover stead-fastly refusing to take advantage of a promising situation on grounds of pure integrity, and already Hardy makes it clear that Giles in *The Woodlanders* is, along with the rest of the Hintock folk, almost an anachronism, a product of a bygone era. Although Fitzpiers's adultery with Mrs Charmond has been revealed, and Grace is currently under the impression that it can be considered as grounds for divorce, in both her eyes and those of Giles it is a heinous offence for them to kiss each other while the legal knot is as yet untied. Their mutual affection grows in spite of the lack of physical expression, but so un-swerving is Giles that even when bad weather has forced Grace to shelter in a woodman's hut Giles will not step inside the doorway with her. It is to Hardy's credit as a writer that he makes perfectly credible the extraordinary lengths to which Giles goes to pass food into Grace through a little window, and his dogged refusal to come inside when the rain becomes a torrential downpour. Giles is not rewarded for his heroism, unless it be in the eyes of posterity, for he dies of exposure; Marty South, his devoted and unnoticed adorer, speaks his epitaph : 'You was a good man and did good things.'

Hardy's own attitude is ambivalent. He shares, and wishes us also to appreciate, Marty's belief in Giles's innate goodness. But Giles verges on being more naïve than intelligent ('too stupid to come in out of the rain', indeed) and his death implies that Hardy believed, however reluct-antly, that there was no room in the modern world for old-fashioned and ingrained morality. Grace was really as unsuitable a mate for Giles, because of her education, as she was for Fitzpiers, because of her childhood upbringing; in a world of changing values, it is hard for anyone to find another person of their own level. For poor Giles, in spite of his virtue, happiness was out of reach.

Unfortunately, his sterling character is memorable for its unique-ness. In tinny imitation Zola depicts in *Une Page d'Amour* a widowed mother who falls in love with a doctor and after succumbing once immediately breaks up the relationship, under pressure from her daughter. The child, Jeanne, is so jealous that she falls mortally ill when her mother is with the doctor; overcome by remorse. Hélène accepts the advice of a priest, and marries a good man for whom she has no love at all. Zola appears to be attacking many things in this curious novel, with its platitudinous story-line and surprising moral, but one is left with the feeling that he was unable to resolve a complicated situation that posed more problems than he imagined. He allows a hitherto exemplary *honnête femme* to fall, thereby inferring that such women profess moral standards they cannot in fact live up to; but having approached the abyss, he rushes back, avoiding the issue of what really would have happened to Hélène and the doctor (would they live together? would the doctor get a divorce? would the affair simply peter out?) by using Jeanne's illness as an escape-mechanism. The implication is surely that he is unwilling to look squarely at the real issue involved, the possibility of an *honnête femme** stepping over the dividing line and turning into a kept woman; he finally puts his heroine in the very situation that he acknowledges leads to incompatability and potential adultery in his other novels of the loveless marriage. Moreover, the lover returns unscathed to his wife. It is difficult not to interpret Zola's attitude as one of vested interest in the continuing existence of the *honnête femme* and the bourgeois marriage. The lower orders might behave in a depraved fashion, and the Count Muffats of high society might also frequent the dressing-rooms of actresses; but a good woman, though she falls once, must be redeemed. Any alternative does not bear thinking of. Better a dead daughter than a loose-moralled mother.

Unlike Zola, Meredith is not at all afraid to examine the issue of the extra-marital union, but he recognises in one of his earlier books, *Diana of the Crossways*, that a writer may hold personal views which

---

* The familiarity of the concept of the '*honnête femme*' could lead one to suppose, equally, that there was no need to define or discuss it, or that the very banality of the term should indicate a rich and interesting history. Though the scholar may accept that the first alternative is not his to choose, he may be disappointed in his efforts to pursue the second; while there have certainly been attempts to define and portray the *honnête homme*, she seems in fact to have earned the contempt due to familiarity. One work, René Guerdon's *La Femme et l'amour en France* (Paris, 1965) goes somewhere along the way to explaining the notion of *honnêteté* itself, ascribing its origins to the Renaissance dissemination of the Platonic ideal of reasonable and unselfish love. Balthazar Castiglione's *Cortegiano* (1537) lays down the guide-lines for combining social success with virtuous behaviour, and is still the essence of the *morale mondaine* of the seventeenth century. Guerdon concludes that *l'amour* in France was subsequently divided between sensuality and *honnêteté*, the former being associated with the male, the latter with the female. The emergence of the *femme du monde* of the eighteenth century, with her sharp wit and disdain for sentimentality, aroused in the male a nostalgic desire for a less worldly female, which need Rousseau answered in his paradigm Julie. Thereafter, the nineteenth-century feminine world was split between the *demi-mondaine* and the unimaginative but faithful bourgeois wife – the *honnête femme* herself.

Perhaps this résumé does not do justice to Guerdon's account; but nor, I think, does his account do justice to the concept, whose origins appear to be shrouded in the rags of common usage and, in France at least, universal acceptance.

society is not yet ready to accept. Thus Diana's story is one of a series of *adultères manqués*, in spite of her beauty, wit, intelligence, independence and political awareness (she is a model New Woman of English society). Partly prompted by the distress she feels when her best friend's husband makes a pass at her, and partly anxious to retain ownership of her house (a motive Meredith is critical of) Diana makes a hasty and loveless marriage which she almost immediately terms an act of insanity. She continues to lead an independent life in London, conducting something like a political salon, and in the process gets her name linked with the influential Lord Dannenburgh's. Diana is in fact perfectly innocent, but the incident is used to show the difficulties faced by the New Woman in a society still bound by convention. 'Such are men in the world of facts', writes Meredith, 'that when a woman steps out of her domestic tangle to assert, because it is a tangle, her rights to partial independence, they sight her for their prey, or at least they complacently suppose her accessible . . . The world is hostile to the face of an innocence not conventionally simpering and quite surprised; the world prefers decorum to honesty.'[15]

Diana then falls in love with an aspiring political leader, Percy Dacier; aware that they cannot live together in England they nearly run away to Spain, but Diana is forced to stay and nurse her life-long friend Lady Lukin through a severe illness. The relationship with Dacier cools, and is completely killed when Diana leaks a political secret to the press. Her husband dies, and she finally accepts the hand of a long-time suitor for whom she feels only a sage affection. However, Meredith allows love to burgeon with the sudden arousal of sexual attraction between Diana and her fiancé. She puts a kiss on his arm, and suddenly realises she is 'dealing with a lover, a man of smothered fire, who would be electrically alive to the act through a coat-sleeve'. A union sanctioned initially by 'grey-toned reason' turns into the 'perfect mating'.

The mechanics used to avoid an adulterous situation are unfortunately reminiscent of Zola's manœuvres – the sudden illness of a dependant, and the final acceptance of the marriage yoke. But one is aware of a difference of attitude between the writers : Zola seems, as we have said, to be personally afraid to grasp the nettle because of the implications its prickles would have for the society he inhabited; Meredith was working towards an idea of redeemable adultery, but could not at the point of writing see how it could work in English society, and especially for a man whose career must necessarily be confined to the English political scene. The Diana–Dacier liaison, Meredith acknowledges, is too flouting of public morality and must be abortive; it is only later, with Aminta and Matey, that adultery will find a way. But here and in other novels he clarifies for himself and his reader a good many sound and unsound tenets of social belief. For example, he relates the subjection of women like Diana to the artificially class-based inequality fostered by the Conservative Government and its desire to maintain women in the role of sex objects : 'Conservatives know what they are about when they refuse to fling the last lattice of an ancient harem open to air and sun – the brutal dispersers of mystery, which would despoil the ankle of its flying wink.' Diana is martyr to this cause, getting her fingers burnt when she tries to play at being Dacier's equal; for the game is a fierce one indeed. The men are in fact terrified of the female invasion; when another equally in-dependent lady ventures into the all-male sanctum of the Courts, the male reaction is one of fearful suspicion : 'Is she moral? Does she mean to be harmless?' They seem to be torn between what the women themselves might do, and what they, the men, might do when the unexpected female presence arouses unhallowed emotions. Men might in general be over-anxious and insecure, but Meredith himself was not one of them; and there must have been not a few like-minded readers eagerly awaiting the gospel – *Diana of the Crossways* was an immediate, three-edition success.

So far the considered pressures against an adulterous relationship have been external to the lovers; there is also a group of books in which the more one examines the non-consummated affair, the stronger grows the conviction that the potential lovers were applying to them-selves some internal stricture – that they actually willed, half-con-sciously or unconsciously, the perpetuation of the pre-physical relationship.

Outstanding amongst these novels is Fromentin's *Dominique*, in which the temptation of a love affair 'impossible et coupable' must be resisted before Dominique can settle for the state of stable bliss. As a very young man, Dominique cherishes a first-love adoration of his friend's sister Madeleine; but she is three years older than he, and of superior background. He does not aspire to marry her, but appears content to worship from afar. Madeleine soon makes a suitable *mariage de convenance* which arouses no jealousy at all in Dominique, for Madeleine's husband represents 'l'empire de la raison avant même celui du droit'. Dominique has a very clearly defined system of priori-ties. However, Madeleine's husband is often away, and Dominique is often at the house; their relationship develops in spite of all, until honesty forces them to acknowledge the *idea* of scarcely mentioned temptations, which are referred to as abominable, and pushed aside with averted eyes. The culmination in a mutual avowal that they do in fact love each other is more than they can allow; they separate, for ever.

What of course is really interesting are the motives behind the actions. We get a first clue on the day of Madeleine's wedding, when, shrouded in white veils, she reminds Dominique very poignantly of his own youth, 'virgin, veiled, and gone forever'. The virginity of youth is a symbol of purity; purity attains the status of an absolute equated to ultimate goodness. Dominique never really wants to have a physical relationship because of his innate conviction that passion equals bad equals wretchedness, while reason equals good equals happiness. Madeleine has to be unattainable, not just because *illicit* love is destructive of the person and ultimately of society, but because Dominique is unable to hide from himself the fact that the love he feels for Madeleine is rooted in passion and must therefore lead to a passionate marriage. But this is a contradiction in terms : passion (bad) is not part of marriage (good). We are reminded of Descartes, of Bataille, of de Rougemont; passion is bad because love is in its extreme form self-destructive, and can only subsist by remaining unconsummated. What closer parallel to the sleeping bodies of Tristan and Yseult separated by the sword can there be than this description of the Madeleine–Dominique relationship : 'I felt that our destinies were close and parallel, but always irreconcilable; that we would have to live side by side, but separate . . .'[16] Madeleine's bridal whiteness becomes more than just a reminder of a lost virginity; women are the symbol of what men would have been had they never succumbed to passion, the female *must* represent the innocence and purity of the whole world, lost irrevocably to the male, but ardently sought.

It was at this time that mariolatry enjoyed a second vogue in France;* it is not unrelated to the image that Madeleine acquires. In order to crush underfoot the demon of passion sometimes aroused even by virtuous women, all women must be angels of foresight, on guard against any attack on their purity. Madeleine is thus remote, cloistered, veiled in innocence, impervious to the most speaking glances. The dreaded *mariage de convenance* is suddenly seen in a new light, for we are gladly assured that there is no passion between Madeleine and her husband. Her husband does not sully her any more than Dominique hovering outside her door at midnight, but not going in because 'une faute la tuérait'. (The prosaic reader is moved to remark that it might on the contrary do her a great deal of good; but it would certainly upset Dominique's assumptions to a degree he could not stand.) The point being reached where something has to happen, Dominique retires from the fray, pretending it is for her sake, but in

---

* The *Initiation Théologique* speaks somewhat wryly of a 'renaissance mariale qui . . . prend des formes surprenantes . . . un jaillessement charismatique . . . Le début du siècle se caractérisait par l'absence d'ouvrages marials. De là on passe soudain, vers 1840, à une prolifération plus affligeante encore.' (pp.270–1)

D

reality to save his own illusions. He converts his threatened ideals into a new, acceptable situation – the marriage based on 'the noble, the legitimate, the evident' – a passionless conjugal existence of his very own.

He thus, through his constancy to a philosophical idealism, avoids the dangerous trap of psychological idealisation – the process by which we descend from the clouds of idealism, clothing our clay-footed loves in mantles of glory, only to find that everyday life with the supposed angel is a disillusioning process. If only Adolphe had learnt from Dominique before becoming so inescapably enmeshed with Ellénore!

In spite of Emma's later history, her first episode with Léon has enormous similarities with the Madeleine–Dominique relationship, as well as sliding smoothly as a jelly out of the de Rougemont mould. There is an initial obstacle of the great social gulf between them, which makes even conversational intimacy impossible, as well as psychological 'vagues abîmes'. This creates some delight in the impossibilities of the situation and even the temporary setting up of false obstacles : Emma feigns an uncharacteristic absorption in domestic matters, and an even less believable affection for Charles. Her inaccessibility inspires in Léon a discarnate passion, 'dont la perte affligerait plus que la passion n'est réjouissante,* while Emma feeds her love for Léon by an imaginative life that is stronger than her real life with either Charles or him : 'She was in love with Léon, and sought solitude in order the more easily to be able to delight in thinking of him. The sight of his actual person disturbed the pleasure of this meditation.' But the more Emma notices her love, the more she rebuffs it – no doubt, says Flaubert, through laziness, fear or modesty. The irony indicates his belief in a more subtle explanation, the recognition perhaps that the state of undeclared love is the desired obstacle? Charles is explicitly 'l'obstacle à toute félicité'; there are other vague, indefinable feelings – 'the temptation to run away, somewhere far away, with Léon, to start a new life, would seize; but immediately a vague, dark gulf would open in her soul . . .' Léon's defection to Paris simply allows Emma to indulge in an idealised dream of him, more tall, beautiful and smooth than ever, and also more insubstantial.

But clearly, if Emma is to become the woman she is later in the story, the de Rougemont theory must cease to apply; Flaubert has in fact reversed de Rougemont's process.

Instead of sexual passion leading finally to an idealised love culmin-

---

* Cf. C. S. Lewis, *The Pilgrim's Regress:* 'In the first place, though the sense of want is acute and even painful, yet the mere wanting is felt to be somewhat a delight . . . This desire, even when there is no hope of possible satisfaction, continues to be prized, and even to be preferred to anything else in the world.'

ating in the death of the lovers, Emma begins with the idealised and necessarily unconsummated love, and must, for Flaubert's purposes, get from there to physical depravity. Thus, instead of her love for Léon thriving on absence, it finally withers and dies. This time, 'la passion se consuma [sic] jusqu'aux cendres . . . elle demeura perdue dans un froid qui la traversait'; she would be warmed only by the opposite kind of man – the Don Juan who was Rodolphe.

Since Flaubert presents more than one picture of male–female relationships, the only thing to be concluded for the moment is that he recognised in the society around him the existence of an idealised form of love in which non-consummation, via obstacle and distance, was a necessary element. The importance of this strand in the over-all picture of love in French society of the time is again stressed in the history of the *adultère manqué* between Frédéric Moreau and Mme Arnoux in *L'Education Sentimentale*. The situation really begins with the Arnoux marriage, originally an arranged marriage, though Arnoux has fallen in love with his wife's beauty and continued to love her 'à sa manière' ever after. His *manière* demands total fidelity from her, and complete freedom for him to take several outside mistresses while preserving the stability of the marriage – and even a quite fond and friendly relationship with Marie, who accepts both conditions without indignation.

When Frédéric first sees her and is struck by a *coup de foudre* it takes him little time to learn that she is an *honnête femme* and intends to remain one. He does not however give her up, for the Dominique-type reason that she fulfils an ideal he wants to retain as an ideal.

An inheritor of both a church-propounded cartesian morality, and a *désoeuvrement* and disillusionment common in his post-Romantic generation, Frédéric is unable to find a *raison d'être* in either religion or politics. His desire to revere Marie as a substitute religion is documented in the text of the novel : she is a 'point lumineux'; he esteems her 'par-dessus la passion'; with her he feels 'transporté dans un monde supérieur' and invaded by an 'envie de se sacrifier', a 'besoin de dévouement'. Marie herself has a 'majesté tranquille, presque religieuse', while Frédéric is struck by a 'crainte religieuse' which makes her skirt quite 'insoulevable'. Her name should be breathed in ecstasy and surrounded by incense and perfume . . . She answers to the psychological need, created by disillusionment, to have an ideal always ahead of him – an ideal which must never be seized and squeezed to nothingness. Like Dominique he feels no jealousy of Arnoux, since Marie is truly not an object of desire for him; on one occasion, when he detects a mere look of complicity in her (which he designates 'un début d'adultère'), he throws her back into Arnoux's arms, and he accepts with what is clearly a sigh of relief the satisfaction of the supposedly frustrating mode of life at Auteuil. Marie has now admitted to herself that she loves Frédéric, though he has carefully erected a protective passivity around his own emotions – 'by the very strength of his dreams he had placed her outside the human condition'. The explicit acknowledgement of love between them is seized by them both as a safety valve increasing the distance between them, and they do in fact live out a period of 'innocent' love at Auteuil where the agreement not to belong to each other guarantees their immunity from each other. It is a situation potent with a promise it never really threatens to fulfil.

Marie's motives appear to be mixed : she is partly prey to a hazy and not always active religious inhibition; she is partly quite simply afraid of the consequences (her husband might well throw her out into Frédéric's none too robust arms, or call the law down upon her head), and she has some sense of responsibility for her children. Frédéric's motives, as we have said, more obviously stem from his elevation of the whole affair to a quasi-religious plane, which makes it possible to avoid both loss of ideals and the post-coital *tristesse* Flaubert relates in the semi-autobiographical *Novembre*, and which gives rise to a world-embracing disgust and nihilistic despair. The artificial ideal he turns Marie into is, like the super-pure Madeleine, the self-propagating answer to the *cri de coeur* sent out by a lost generation.

Here there is a distinct link with the personal nihilism experienced by Thomas Hardy – except that Hardy does not try to set up an artificial ideal; he looks at substitutes for the other, but they always prove unsatisfactory.

In *The Return of the Native* Eustacia only marries Clym because she associates him with Paris and hopes he will take her there; Clym marries her because he is attracted by her beauty and ignores their incompatibility; Tamsin marries Damon because of the shame of being jilted by Clym, and Damon marries her in a pique at the thought of being rejected by two women. However, Eustacia and Clym retain almost all of their previous attachment, and while there is a familiar Hardy message in this – that if marriages were dissoluble a great deal of trouble and tragedy might be avoided – there is much below the surface to indicate that Hardy was also working out his perhaps unconscious convictions that possession of the beloved bodes no good for either party. In their search for some kind of ideal, the characters spurn the available and yearn for the impossible; when the impossible becomes theirs, they spurn that too, and return to the unavailable. They seem in fact only to appreciate the beloved when he or she is loved by someone else, just as Fitzpiers only began to love Grace when she was loved by Giles. Thus they are able to live in some kind of hope. Miller writes : 'In a world without God, no attempt to replace God will succeed . . . his characters are possessed of a longing for

God, of something like God, to give order and meaning to their world
. . . their disillusion when they obtain possession of what they desired
is a negative religious experience.'[17]

Angel and Tess's love also remains unconsummated, not only on
their wedding night, but even upon Angel's return from South America.
The mental obstacle, which had been Angel's inability to forgive Tess
for having been seduced in her past, Angel has overcome, only to be
faced with a truly insurmountable barrier – the fact that Tess has now
been living in sin with Alec d'Urberville in a protracted relationship.
Drastic measures bring a brief few days of happiness and unity to
Tess and Angel, but the end to it all is already inherent in the measures
themselves. (Tess has murdered Alec, and the police are out for her.)
Tess herself is sadly aware of the impossibility of any fulfilment of
their love : 'This happiness could not have lasted. It was too much.
I have had enough, and now I shall not live for you to despise me.'

Within this framework, legal marriage and adulterous love are of
equal significance, both being interchangeable as the source of love
or the source of the frustration of love. In *Jude the Obscure* the word
adulterous is used only once, of the too elaborate nightgown Sue refuses
to wear on her *wedding night* with Phillotson. However, the legalities
of marriage, and the binding nature of promises to marry, or even of
isolated sexual encounters, are taken seriously, to the point of exaggeration – as if to constitute the required barrier. Once again the symbolic sword is laid between the lovers; is it pure coincidence that the
only play tackled by Hardy was a re-working of the Tristan and Yseult
legend, entitled *The Tragedy of the Queen of Cornwall*? As Miller
sums it up, 'the only happy love relation for Hardy is one which is no
union, but the lover's acceptance of the gap between them . . . the
only permanent and (ironically) happy relationships are those which
are no union at all, but for one reason or another prolong indefinitely
the time before possession.'[18]

Although few threads have so far been drawn together, it will be
clear that the frustration of love has not been due, at least in any
direct way, to male inadequacy. But in the unconsummated opportunities for adultery in Turgenev, the theme of the strong woman/
weak man that began with Tatiana and Onegin is perpetuated as the
main reason for the fruitlessness of the affairs. The question of legal
and non-legal unions is less interesting to Turgenev than the basic
desire to avoid the whole issue of marriage as a personal confrontation
between two people. Thus the existence of Fedya's wife in *A Nest of
the Gentry* is really only a necessary device to allow Fedya to avoid
marriage with Lisa; in *On the Eve* the course of true love does run
smooth, but the hero here is a non-Russian; in *Fathers and Sons* the
hero is rejected by a stronger woman; in *Smoke* the strong Irena ulti-

mately rebuffs Litvinov, who equally fails to meet the challenge offered by his pallid but strong-minded fiancée; and in *Torrents of Spring* the weak hero is yet again caught between the two strong women. Most of these situations lead only to the frustration of the love initially involved; the Russian male is portrayed as a self-doubter who cannot, or dares not, carry through a full relationship for fear of his weakness being shown up. Turgenev gives a clue to this sense of inadequacy in his short story where one of the female characters says, paraphrasing Lermontov but with much poignancy, 'There are no heroes in our time . . .'

Freeborn has argued that for Turgenev the self-fulfilment possible in the relationship between a man and a woman 'comes too close to the divine for it to be countenanced in earthly terms . . . It is an article of divine bliss that is naturally accompanied by a feeling of guilt at having usurped more than humanity is permitted to experience. Death alone offers the true possibility of reconciliation.'[19] This of course echoes Hardy: but Hardy seems an isolated figure in his grapplings with the universe, whereas Turgenev, though original, stands rooted in a tradition which was lived out even by his own mysterious relationship with Pauline Viardot. The sense of inadequacy which haunts the Russian male when he confronts the strong blameless female who has not betrayed the peasants or lost her sense of purpose is an overriding factor in Russian sexuality. Is there also a related possibility that the exaltation of Romanticism, imported via George Sand, was in fact as foreign to the Russian emotional character as Bogomilism was to their spiritual nature, but that no one dared to say so? That it created in the Russian a feeling of self-doubt based on the fear that he would not be able to reach such heights, and thus led to his anxiety to avoid a position in which he would be bound to fail?

If this supposition contains any truth, we are left with the inescapable conclusion that the Russian would-be Romantic – that product of the French-educated, tending-towards-effete, intelligentsia – avoids passionate love because it represents an ideal he feels personally unable to attain, while the French anti-Romantic (e.g. Dominique, Frédéric) sees his ideal as actually threatened by the fulfilment of romantic love. In both cases the argument rebounds upon the male, while the female appears as merely a projected image of the aspirations and conflicts which gnaw at him. She comes less, not more, into her own when she attains the status of wife, for the accounts we have of the marriage-ideal are solely for the purpose of offering an acceptable alternative to the passionate love rejected by those who unconsciously but desperately wanted their bid for an adulterous relationship to fail.

A contented working arrangement is arrived at by Tatiana's parents;

one encounters the occasional lively and harmonious marriage in the novels of Trollope; but on the whole amicable conjugal relationships – in literature at least – serve only as a background or culmination to some other drama of courtship, seduction or adventure. Detailed and deliberately informative studies of successful marriage are rare; particularly in a field limited to writers making a feature of adultery. Such precedent as there is seems to be confined to Rousseau's *Nouvelle Héloïse*, and to be taken up in the French novel by only two writers – Barbey d'Aurevilly and Fromentin.

Barbey's ideal of married bliss leaps from the pages of his novels : the wedding itself should take place in a church, 'devant Dieu', and is indissoluble 'en vue des enfants'. (It is implied that the rule is universal and hence should apply equally to childless marriages.) A study of the attributes variously applied to it show it to be *chaste, pur, amoureux, ardent, calme, tendre;* also simple gracious, faithful, innocent and nature-loving. It is above all not passionate.

Thus it provides a noble forerunner to the Fromentin ideal, though twenty-five years separate the two authors. The marriage of Dominique and his wife (a lady so modest as to be nameless) is based on self-control, retirement from the world, the relinquishing of all worldly ambition, and service to the surrounding rural community. Its virtues are modesty, prudence, reason, simplicity, discretion; a sense of duty and responsibility, and a determination to be equal to one's task and sufficient to one's desires. Its activities consist of the cultivation of the soil, the maintenance of the roads, and the habit of doing good, in conjunction with one's wife. All is to be performed 'non pas comme une servitude, mais comme un devoir de position, de fortune et de naissance'. (The domestic harmony of the poor is not discussed.) The rewards of the union are finally *certitude, repos* and self-respect.

These two examples from the French are strikingly paralleled by the two pictures of domestic harmony finally achieved in the epilogue of *War and Peace*. As we shall see in greater detail in the following chapters, Tolstoy came to be as adamantly opposed to romantic love as any French writer; yet he shared the Russian reaction against arranged marriages. After examining the conflict between marriage-for-money and marriage-for-love through the experience of several couples, he arrives at a delicate resolution : marriage without love is unworthy; but love, while necessary, is still a dangerous emotion; therefore, as soon as the marriage has taken place, the romantic love which brought it about must be transformed into a more acceptable form. Thus Nicholas and Mary achieve a contented and solid marriage, because Nicholas works hard on the estate and enjoys it; Mary finds happiness in the love of her husband, children and relatives, but is spiritually nourished by an intense inner life. This also has the good effect of elevating Nicholas's somewhat earthy nature. Nicholas's daily discovery of fresh spiritual treasure in Mary leads to ever-increasing harmony, which successfully eliminates all traces of romantic love : Mary's aspirations are spiritual, Nicholas's affection is prosaic but they represent the two forms of love acceptable to Tolstoy.

Comparable is the recipe for a happy marriage adopted by Natasha and Pierre. Natasha lacks Mary's deep spirituality, but makes up for it by channelling her entire life into the approved mould of total devotion to husband and children, and utter absorption in their needs. Pierre also must belong exclusively to the family, even pursuing his intellectual interests at home and going rarely to town. Tolstoy's absolute approval of Natasha's form of married life is contained in his view that the sole aim of marriage is the production of a family, while Mary is the answer to man's complementary need for spiritual uplift.

To the serene regularity of Barbey and Fromentin, Tolstoy prefers a bustling activity, yet he insists more than they on the value of spiritual resources. In the imperiously organised pattern for domestic harmony which is for Tolstoy the symbolic microcosm of universal harmony, harmony between man and man, man and nature, man and God, lies not merely the repudiation of romantic love, but a vital though perhaps oblique reflection of Goethe's famous dictum : 'The classical is healthy, the romantic sick.' The Happy Marriage is seen above all to be a rejection of passion and a vindication of reason, order and will.

3 The Order Broken:
The Course of Love

The essence of adultery is contained in the modern term 'two-timing', which tersely sums up the simultaneity of the double relationship. Yet an affair of the past can sometimes be so present to the mind of a lover or spouse that the passage of time is ignored and yesterday's involvement shows its power to touch quite deeply today's commitment. Such is particularly the case when the past affair is seen as having some kind of 'sullying' effect, as though all the perfumes of Arabia were indeed helpless to wash away the blemishes on a soul fallen from grace.

The point is made clearly in *Tess of the d'Urbervilles*, when Tess's disclosure of her past seduction by Alec d'Urberville causes Angel Clare to desert her a few tortured days after her wedding-night confession. Angel experiences a gamut of emotions, each of which convinces him of the impossibility of living with Tess any longer. His first reaction is that he has been deceived – Tess is not the woman he imagined he had been loving, but 'another person'. Then he ponders the connection between her 'fall' and her family's decline : both seem to bespeak a related decrepitude. Thirdly, he insists that Alec is her 'husband in nature' – as though the first act of intercourse set up an unseverable tie as serious as marriage (though only for the woman in the case . . .). And finally he is persuaded that if he were to remain, his and Tess's children would grow up under a 'taunt' whose sting would hurt more as they advanced in age and understanding. Convinced by his own logic, he leaves; his ensuing approach to Izz Huett will be remembered from Chapter 2.

This episode shows vividly the reaction of a man discovering what effect the past can have on the present; however, Angel's extreme reaction cannot but make us ponder further the relationship not just between the past and the present, but also between the idea of purity and the act of defloration. What are the psychological effects of loss of virginity? Is purity only a physical attribute dependent on an intact hymen, as Hardy certainly implies? Does the first act of physical intercourse set up some emotional bond between the partners, irrespective of the affection which may or may not have motivated their union?

They are difficult questions, and ones the nineteenth-century novelist can only hint at, not even stating the problem explicitly, let alone provide answers. Our contemporary Kinsey discusses regret after pre-marital coitus, but not the specific situation of the first time. His conclusions are nevertheless the most helpful in an unsatisfactory situation, for he states : 'The psychological significance of any type of sexual activity very largely depends upon what the individual and his social group choose to make of it. The disturbances which may sometimes follow coitus rarely depend on the nature of the activity itself, or upon its physical outcome.'[1]

If this is taken in conjunction with Henriques' view that Western attitudes to pre-marital sex have always been ambivalent, but that the nineteenth century reveals an intense but pressing obsession with virginity, then all we can say is that Angel is nothing more or less than a man of his own time, thoroughly undermined in his male pride by the notion of his bride not being *virgo intacta*. In reacting as he does, of course, he effectively allows himself to be used by his author and creator as a hindrance to marriage; and this, as we know, was what Hardy was really after.

In yet another Hardy novel, *The Mayor of Casterbridge*, the public knowledge of a past adulterous affair is used as effectively as Angel's inner anguish to destroy a marriage which otherwise boded well. Lucetta has married Donald Farfrae; but the townspeople, suspecting Lucetta's sexual relationship with Henchard many years ago (when Henchard believed, if falsely, that he was married to Susan), seize the opportunity to get up what they call a skimmity-ride – that is, a procession in which effigies of the two offending figures are seated back to back on a donkey and paraded through the streets to the accompaniment of hoots and jeers. Lucetta cannot mistake the dummies of herself and Henchard. Horrified and shocked, she faints, falls, miscarries her baby, and becomes dangerously ill. After a desperate night during which she tries weakly and vainly to tell her husband the secret of her past, she dies. Thus, although we have no clue as to whether Donald would have reacted as Angel did on discovering the truth, it is clear that Lucetta fears he might; she operates *as though* Angel's objections were all valid and generally applicable.

While it is not part of Hardy's purpose in either of these novels to show the inner workings of the adulterous liaison, both works are interesting for the emphasis they lay upon the way a past relationship can be used as a powerful weapon in the destruction of a love newly grown up. It is a further twist to a theme that is becoming familiar –

the Hardyesque pessimism which seeks to frustrate all potentially fruitful encounters.

Less melodramatic and more subtly worked than the fates of Tess and Lucetta, the outcome of a relationship severely affected by a previous adultery becomes in James's *Portrait of a Lady* one of a dogged endurance of a disillusioned and joyless existence. By the time Isabel has met and married Gilbert Osmond, the latter's most significant affair is over and done with; yet the past adultery overshadows the present marriage in the complicity of Osmond and Mme Merle. Osmond, born American, but having cast off his native inheritance for the sake of European values, marries Isabel because she is wealthy, measures up to his standards of taste, and can look after his daughter Pansy, both practically and financially. He acknowledges that Isabel has 'too many ideas' which will 'have to be sacrificed', but feels confidently equal to the challenge. The American Isabel is positively attracted by Gilbert's lack of accoutrements in the way of money, title, property, etc., and by the notion that she can supply something, be 'of use' to him. She takes pride in surrendering all she has to the marriage in the mistaken belief that Gilbert is 'better than anyone'; and not least important she is physically attracted to him : Gilbert is an admirable lover. Mme Merle* was also born American, but has had a European upbringing, so that Isabel feels, significantly, that she is the product of a 'different moral or social clime'. Mme Merle engineers the marriage between Gilbert and Isabel, since she is the mother of Pansy, but of this, as of the relationship between Mme Merle and her husband, Isabel is unaware.

But Mme Merle is certainly not the first reason for the breakdown of the Osmond marriage. There are several intrinsic factors which presage its essential collapse in spite of the maintained appearances : Gilbert discovers that Isabel is a great deal less malleable than he anticipated – more 'not what he had believed she would prove to be' than he had dreamt of. He accuses her openly of having too many ideas that are in direct conflict with his own conception of 'high prosperity and high propriety' within the aristocratic tradition, while Isabel on her side is horrified by the moral looseness of the society they move in, and will not accommodate it. She comes to believe that Gilbert actually hates her because she gives him the sensation of having been too confident, of having made an error of judgement.

However, Isabel also comes to suspect the depth of the relationship between Osmond and Mme Merle; her wavering feeling for her husband founders on her deep distrust – an emotion far stronger in her breast than jealousy or resentment. The bitter acknowledgement that

* Could James be indulging in name symbolism? A *merle* is after all a blackbird.

she has been used by them simply makes her envy Ralph his imminent death. Having absorbed during her strict American upbringing a non-religious belief in the permanence of marriage, plus a commitment to personal honesty between people, especially partners, her dis-illusionment is profound; but so is her sense of obligation. In spite of the hostility between herself and Osmond, and the proffered possibili-ties of escape with either Caspar Goodwood or Lord Warburton, she determines to continue with the marriage. Gilbert is easily persuaded, since he is so integrated in the European tradition that he accepts completely a form of marriage which presents superficial unity while masking almost total internal division. So long as the form is observed, he is satisfied. Isabel is personally repelled by such lip-service, but she endures it for three reasons. First is her moral adherence to the in-dissolubility which James uses symbolically as an image of a person's commitment to life itself. Secondly, she feels she is partially guilty for the failure of the marriage, in that she allowed herself to deviate from the path of total personal truth to herself; admiring Osmond, respon-sive to his charm, and impressed by his taste, she had minimised her own self, her independence, her strongly held ideas, her moral outlook during the period of their early attraction, but had not been willing to forgo them when the first conflict arose. She thus feels bound to make reparation to him for not being what she seemed, by observing, now, the form that is all he requires. Lastly her resolve to be a parent to Pansy – again a value inherited from her American back-ground – requires that she stay, and stay to oppose the financially advantageous match Osmond and Mme Merle are planning for their daughter.

So, while James is exploring in this novel the various forms a mar-riage can take much more than he is concerned with the details of an adulterous relationship, his standpoint in relation to both situations begins to emerge. Marriage for him is *in itself* a rarely achieved ideal which he sees in terms of high aspiration and deep personal commit-ment; it is glimpsed in the hopes of Touchett for Isabel and Isabel for Pansy. But while lesser forms of marriage are vividly portrayed in the Osmond, Gemini and elder Touchett unions, James does not judge them; he merely makes them less worth while, less admirable. And similarly, he does not actually condemn the pre-adultery of Osmond and Mme Merle, at least by any absolute standards. What he does do is show the dishonesty required to maintain their psychological liaison, and the effect on Isabel of its discovery. It makes concrete Gilbert's lack of love for her, and sets the changing course of their relationship; after its discovery things will never be the same again.

James's perceptions in this area are both fascinating and predictive; they will be developed with even more attention in his later works;

however, the novel *par excellence* dealing with the effects of an adultery which has taken place before the story opens is of course Hawthorne's *The Scarlet Letter*.* It must be stated from the outset that there is some difficulty in assessing this work – from the point of view of the present study – partly because of its historical placing (it takes place three centuries before the date of publication) and even more because of the ambiguity of the genre, which is vastly more complicated than that other hybrid, *Evgenii Onegin*. It has not been considered essential hitherto to take into account the *forms* of the novels under discussion; but the very fact that *The Scarlet Letter* does not fit in with the conventional realism of the nineteenth-century novel makes it require some clarificatory comment. Joel Forte, for example, has classified it as a romance – and certainly there is a lack of concern with the possible, probable, or everyday courses of experience. Yet there are glimpses, when one looks at the realism of Governor Bellingham's Boston, and of *some* of the characters, of the straight historical novel. It could be equally classed as a sentimental novel, in view of the analytic treatment of Hester and Dimmesdale; but there are also strong overtones of the Gothic horror story – witness the episode of the witches, and the whole treatment of Chillingworth. Some may see it as an allegory; Daniel Hoffman goes so far as to endow it with the qualities of a myth. Both James, in writing on Hawthorne, and Hawthorne himself contribute indirectly to this last interpretation. Commenting on the thinness and blankness of the American cultural heritage, Hawthorne says in the Preface to *The Marble Fawn:* 'No author, without a trial, can conceive of the difficulty of writing a romance about a country where there is no shadow, no antiquity, no mystery, no picturesque and gloomy wrong, not anything but a commonplace prosperity in broad and simple daylight, as is happily the case with my dear native land.'

The irony bespeaks an ambivalence, from which can be postulated a desire on Hawthorne's part to set up and explore an instant myth – a gambit which would allow him both to fill a gap in the American cultural heritage, and also to discuss sexual issues without flouting either American literary tradition or Bostonian morality. Thus while the story is firmly grounded in the historical past – it was simply a fact that adulteresses were in some states required to wear the scarlet letter on their breasts as a punishment for their sins – Hawthorne goes beyond verisimilitude to a more fecund ambiguity : it is finally suggested that the A in Hester's case might stand for Admirable as much as for Adulteress. And on ambiguity Hawthorne builds not so much

---

* Fiedler's view of the repression of overt sex in the American novel is supported by the fact that *The Scarlet Letter* is frequently called the only major novel of adultery in the literature – but the word itself is never used in the text.

a mythology as a series of mythologies ranging over the areas of sexual passion, witchcraft, diabolism, Puritanism, pagan innocence and feminism. (The term myth is used loosely here, in the sense of a story that expresses the rules of conduct of a given society or religious group, issuing from whatever sacred principle has presided over the formation of that group. *The Scarlet Letter* markedly conforms to the convention that the origin and content of myth are obscure.)

The exploration of these quasi and incomplete mythologies is shot through with Hawthorne's own perplexities. Myth does not equal answer-machine; thus many of his symbols are ambiguous. For example, the symbol of the sexual-passion myth is the colour red, first seen in the rose-bush at the prison door; but Hawthorne cannot be sure himself whether the bush springs from the wilderness (itself a symbol of paganism) or from the sainted Ann Hutchinson, whether it it a 'sweet moral blossom' or a weed associated with a dark tale of 'human frailty and sorrow'. The red of the flower is first transferred to the red of the letter A, sign of shame and disgrace, but then to the embroidery which is a manifestation of Hester's art. In the course of time the scarlet letter becomes a sign of wisdom and knowledge that only the scarlet woman can dispense, but which is recognised as beyond that of the ordinary community, and of infinite value to them. When Hawthorne finally suggests that A might stand for admirable, he appears to be demonstrating the paradox of good issuing from that which was thought to be evil – as well as his own inability either to accept unredeemed passion or to totally reject it.

The destiny of Pearl presages his ultimate decision. Pearl in the early parts of the book is as ambiguous as the rose-bush : sometimes she is a 'lovely and immortal flower', sometimes an 'imp of evil, emblem and product of sin'. But later, through Dimmesdale's confession, she is given an acknowledged father and thus a defined, though bastard, reality. Though Dimmesdale dies, Pearl continues to become more and more substantial in the symbolic fatherland of England, until she finally marries and produces her own real, legal, and totally acceptable child, and thus unites herself to normal society. In his later books, as Fiedler is quick to point out, Hawthorne projects the example of Pearl by portraying couples whose redemption is assured when they choose marriage before passion.

The mythology of pagan innocence with its concomitant of moral wilderness is symbolised by the forest, source of Hester's beyond-civilisation knowledge, and sympathetic shelter for her passion with Dimmesdale. For the strong Hester, the forest is a place of truth, but the weaker Dimmesdale cannot accept the alienation entailed by un-civilised knowledge; he will only go deeper into the forest-world of the unconscious which is death. Hawthorne is sure that the forest is the source of Hester's strength and knowledge, but he sees that no ordinary being can go into it unscathed; he sets beside Hester's forest-experience the trial-by-shame of her moral isolation and self scourging, and finally rejects even for her the passion justified and celebrated by pagan innocence.

The mythology of diabolism provides still more parallels between morality and sexuality. It is first used most deviously by Hawthorne to imply the communal sexual guilt of the whole town; that is, he points to what he cannot tell overtly in fiction except through the mad accusations of the witch figure, Mrs Hibbins. Although her claim is only to have seen devil-worshippers amongst churchgoers, her implication is that they are more to be censured than Hester, because they add hypocrisy to depravity. And in another parallel between diabolism and sexuality, the idea of demonic possession of one soul by another is used to demonstrate the intimate bond between cuckold and cuckolder, simultaneously with the idea of the thrall of passion *and* guilt. If Chillingworth stands for Dimmesdale's Calvinistic heritage tormenting him with the consciousness of his guilt, his role is only made possible by the existence of sin in the first place. Dimmesdale both loves and hates Chillingworth; Chillingworth's power over him is equalled only by Hester's. Thus Chillingworth becomes another ambivalent symbol of man's turning towards, and away from, passion.

The mythology of Puritanism is ambiguous in that Hawthorne cannot completely accept the Puritan rejection of the flesh even though he sees it as the only safeguard against passion. The Puritans of the story retain a certain Elizabethan lustiness, although they lack compassion, and through this, sympathy in presentation. But the history of their denial of sexuality over the centuries will make them paler and thinner; they will come to forget gaiety and will wear the 'blackest shade of Puritanism'. Fiedler interprets their decline as Hawthorne's recognition of the attenuation of sex in America, a paradigm of the fall of love in the New World. Hester then represents, in this context, as ambiguously as ever, the statuesque ripeness of the earliest New England woman, a relic of the Merrie England Hawthorne cannot quite regret, and can even be taken as a visible sign of the feminine principle which the Puritans attempted to stamp out of their religion and social ideas. By her fall and redemptive powers she unites within herself both Eve and Mary, the Fallen Woman and the Divine Mother.

Lastly, Hawthorne was concerned with the nineteenth-century feminist movement, and tried to relate the status and role of women to his creation of a cultural mythology : Hester ponders the need for the reform of society and of the role of men, so that women may have a 'fair and suitable position'; she sees that she herself may have been able to herald the coming revelation had she not fallen. But, as

Fiedler points out, these 'prophetic anticipations of female discontent' are not dangerous because of Hester's isolation from the community. By contrast, Zenobia's feminism in *The Blithedale Romance* is punished vindictively.

In conclusion to *The Scarlet Letter* it must be stressed again that only imaginative speculation can help to seize a meaning Hawthorne himself was chary of declaring forthrightly. However, it is not inconsistent with the story to see its contribution to the adultery theme as essentially ambivalent *because* of Hawthorne's inner conflict between passion and Puritanism. He ardently desired to examine what he could resurrect from the New England subconscious and the overt heritage of the Puritan repression of passion; but having done so once, he quickly put it back where it would do no damage, and proceeded to resolve the conflict by setting up neatly categorised Dark Ladies and White Maidens while eschewing for ever the real issue of the role of passion and adultery in civilised society.

In point of fact, the Dark Ladies and White Maidens seem to be to the American male what the voluptuous mistress and the *honnête femme* are to the French : fabricated symbols of an unreal division created and imposed by the need for security from the dark forces of passion. Paradoxically, each of the male authors just discussed – Hardy, James and Hawthorne – have only emphasised in their different ways the power of the adulterous woman, and of the passion she unleashes, by their admission that the effects of an anterior liaison may be unforeseeably far-reaching in time and influence.

In contrast to these long-term effects, the immediate reaction of the just-fallen woman brings into concentrated focus the specific relationship between gratification and guilt. The degree of happiness in an adulterous relationship would appear to be in inverse proportion to the weight of culpability and remorse pressing upon the participant. In other words, if guilt can be eliminated, happiness is at hand; and this seems possible at least in the initial stage of the relationship. Guilt is the last emotion in the world to trouble Emma Bovary, and in the early days of her second, consummated affair with Léon, she and he are both happily and genuinely in love. There is a pleasing fusion of reality and make-believe in their meetings, when they think of themselves as living in their own house, and having to stay there till they die, like two eternal newly-weds. Perhaps this brief period is even the only time Emma is truly happy in the whole book. Her delight is matched by Sévérine's, in *La Bête Humaine*, and her sense of blamelessness by many : by Thérèse Raquin who is disturbed by murder but not at all by adultery; by Maupassant's Christiane who refuses to think, suffers not at all, and regrets nothing; and by his Mme de Guilleroy, who keeps accusing herself of being 'a lost woman', but fails to find in herself any echo of suffering response to this attack from her conscience.

There are others, like Mme de Dambreuse *(Education Sentimentale)*, and Mme Marelle and Madeleine (both in *Bel-Ami*) whose entire way of life depends on affairs conducted with such discretion that it would be naïve to raise the question of guilt; and some who feel a positive and complete moral justification. Such a one is Nataly in *One of Our Conquerors:* 'I do not feel the guilt! I should do the same again on reflection . . . I do believe it saved him. I do; oh! I do, I do . . . He had fallen into a terrible black mood. He sinks terribly when he sinks at all.'[2]

Charlotte and the Prince in *The Golden Bowl* try to believe in a similar justification, but the level of their argument has to be a great deal more sophisticated than Nataly's. At an early meeting, when they are simply drinking tea and talking, Charlotte says, 'This is what they must like to think I do for you? – just as, quite as comfortably, you do it for me. The thing for us to do is to learn to take them [the unwitting and trusting spouses] as they are . . .'[3]

The Prince argues with accomplished and wilful duplicity that it would be naïve, even 'ungracious', not to develop between them 'an exquisite sense of complicity'; and from there they proceed to the assertion : 'We're happy and they're happy. What more does the position admit of?' It is evident that both need to convince themselves that they are faultless, with all the subtlety their fastidiously immoral consciences can muster. James insists upon the strength and complexity of their determination not to feel a guilt which might demand of them a renunciation they are unwilling to concede.

By contrast, some women are consumed almost immediately by a remorse whose sources are not always analysed. Mme Walter *(Bel-Ami)* is victim to an access of frightful remorse, and proceeds to heap reproaches and curses on her lover's head, though after a time her infatuation overcomes her guilty feelings. Anna Karenina is straightway stricken by moral shame and physical disgust : she begs forgiveness, but there is no religious contrition in her plea, as Tolstoy makes clear : 'She felt herself to be so criminal and guilty that it only remained for her to abase herself and beg forgiveness; but there was nothing now in life except him, and so to him she directed her prayer for forgiveness.'[4]

It is difficult to draw any useful conclusion from these scantily-documented and somewhat arbitrary accounts; perhaps in the long run they only say something about the author. It cannot be without significance that the women who feel no guilt are products of a society under censure from the writer, so that the sense of righteousness is just another black mark against them. Such is also James's view of the dark-haired Charlotte, with her 'habit, founded on experience, of not being afraid'; while Meredith's sympathetic presentation of Nataly's slightly foolish role-playing reveals his own idealistic compassion for the 'genuine' if illegal union.

As for Tolstoy and Anna . . . the scene described gains all its power from the agonising conflict in the author's heart over his own creation. He loves Anna too much not to grant her the indulgence of remorse : but he is adamant in his hatred of her sin. More than all the others put together, Tolstoy tries to work out his own torments through his heroine. Hence Anna's frightful self-loathing – and her determination to continue along the primrose path.

If however, only some women, but no men, bear the brunt of remorse-ful self-accusation, the effect of the shock of discovery upon the deceived spouse is generally much greater than, in some cases, one would expect.

For example, Nana comes to hear of the Countess Muffat's discreet affairs before the Count, and is genuinely offended : 'An honest woman deceiving her husband! Impossible! What a business! It's too dis-gusting!'[5] But the effect on the Count – in spite of the fact that his liaison with Nana is well developed – is utterly devastating. He wanders the streets weeping, and undergoes a rapid reconversion to a frenzied faith in God, which quite fails to console him.

Karenin, also as we have seen, feels that his entire life, which Tol-stoy labels 'artificial', but which is all the man knows, is broken; but it is in the *Kreuzer Sonata* that discovery has its most dramatic outcome; since it is this time accompanied by the presence of the lover – a genuine *delicto flagrante* situation – there is little time for feeling : the husband acts fast, killing his wife. However, just before the job is done, he is struck by the realisation that he is seeing her as a human being for the first time : 'I looked at the children, and at her bleeding battered face, and for the first time I forgot myself, my rights, and my pride; for the first time I saw her as a person.'[6]

It seems then, that apart from the rush of feelings which range from rage to bereftness, the husband who discovers the unsuspected is also likely to endure a moment of truth born of the realisation that he himself may be the cause of his wife's desire to find consolation outside the marriage. The theory receives a nice twist in Muffat's case, since having found out about the Countess, he goes to Nana, only to discover her in bed with someone else. He then endures another crushing bolt of awareness, recognising the low value he has set upon the mere mistress; if he had *really* loved her, she would not have betrayed him.

The wife's discovery of her husband's infidelity is a more common situation, and invites a variety of reactions. What might have been thought to be a cliché turns out to occur with any degree of conviction only once – Lillie, upon finding a letter from Mrs Larue to Carter, faints, recovers, and declares she never wants to see her husband again. Unfortunately, from our own as well as his point of view, Carter is killed in battle before Lillie's affirmation can be put to the test. Lillie's extreme delicacy indicates that she might, for reasons of genuine aversion rather than resentment or desire to punish, have carried out her resolution; after all, the novel represents the view that sex is dirty enough inside marriage, but quite, quite unacceptable outside.

Most women are however made of sterner stuff; although Dolly refuses to speak to Stiva for a few days, and threatens to leave home, she has no real intention of carrying through her commination. She soon comes to realise that the running of the household and the care of the children necessitate at least minimal communication with her erring spouse, and finds herself heavy-heartedly but inevitably carrying on. Mme de Camors, on the other hand, *resolves* to carry on, and manages to find some consoling occupation in the busy dusting and rearranging of the furniture, though underneath the starched apron there does beat a chagrined heart : 'She tasted the bitterness of her desolation to an almost unbearable degree.' Her admirable resignation is matched only by Hermangarde's – that woman 'of too divine a stamp for this accursed earth'. Barbey writes : 'Until now she had had no more than gnawing suspicions. Now . . . she had the dull certainty of accomplished unhappiness. She would start to live again without self-pity, her lips closed in a resigned smile, and a sword plunged up to the hilt in her breast.'[7]

The wives show definite spirit in their determination to fight back, though their methods are quite varied. The Princess Grigorev accepts easily enough her husband's extra-marital affair so long as the appearances are maintained; but she does object to his entertaining Elena in the drawing-room when she herself is sick upstairs. Having successfully fallen in love with Baron Mingen, the assiduous but hitherto rejected aspirant, she allows him to overcome any scruples she may have been supposed to entertain by accepting the arguments he has picked up from the Prince, originally designed to justify the latter's relationship with Elena. The Prince feels considerable chagrin at the turn of events, and confesses that he really cannot accept the position of the *mari trompé*; but his friend's advice to resort to reasonableness, glasses of water and long walks is not well received. Very clearly, the double standard was a tenet of the highest society that was not easily broken.

Maggie Verver's reaction to certain knowledge is the most complex of all; we see it through Fanny Assingham's astute but not always wise eyes : ' "It isn't a question of recovery. It won't be a question of any vulgar struggle. To get him back she must have lost him, and to have lost him she must have had him." With which Fanny shook her head, "What I take her to be waking up to is the truth that, all the while, she really hasn't had him. Never." '[8] Fanny is, of course, perfectly correct. Maggie has not really 'had' the Prince – not because of the existence of Charlotte, but because of her unbelievably childish attachment to her father. (She keeps a room for herself, one for her baby, and a whole wardrobe for both in her father's house as well as her own.) Fanny is also correct in her assertion that Maggie's naïvety extends to the point of being sincerely unaware of what Fanny calls Evil; the first step in her restoration of Amerigo to herself must be the opening of her senses to 'what's called Evil . . . the crude experience of it . . . the harsh, bewildering brush, the daily chilling breath of it'. This is in fact all we are told of what Maggie can be expected to undergo as she detects the truth of the Charlotte–Amerigo relationship; the rest of the novel is devoted to the steps she takes. However, it must be admitted that Maggie has to endure her moment of truth, just as Karenin does; and in this sense the discovery of betrayal becomes like a challenge. Ignorance may be a form of bliss, but it is an unworthy one; knowledge of the truth presents a challenge which can be met or ducked. If it is met, it will be with a range of attitudes, from heroism to spite, resignation to resistance, tolerance to horror. The appropriateness of the attitude comes out in the development of the relationships.

One rather pathetic, or chastening (depending from whose point of view it is seen) aspect of the course of an adulterous affair is the anticipated display of male disdain for the fallen woman. Many women, notably Anna, fear it, but few in fact get it, as Anna, to Vronsky's credit, does not. The sole example – and it is a nasty one – occurs when M. de Camors early in the story seduces the wife of his best friend. Her reaction can be compared to the cry, 'Now you'll think I'm awful.' And yes, indeed, he does. 'Women like you are not made for perverted love like ours . . . your charm should lie in your virtue; when you lose that, you lose everything', he says savagely, no doubt deeply chagrined at the ease of his conquest. For virtue seems to be a quality conferred on the French wife by a deeply insecure male population, anxiously desirous of believing in the inseductibility of *certain* females – to whose ranks belong the ones they themselves marry.

On the whole, the male seducer of the novels does not despise his victim; but this is because the author is rarely brave enough to broach the subject of the fall of the *genuine honnête femme*. However, desertion by the lover soon after the affair is also rare, so long as one does not count the liaisons doomed in the nature of things to brevity, like Stiva's peccadillo with the governess. Yet fear of desertion is built into almost every one of the liaisons under discussion, notably those of Anna and Muffat, and also the case of Chad's desperately dependent mistress in *The Ambassadors* – especially as the adulterous liaison is not often nipped in the bud, but rather tends to drag on for a considerable time. During this period it must constantly strive to keep various enemies at bay, particularly dreariness, isolation and anxiety. These hags need not be found together, though they often are; and when they are it is difficult to tell which of them caused, or was caused by, the other.

The pre-eminent example is of course the Anna–Vronsky partnership, particularly during their stay in Italy. However, if we try to trace the course of their love, we must take note of Tolstoy's signposts; the first drop of acid that falls on their relationship occurs as early as their first sexual encounter, when Anna is rendered speechless by her sense of degradation while Vronsky feels like a murderer who has just killed the first phase of their love. But there are other stages to be lived through – notably one of 'misery for all three', when Anna lives in the same house as her husband but is totally estranged, and meets Vronsky away from home, in a situation which is only made tolerable to all three by the hope of change – Karenin hoping the passion will pass, Anna and Vronsky hoping for a resolution, but unable to predict what it can be. Here is the first mention of Anna's fits of jealousy, whose only effect is to alienate Vronsky from her : 'Now she loved him as only a woman can for whom love outweighs every good including life itself – and he was much further from happiness than when he had pursued her from Moscow. Then he had thought himself to be unhappy, but that happiness lay ahead; now he felt that the best of his happiness was already behind him.'[9] Vronsky is in the process of discovering the deadening hopelessness of the human psyche when the old desire is satisfied and no new one comes forth to take its place.

And yet its misery is matched by the anguish of a situation where hope exists, but the uncertainty of the how, where and when that hope will be realised is a constant torture. Betsy fears that the unsettled state of affairs will make Anna pine away; when she with difficulty persuades Karenin to grant a divorce, Anna cannot accept it because of a new and unexpected reaction : when divorce seemed unattainable she longed for it; when it is put within her reach she feels too guilty to seize it. The urge for self-punishment becomes an emotional by-product when the adulteress is possessed of an active conscience. The removal to Italy greatly eases this torment for Anna, for the greater the distance from the scene of the crime, the less significant does it appear to become. But Vronsky, whose conscience had not been troubled at all (Karenin was merely a 'superfluous hindrance') now discovers a new burden to weigh him down; though Anna is on the whole less jealously possessive in Italy, because she feels more secure, Vronsky smarts from the dreary ennui of having nothing to do with his time. While Anna is 'unpardonably happy', and frequently experiences a rapture so intense it is terrifying, Vronsky finds that he is getting 'only a grain of happiness from that mountain of which he expected so much . . . Sixteen hours of every day had somehow to be filled in.' The lack of outside interests is partly caused by Anna's dependence on him, partly by their irregular position. The strain of maintaining by silence Anna's non-existent honour had begun to tell on him in Moscow already; the extreme of social isolation in Italy is both more than he can endure, and a destructive influence on their relationship. He has to substitute for family, children and friends as well as be both husband and lover. The unnatural environment, the imbalanced relationship, inevitably corrode Vronsky's ability to give, while driving Anna to demand even more. Yet the fact that her demands are insatiable does not prevent her feeling insecure when they are not met; insecurity breeds fear, fear makes for possessiveness, possessiveness creates irritability and hyper-sensitivity (Anna interprets Vronsky's desire for a child as proof of his indifference to her beauty) and finally the despair that causes Anna to throw herself under the train. Tolstoy has not spared her a single one of the gamut of damaging emotions adultery can bring in its wake; but even while we grieve for Anna, we must look to see how universal is this apprehension of the course of an affair.

Deception, isolation, ennui and guilt – these were the marks of the Anna–Vronsky story. Deception is a necessary condition of adultery, of course, though its intensity may vary from the deliberate winking of the eye – as in the case of that upper stratum of society where discreet adultery is the norm – to the hideous feeling of being caught in a cleft stick which marks the double life of Ryno Marigny in *Une Vieille Maîtresse* : 'To tell the truth, tell everything, would have been to burden Hermangarde's spirit with much crueller and more terrifying fears than those which were germinating there now . . . he lowered his head and was silent . . . and she, poor unfortunate, was also dumb, overwhelmed by her husband's silence . . .' It leads to a paralysis of feeling between them :

They were dumb, closed in, constrained . . . and there were profound changes : the utter shattering of their intimacy . . . In love as they were, but repressing their feelings, they exhausted their strength in this feverish, stifled relationship. Sometimes the desire to break the ice, or love, pity or remorse, would urge him to take her in his arms and reveal his heart to her . . . but the thought that she would not believe him prevented him. And yet, it was true, he had never loved her so much . . .[10]

The deceit involved in betraying a wife he still *wants* to love with a mistress who holds an irresistible sway over him puts Marigny in a dilemma with particularly sharp horns, but it does not persuade him to give up one for the other. Marigny exemplifies the apparent fact that while the need to practice deceit is a constant and often painful feature of the adulterous liaison, it is not of the fear of discovery that such relationships die. The death-knell is more likely to be sounded after discovery has taken some of the exciting danger out of the clandestine meetings.

Emma, for example, operates by manipulating the combination of Charles's blindness and her own craftiness. The demise of her affair with Léon has nothing to do with anticipated discovery, but rather with its innate unsatisfactoriness, and in this has something in common with the destruction of the Anna–Vronsky liaison. Both couples are for a time happily in love, and both relationships deteriorate under pressure from the female. In the case of Emma, she imperceptibly, at first, replaces their genuine and satisfying physical love with her old imaginary passion-love, whose extreme, vague, and joyless aspects alienate and even frighten Léon. But, more important, he revolts against the 'devouring' of his personality, which every day grows greater, and creates a resentment of Emma's 'permanent victory'. She tries more and more to draw him away from his real world of work and friends, and only her pride prevents her having him followed in an attempt to watch over his entire life.

But at this point her similarities with Anna end. For Anna, the despair is born of the insufficiency of her closeness with Vronsky; but Emma understands that no human relationship will ever make her happy, that *nothing in this life* has ever, will ever, give her happiness. She dreams yet again of a more perfect lover, with the heart of a poet and the form of an angel – and admits that his realisation would still leave her with an unsatisfied desire . . . even 'the sweetest kisses only leave your lips with an unfulfillable desire for an even greater pleasure'. Personifying uncannily the de Rougemont language, she burns, and is burnt by, the flame lit by her adultery, even though in the actual presence of each other she and Léon bore and disgust one another. All she now gets out of their times together is a jaded weariness.

Emma, in fact, according to Flaubert, finds in adultery all the plati-
tudes of marriage.

She retains the passion which is more important to her than Léon
by substituting for him, in her thoughts, another man, a phantom, who
lives in a country yet more unreal than their earlier dreams, one which
is bluish in the moonlight, and has silken ladders leading down from
flowered balconies.

In this fantasy-country the phantom lover comes and carries her
away . . . the intensity of her imaginative life leaves her flat and
brisée – broken, half-dead. For Emma the death-wish *is* at the end of
passion. Her desperate need for money simply provides Flaubert with
a credible mechanism for ending his story which Emma herself does
not need at all. For Léon, whose youthfully romantic days have long
since fled, the end of the affair is a welcome release from a cloying
relationship he has come to resent because it so isolates him from the
enjoyment of normal companionship. But unlike Vronsky's situation
the stigma of social ostracism is not for Léon the cause of the isolation.
Flaubert's anger is directed to the castigation of romanticism; Léon
is no more than a victim caught up in Emma's death-dance with passion – a partner who is made to follow the steps further than he wants
to go. The course of their affair is a progressive withdrawal from
reality, from life itself. And while Léon finally makes it back to the
real world, Emma finds her true goal in suicide.

Romanticism in this sense however had never such a grip on the
English imagination, and the preoccupations of the English affair are
quite other. In *One of Our Conquerors* Meredith gives a particularly
sympathetic account of Nataly and Victor's life together, which differs
basically from Anna's and Emma's stories because he deals with something which is practically a marriage. Victor has simply cast off his
first, unloved wife, and on the whole she makes very little trouble for
him. He is loving and faithful to Nataly, and able also to continue
a perfectly normal, not to say successful, business life. But Victor's
imperviousness to the infrequent society snub also makes him insensitive to Nataly's sufferings, which are very real. Cast off by her own
family, goaded into leaving two successive country-houses when people
find out about her, she is forced into complete emotional dependence
on Victor. 'Only Victor, none other, stood with her against the world'.
The story's interest shifts to the daughter of the union, but throughout it all Nataly looms in the background, dependent, unhappy, and
longing for the life of seclusion Victor's business interests cannot allow
– and which was the cause of breakdown between Anna and Vronsky.
Nataly and Victor survive to win forgiveness and good will from
Victor's first wife, but the path to it is, for Nataly at least, fraught
with a loneliness Victor never feels. Meredith demands sympathy and

understanding for Nataly, convinced as he was that it was always the woman who bore the brunt of the illegal union.

On the other hand, the loneliness ensuing from the bachelor existence led by the hero of *En Ménage* after he has turned out in high dudgeon the wife found in *flagrante delicto*, is also not without its pathetic side. André sees quite clearly that it is not so much physical satisfaction that he is missing, but the *society* of a woman – the rustle of her skirt, the tinkle of her laugh, the murmur of her voice. He begins to wish he had accepted what Karenin also could not accept – a union based on mutual indulgence, so common in Paris – but which he has prevented by his instinctive reaction to turn her out.

So great is his loneliness that when Berthe comes to see him on business he sweeps her into his arms, into their bed, and back into the conjugal nest. It is not said that they live happily ever after; Huysmans sees all long-term relationships, whether in marriage or concubinage, as roughly the most convenient way of obtaining the right number of buttons on one's shirts and adequate satisfaction of the *crise juponnière*; but either is preferable to the alternatives of the prostitute, the paid mistress, or the loneliness of bachelordom. That dreariness is unfortunately inevitable in any walk of life is the burden of French nihilism; when one's *illusions* are *perdues*, one simply makes the best of what is to hand.

In considering the course of the adulterous affair, we have so far seen examples of some of its characteristics: deception, guilt, ennui, and isolation or loneliness. We have not yet considered the question of jealousy, which, like guilt, draws an interesting dividing-line between those who feel it and those who do not. André's reaction upon discovering Berthe in bed with her lover shows what jealousy does when taken unawares – its tendency to lash out, to reject the offending partner, to feel full of moral indignation and wounded pride.* It is also the case that André comes to regret the hastiness of his action, and bolstered by the philosophy 'What does it all matter?', lives to see the day when he takes back his erring wife.

Nevertheless, his instinctive sense of outrage and anger is a stereotype in the French mentality. It is the reaction which Mme Arnoux so fears from her husband that she thwarts every attempt on Frédéric's part to make bodily contact with her; and it is partly what makes the sophisticated Bel-Ami set the police on to his wife, so that they can

---

* André is a prime example of a husband who feels jealous over a wife whom he does not love, for wounded self-esteem can be the root of jealousy as effectively as the sense of loss. Nevertheless, Stendhal regarded the phenomenon as the height of stupidity.

discover her in bed with the Cabinet minister and charge her with a punishable offence.*

But the French stereotype does not tell the universal story. Jealousy is a relatively rare emotion in Russian literature, and even more rarely is it endowed with grandeur. The stock cuckold, Pavel Pavlovich, in Dostoevsky's *The Eternal Husband*, is introduced as a petulant fool, such concern for his rights as he does show being the main source of a satirical ridicule in the story. The New Man rejects jealousy as unworthy, and while Prince Grigorev, a Frenchified aristocrat, does not like being a *mari trompé*, his basically Russian outlook is revealed after all when he sends his wife away with her lover (although in separate compartments of the same train) to conduct their affair abroad.

In this light, Tolstoy is the exception; his feeling for jealousy is both more acute and more complicated than any other author's. Both the deceived husbands, Karenin and Pierre Bezukhov, conform to the Russian character by displaying an innate lack of jealousy. Karenin is of course gravely disturbed by Anna's infidelity, but his reaction is to shut himself away, to pretend that neither he nor anyone else has noticed. He punishes Anna only in the most private of all ways – for example, by not letting her see Seriozha. But the fact that he *will* not punish Anna, that he fails to make a sufficient stand, is the root of Tolstoy's contempt for him – a contempt he translates artistically by depicting him as essentially dried up, inhuman, scarcely alive. If Karenin had been able to go through with the idea that briefly presents itself to him – that of fighting a duel with Vronsky – he would have earned his author's approbation; he would have been seen to be defending what Tolstoy vehemently approved of and detested to see threatened – the image of the faithful wife and mother as the basis and kernel of stable family-life. But he only toys with the idea, knowing all the while he will not go through with it. Abominating culpable inaction, Tolstoy pours scorn on all Karenin is.

Pierre, on the other hand, is a favourite of his creator's, his high standing shown partly by the fact that although he most properly, in Tolstoy's eyes, loathes his depraved wife (her depravity being at least partially contained in her lack of jealousy *vis-à-vis* Pierre) he nevertheless challenges Dolokhov to a duel. As with all Tolstoy's characters, there are cogently powerful motivations for Pierre's action. His idealistic nature is distressed by the notion of being united to a woman he

---

* It will be recalled that in France adultery was illegal. Nevertheless, it was not easy to catch lovers (see *Bel-Ami*, p.328):

  – Vous avez jusqu'à neuf heures, n'est-ce pas? Cette limite passée, vous ne pouvez plus pénétrer dans un domicile particulier pour y constater un adultère.

  – Non, monsieur, sept heures en hiver, neuf heures à partir de 31 mars.

despises – a depraved, incestuous, immoral, and meretricious woman; yet the suspicion of her infidelity tortures him like the coming to a head of an aching boil. By challenging Dolokhov to a duel he feels, quite illogically, that he is comfirming his suspicious and taking the step needed to lance the boil; and finally, once launched, he fears to look ridiculous in the eyes of the world by withdrawing. Underlying these reasons there is also his desire to be free of Hélène, which the duel, by revealing her infidelity, will ensure. The psychology is perfect; yet Tolstoy's personal convictions are never far from his most consummate artistic creations. In this case he sets a personal seal of approval on Pierre's show of jealousy which he angrily withholds from Karenin's paralysis.

It is of course true that Anna's jealousy fits are wholly unadmirable, and in fact destructive of what is left of her relationship with Vronsky. But Tolstoy, like the Old Testament teaching on anger, distinguishes between a just and an unjust jealousy; the jealousy of the betrayed husband is not only just but necessary – necessary to the maintenance of family life. According to at least two of the characters in *War and Peace*, André and Dolokhov, woman is essentially vain, selfish and trivial, reprehensibly incapable of acting as the regenerative and elevating influence man needs and seeks. Neither of them, they claim, has succeeded in meeting an incarnate version of the bridal purity they both seek. What they are really saying is that the perennial sense of guilt harboured by the self-accusing Russian male can be partly assuaged by casting the blame elsewhere; thus, it becomes the woman's fault that he is as he is, since it is she who has failed to elevate him to the heights he recognises but does not attain. To man then must be left the task of ensuring the respectability of the female; and with perhaps unconscious bitterness, Tolstoy deliberately condemns the man who fails to insist upon the establishment and retention of his only source of redemption in a depraved world : the family circle guided and inspired by the one woman who has redeemed herself, the Mother.

In fact the earliest ground on which Tolstoy despises Karenin is his failure to set up a proper family life in the first place : Anna is a mother, but only just; their life together scarcely portrays the kind of family life Tolstoy was thinking of (best seen in the epilogue of *War and Peace*). Dolly, on the other hand, reacts correctly every time : she is suitably upset by Stiva's threat to the family happiness, but she does not in fact *do* anything except continue to maintain the household, and by taking Stiva back, helps him to keep as close as he can to the ideal – always given that he has perennial bachelor tastes. But so long as Dolly is there, and the family circle is not disrupted, the correct order of things is held in balance. There is no real threat.

Here then is the source of Tolstoy's championing of the jealous husband and his anger at the tolerant one. And in his equivocal treatment of the emotion harboured by Anna on the one hand, and the husbands on the other, he appears to see jealousy as a two-headed eagle, capable both of gnawing at the vitals of a love-relationship, and standing as a symbol of male dignity and dominance.

Moreover, it does seem to be the case that Tolstoy's attitudes to jealousy are more commonly echoed in the French novel than in the Russian. But here we must insist on the distinction between how his characters behave, which is with complete fidelity to the Russian character, and how Tolstoy thought they ought to behave, which was with fidelity to a rather personal ideal of his own.

The writers of the French school did not face the same difficulty. Zola, for example, seems to be comfortable within the national tradition when he also depicts contempt for the *mari trop complaisant* in *La Bête Humaine*. With the conjugal relationship reduced to silent toleration of each other, Roubaud and Séverine drag out their life of mutual contractual obligation to each other; but Roubaud displays a passive acceptance of his wife's infidelity with Jacques, so strange to Séverine's mind that she interprets it as part of a progressive moral gangrene attacking his whole being. When he comes upon the couple together he does absolutely nothing; even Jacques feels a mixture of pity and scorn for this *'homme fini'*. Jealousy is in this context seen as a manly and protective reaction in a stratum of society rife with promiscuity : Grandmorin rapes every young female he comes in contact with; Becqueux has a 'femme' (wife or woman?) at each terminus of the railway line; Duvergne assumes that if Jacques can be Séverine's lover then his turn will surely come, and Grandmorin's sister, who occupies a high place in Rouen society, has many affairs managed with sufficient discretion to prevent scandal. If it were not for the fear engendered by the jealous husband, implies Zola, the society would be fragmented by a plethora of irregular relationships.

However, despite the temptation to be drawn into a few inescapable comments on what appear to be certain national tendencies, it must be stressed that the role played by jealousy is essentially a very personal one. Husbands who have any stakes at all in the fidelity of their wives – whether it be because they love them, because a virtuous wife is necessary to their position in life, or because some part of the male's self-image is vested in the notion of his wife's decorum – are to a greater or lesser degree shattered when they discover the truth, and are riven by the pangs of jealousy. Husbands who have accepted a true *mariage de convenance* and assume that the wife will go her own way, demand only discretion – hence the difference between Count Muffat, who sincerely believed his wife to be faithful, and M. de Dambreuse, who never dreamt that his was. Hence also the series of *maris complaisants* in *Bel-Ami*, as opposed to the anger of Bel-Ami himself, who had chosen to believe that Madeleine's interests in other men were genuinely professional and was proved wrong.

As for lovers, they are inclined to accept the existence of conjugal rights, and very rarely feel jealous of the husband : Rodolphe and Charles (who is emblematically the kind of husband who never knows what is going on) are the best of friends; Bel-Ami sits down to lunch with Mme de Marelle and her husband with only the most transient flutter of a qualm; Dominique utterly accepts that Madeleine should have a husband (though his reasons go deeper, as we saw); and Vronsky's offhand disdain for Karenin is nowhere near jealousy. By the same token, Grace is not jealous of Mrs Charmond, since she cares little whether Fitzpiers loves her or not, and finds her security in the loyalty and affection of the Hintock folk. Her father, however, feels deeply disturbed and jealous on her behalf, since he feels half responsible for the marriage – that is, he had as much interest and concern vested in it as many a husband.

After a jealous outburst, one might suppose a magnanimous pardon to be a possible follow-up; but the fact is that, with the exception of Barbey d'Aurevilly, almost no writers consider the concept of forgiveness with any seriousness. The pragmatic M. de Camors genuinely appreciates the determination of his deceived wife to put a cheerful face on things in the hopes of improvement, but their façade is scarcely a reconciliation. Only Marigny has to contend with the burden of a wife's suffering resolve never to offer reproaches, and he writes accordingly: 'For Ryno . . . this magnanimity of silence, this grandeur of touching reserve was a kind of torture, both inexorable and deserved, which would last a long time. Why, indeed, should it cease? The wrong he had done was irreparable. Hermangarde might forgive them . . . but in the act of forgiving she would remember. She would not forget.'[11] The author comments that this point – when communication has become impossible – is the sign that the marriage is truly broken. The modern counsellor would certainly argue that inability to communicate is indeed a marriage-breaker; but Barbey is saying something more.

Ryno and Hermangarde cannot communicate because forgiveness is both essential and impossible to their relationship. Only confession, contrition and forgiveness can loosen the lines of communication that have seized between them; but beyond the fact that unilateral forgiveness makes for a psychological and moral imbalance which will always provide difficulty for the one needing to be forgiven, Barbey, and his creation Ryno, are of the race of men who find unacceptable the notion of male self-abasement. With the woman in the position of granting or withholding pardon, she becomes too much like a superior.

Terrified by the dread of not being in control, Ryno stops short at the point where his mastery comes into doubt – even if, as is here the case, it means the total breakdown of a marriage he still has some yearning for.

It is as much on the impossibility of forgiveness as on the practice of adultery itself that the marriage founders; and in spite of the inherent universality of this fact the profound unease it arouses is perhaps the reason why the theme is not approached in any other novel.

From this brief speculation then, we move on to what the case of Ryno and Hermangarde stopped short of revealing about the course of an affair : the shoals encountered when, for whatever reason, it appears that the female really has gained the upper hand.

To warn against domination by a woman is the motivation of the last part of *Nana*; Zola depicts early in the novel the growth in Muffat of some kind of real love for Nana, but shows that she is incapable of returning it. His affection is misplaced; in Zola's hierarchy of females no honest women are to be found in Nana's milieu, and there is no possibility of a prostitute being rescued from her evil ways by the ennobling power of love. Zola's compulsive realism makes him see society as not only socially static, except for what prestige money can occasionally obtain, but also *morally* static : different social strata have their own codes of morality, and they are not interchangeable. In allowing himself to become pathetically and desperately dependent on Nana, Muffat is breaking certain shibboleths which, if universalised, would result in the total upheaval of the only form of society Zola and his public knew. There is more than a suggestion of class-warfare in Nana's savagely successful attempt to make Muffat dress up in his official robes and spit on them, while she kicks him along; and in his depiction of Muffat's humiliation Zola intends more than the hint of a warning.

The message is made even plainer by the activities of Muffat's wife, who uses her knowledge of her husband's helpless involvement with Nana to wreak her own form of vengeance. We have seen Hermangarde's silent reproaches and visible martyrdom, and Mme de Camors' much more efficient attempt at pretended cheerfulness. But the Countess goes the other way, abandoning her former discreet cover of dignity and devotion to espouse a life of frivolous and expensive pleasure, and wielding an upper hand which puts Muffat, for the first time, at a disadvantage to her. Thus the loss of masculine dignity and superiority that Zola sees as a product of the adulterous liaison has a deeper significance related to the delicate balance of power between the sexes. Muffat lies in a crumpled heap at the bottom of a parabola, whose two ascending and ambitious arms are the two women with whom he is involved. Nana and the Countess equally and separately threaten the very immobility of the social strata on which depends Zola's whole view of society, and man's age-old picture of himself as the manipulator, the user, the disposer.

However, although the betrayal of the Countess Muffat by the husband is not without consequence in the way she conducts her own life, she makes no attempt to interfere with Muffat's activities. James's study of Maggie Verver in *The Golden Bowl,* on the other hand, depicts a deceived wife who bends her every power to the end of restoring her wandering husband to herself. In attempting this, James and his heroine are unique; we shall see later what success the campaign has. For the moment we must be content with the fairly considerable light James throws upon the course of an affair, seen from the viewpoint of the deceived wife.

Maggie begins by making two constatations : firstly, that there is something between her adored husband, Prince Amerigo, and Charlotte Verver, née Stant, who had been Maggie's girlhood friend and has married Maggie's widowed father. Secondly, Maggie acknowledges instantly that she herself is partly responsible for the Prince's defection, because of her continued, excessive enjoyment of her father's companionship, quantitatively more available to her than her husband's. The anxiety and doubt aroused by these discoveries affect the way she responds to Amerigo, but contrary to what one might expect, it is a process of enhancement, of deeper love and greater sexual desire. 'She had never doubted the force of feeling that bound her to her husband; but to become aware, almost suddenly, that it had begun to vibrate with a violence that had some of the effect of a strain would, rightly looked at, after all but show she was, like thousands of women, every day, acting up to the full privilege of passion.'[12] Having understood both the fact and the significance of this heightened feeling at work in her, Maggie resolves to hold out to her husband 'the flower of participation . . . the idea so needlessly so absurdly obscured of her *sharing* with him whatever the enjoyment, the interest, the experience might be'. Paradoxically, the one thing that can deflect her from this purpose is his sexual power over her. Just once 'she gave up, let her idea go, let everything go; her one consciousness was that he was taking her in his arms'. But after this instructive moment she is strong, treading successfully the difficult path of full passionate response without loss of self-control.

Maggie's third constatation is that the restoration of the marriage must not be achieved at anyone's expense, that each of the four people involved – herself, the Prince, Charlotte and Adam Verver – must retain their essential selves undamaged, without loss of self-esteem. Therefore, she does not denounce Charlotte or the Prince to their own faces or to anyone else's. She goes no further than to let the Prince understand she is aware of something; she will not tell him how much – or how little – she knows. And she impresses *tacitly* upon him, while always saving his face, a sharp sense of his own wrong. He *never* endures scorn, humiliation or even moral righteousness. On the other hand, she coolly and deliberately exploits the lovers' terror of being exposed; pricks them to compunction; holds them in agonised suspense; keeps them in the wrong; and steadfastly refuses to engage in any verbal battle, which they of course would win, because they are cleverer. None of this is achieved without anguish on her own part. During the whole course of the affair she feels 'very much alone', but her pain is most acute when she is forced to acknowledge that Charlotte and the Prince are silently fighting back. Her father suggests that he and she make a trip to Spain together; she is aware that Charlotte and Amerigo are awaiting her decision with bated breath. Amerigo again uses an embrace to try to exert his sexual power over her (James calls it 'unfailing magic'); it is a test in which Maggie discovers that her concern for their marriage is fractionally more powerful than her overwhelming desire to yield to him. 'To this, as they went, every throb in her consciousness prompted her – every throb, that is, except one, the throb of her deeper need to know where she "really was" . . . She was making an effort that horribly hurt her'.[13] She makes herself propose that *he* and Mr Verver go instead, thus setting a test for him. If he refuses, she knows it will be through unwillingness to leave Charlotte. Amerigo is charming about the new proposal, but inclined to hedge; he gets the better of Maggie by suggesting that the proposal should come from Charlotte. Maggie sees that this could result in the arousal of suspicions on her father's part – an eventuality she is determined to avoid, according to her plan that no one must be hurt by her attempt to get her husband back.

It will be noted that Maggie's way of going about things avoids the pitfalls encountered by Ryno and Hermangarde : whatever the Prince does, he will not have to ask forgiveness of Maggie, since her strategy averts the need on his part to put himself in the wrong. That point made, I do not propose to retell any more of Maggie's campaign, nor to comment on the subtlety with which it is carried out and the sinuosity of the style adopted by James to render the secret despairs, the minute victories, the unspoken parries, the agonies of uncertainty endured by the three protagonists. (Whether Adam Verver is, as he appears, unconscious of it all, we never really know.) What emerges from this section of the story is simply that an adulterous liaison *can* be countered by a betrayed wife; that betrayal is not the final deathblow to a marriage, though it may be a first thrust. And while the components that have appeared in the novels as the by-products of adultery – the deception, the ennui, the isolation – are destructive of the lovers' relationship, the resolution and the integrity which motivate Maggie are positive qualities, almost creative in their power to build anew the damaged bonds between Maggie and the Prince.

This chapter has so far attempted to look at the course of the adulterous affair from the liaison of the past to the immediate reaction of the adulterous wife to her first extra-marital sexual encounter; from the shock of discovery experienced by the trusting spouse to the various emotional components of the affair itself, including such variables as loss of self-esteem, jealousy, forgiveness, female dominance, and the paths open to the deceived wife. In short, we have been preoccupied with the components of the triangle – or the quadrangles, as they sometimes turn out to be. There is however another factor ('the neglected question', as one of the novels is actually entitled): the child who hovers on the periphery of the breaking marriage, often vitally affected by the affairs of its parents and their lovers, but seldom seen by the majority of the novelists to offer any intrinsic interest. There are some, however, who at least see the child as a factor in the relationship, and one or two to whom the welfare of the offspring is a major concern. Pre-eminently we think of Dolly Oblonsky.

Partly because of the time factor – most adulteries occur when the marriage is relatively young – Dolly is the only parent to have produced more than one child; not only is she surrounded by a flock of six, but deep in the country with them, steeped in motherhood, she finds consolation for all her cares. Once again, Tolstoy is far too consummate an artist to cloy his readers' taste for family-life with a sugar-sweet rendition of it. As he himself was well aware, a quiet life with six children is impossible. Nevertheless, the noise and uproar they produce is the only kind of happiness Dolly will ever know; without them, she would be alone with her thoughts of a faithless husband. And in spite of Dolly's fears about the effect of a profligate father, the children seem happy and healthy; it is perfectly clear that their father's adventures do not impinge on them, and that his charm when present is more than enough to compensate for the clouds which occasionally cast a mysterious gloom over the family atmosphere.

By contrast, it is a symptom of Anna's moral deterioration that the intense love she initially feels for Seriozha is gradually displaced by her obsession with Vronsky, while she is almost indifferent to the little girl born of her adultery. She has in Tolstoy's eyes sunk so low in abandoning her first maternal duties that he will not allow her the redemption that is normally possible to every woman who accepts the burdens of motherhood.

E

Most writers join with Tolstoy in seeing the child as a peculiar source of grace; the child of the unhappy marriage is as much a joy and comfort to Mme de Camors as is the baby born of adultery to Christiane *(Mont-Oriol)*. The hint of May's pregnancy is enough to bring out the best in Ellen's nature, so that she retires from the fight for Newland *(The Age of Innocence)*; and it is part of Emma Bovary's disease of romanticism that her baby simply enables her to indulge in her role-playing. She is the doting mother when it suits her, and perfectly indifferent to the child the rest of the time.

However, the effect upon a child of a broken marriage is analysed at greatest depth by James in his deliberate intention stated in the preface to *What Maisie Knew* of 'making confusion worse confounded by drawing some stray fragrance of an ideal across the scent of selfishness, by sowing on barren strands, through the mere fact of presence, the seed of the moral life.' To do this, he does not state adultery to be *per se* morally evil, nor marriage *per se* to be morally beautiful; he rather uses unhappy marriages and extra-marital relationships seen through the eyes of the child, Maisie, to show up selfishness, dishonesty, exploitation and vulgarity, while quite clearly implying that the legal standing of a union may be irrelevant to its integrity.

In this complex novel, conventional morality finds its nearest ally in Mrs Wix, Maisie's nurse, who refuses in the name of propriety to tolerate a *ménage* consisting of herself, Maisie, Sir Claude (Maisie's mother's lover) and Mrs Beale (Maisie's mother). But James shows, through Maisie's perception of her true motivations, that Mrs Wix's real concern is anxious self-interest – if there is another woman to care for Maisie, Mrs Wix becomes redundant, and loses her position.

The rest of the quartet – Maisie's separated parents and their respective paramours – behave with varying degree of selfishness and deceit, all highlighted by Maisie's superb, unconscious, and naïve moral perception and concern.

Ida, her mother, has no love for Maisie, but shares her with her father for six months of the year 'not for any good they could do her, but for the harm they could with her unconscious aid do each other'. She abandons her first lover, Sir Claude, and plunges into a series of affairs. But in order to fabricate a 'moral' justification for her desertion of Maisie, she offers to take the child away to South Africa, knowing quite well that Maisie will refuse the offer, and thus relieve Ida of any vestigial responsibility. Maggie is in fact shattered – but on Ida's behalf – because she instinctively seeks security for Ida, and has lit upon one of Ida's lovers as the one to give it to her. She hopes Ida will go to South Africa not with herself, Maisie, but with this man, unaware that the whole journey is an invention. When she learns that this lover is already a thing of the past, she is overcome with fear and pain, 'a vision ominous, precocious, of what it might mean for her mother to have forfeited such a loyalty as that. There was literally a moment in which Maggie saw – saw madness and desolation, saw ruin and darkness and death.'[14]

Beale Farrange, Maisie's father, sets up with Maisie's governess, using Maisie as a cover; Maisie is willing and happy to be of use, since her mother's desertion has left her with a sense of rejection. She accidentally runs into her father with his newest mistress and he succeeds in manipulating her natural filial feeling for him via recall of past associations. Again her innate generosity shows itself in her desire to give him some token of affection : but his own real anxiety to be rid of her makes Beale invite her to repudiate *his* offer of a trip away. Maisie is in agony trying not to hurt him by refusing his offer. Her exquisite concern is contrasted with his mean-spiritedness, as he deliberately explodes her belief that she is truly loved by her step-parents. He tells Maisie they only want her as a pretext; but again Maisie's selfless innocence frustrates his malice : she accepts joyfully the notion that she is of use to someone.

Sir Claude, Ida's first lover, has more genuine affection for Maisie than anyone else, and tries for some of the time to bring her interests into line with his own. He also dimly perceives some of Maisie's moral beauty. However, he has two vices Maisie has not even heard of – weakness and lust – which finally lead him to abandon the child, even though he knows her first choice is to live with him. Acute enough to be aware of the deadening effect of Mrs Wix's crassly conventional values on Maisie; sensitive enough to feel the life-giving effect of Maisie's love on him; and delicate enough to appreciate the sublime moral sense in the child which will not let her abandon Mrs Wix even though to stick by her means to lose her beloved Sir Claude – aware of all this, he still cannot choose Maisie over Mrs Beale, with her shoddy values and hypocritical double standards.

Maisie emerges as beautifully moral in an absolute way, because she is too young to have got her standards from the world around her; totally innocent amidst the toils of sexual intrigue, she sees the significance of sexual relationships only in terms of the personal integrity or lack of it between the couple. The characters involved are paradigmatic examples of the basic selfishness of lust and its inextricable links with adultery; the hurt and harm the two together often bring in their wake – in this case the abandoning of Maisie to the odious Mrs Wix – is quite abhorrent.

One can only hope the grown Maisie may have the resilience of the heroine of *One of Our Conquerors*. Brought up in ignorance of the *de facto* nature of her parents' union (her father believes that repression and mystery are 'wholesome'), Nesta suffers considerable

shock when first apprised of the truth. She personally survives it well
enough, but a harder test follows when her most ardent suitor needs
also to be told the situation. He reels under the shock, but luckily for
Nesta, rallies, and finally believes he can go through with the marriage. While he is making up his mind, Nesta is accepted for the first
time into the home of her aunts, who have ostracised Victor, but force
themselves to attach no blame to his daughter. Full of what Meredith
calls 'stationary excellence', they try very hard to love Nesta, even
though she clearly fails to conform to their notion of what a young
girl should be – 'round red cheeks, and rounded open eyes, and a
demure shut mouth, a puppet's divine ignorance'.

As Nesta begins to fall in love with the suitor, whom she had previously only entertained in order to please her parents, Meredith
seizes the opportunity to state his own view of the situation :

> Thus was she, too, being put into her woman's harness of the bit
> and the blinkers, and taught to know herself for the weak thing, the
> gentle parasite, which the fiction of our civilization expects of her,
> caressingly and contemptuously, to become in the active, while it is
> exacted of her – O Comedy of Clowns – that in the passive she be a
> rock-fortress, impregnable, not to speak of magically encircled. She
> must also have her feelings; she must not be an unnatural creature;
> she must have sufficient intelligence; for her stupidity does not
> flatter the possessing man. It is not an organic growth that he
> desires in his mate, but a happy composition.[5]

In fact, Meredith gives Nesta chances to escape from the blinkers
by involving her in such experiences as will teach her to think : the
revelation about her parents, the various reactions of her friends and
suitors as the news trickles around, and finally a trip abroad – Meredith's ever-ready escape clause for those suffering from the rigidity of
English society. But before she is, as it were, emancipated, Nesta shows
both how an illegitimate child may feel when she discovers the truth
about herself, and also how people near to her may react. At the close
of the century (the novel was published in 1897) Meredith sees the
situation as painful but not tragic. He is the most optimistic of the
authors who choose to deal with the plight of the child, but also the
only one who looks at the special position of a child brought up
happily enough and threatened only by social strictures. Mostly the
writers who treat the child of the broken marriage see the situation as
one of damage and suffering, the child an innocent victim of the selfish
desires of its parents – unless, as in Dolly's case, the life of the family
can somehow be kept going.

If the child is shown to be one of the fatalities of the continuing
affair, it is not claimed by any writer that the extra-marital bed itself

is one of roses. As we have said, the guilt engendered in all but a few cases has a deleterious effect upon the lovers, and the novelists take pains to portray further miseries as the affair proceeds. In the next chapter we shall examine the final outcome of the various relationships already embarked upon – what has been familiarised to the modern reader as 'The End of the Affair', although few nineteenth-century novelists produce the same result as Greene.

4 The Order Vindicated:
The End of the Affair

What the novelists imaginatively present as the outcome of adultery is highly variable, though a representative judgement finally emerges from the diversity of their creation.

The smallest group, consisting of Turgenev, Chekhov and Pisemsky, scarcely show anything that can be called an outcome in the judgemental sense at all. While it would be inaccurate to say of any of them that they do not treat adultery in their works, they nevertheless exhibit a striking indifference to it compared with other writers. Turgenev, as we have already seen, brushes with adultery in his preoccupation with the frustration of true love. But his *using* of it as a means to an end puts it in the category of a tool to hand, an activity of his society he was able to employ as an apposite mechanism – but not a mechanism he wanted to pull apart to see how it worked. The horror of adultery depicted in *A Nest of the Gentry*, the novel most reliant on this theme, is presented as something quaint and odd, an old-fashioned relic of religious fanaticism. But Turgenev himself neither endorses this reaction nor offers any other moral view; his withholding of judgement is in fact a positive stance of deliberate indifference.

Chekhov similarly uses the theme in numerous short stories, but rarely, despite its frequency, as a central one, and never as a moral issue in itself. In his picture of society love is seldom found in marriage, and is therefore frequently sought outside it. Chekhov displays no reticence at all about the commonness of both casual and deeper extra-marital affairs, but he most often uses the adulterous situation to reveal character rather than to pose a moral problem. The question is always for him one of life's imponderables, but a sociopsychological one rather than a moral one.

Finally, the realist Pisemsky is in no hurry to cast judgement, as M. Ermilov acknowledges fully in his introduction to one edition of Pisemsky's collected works. Elaborating the point, he quotes the critic D. Pisarev:

When you observe the characters in Pisemsky's tales, you realize that when you judge them, you are inevitably judging their social milieu; they are all of them only guilty in that they are not strong enough to keep to their original path; they go whither the others go; it is hard for them, but nevertheless they are not able to protest against that which causes them to suffer. You feel sorry for them, because they suffer, but their sufferings are only the consequence of their own stupidity; they are influenced in the direction of these stupidities by their own society . . . It only remains to us to pity the sacrifices caused by the ugly corruption of things, and to curse those existing perversions.

Thus in *Boyarshchina* Anna Pavlovna goes mad and dies after abandoning her husband, and being abandoned by her lover; but Pisemsky makes no moral connection between her adultery and her death, and there is no justification for imagining her death to be any kind of punishment. The death scene is in fact couched in gently sentimental language designed to arouse compassion for the dead girl, and to insist upon her right to a place in heaven :

Saveli came up and took her by the hand; the sick girl's eyes fluttered. Saveli nearly cried out with joy, for her eyes showed none of their former delirium.

'Anna Pavlovna ! Do you know me?' he asked.

But she only gave a beautiful smile and without answering closed her eyes again. God was asking her for the last time to go to Him and to look at someone who truly loved her.[1]

Rather than condemn the adulteress, Pisemsky's motives lie elsewhere : he appears primarily concerned to show the soullessness of the male members of the upper classes and the lack of spiritual vigour which characterises the lives they lead, and by implication to conclude that neither in the role of husband nor of lover can they provide uplifting or even responsive companionship for their women. If the heroine dies it is because even her love affair (who cares about its legality?) is a failure – and not because a vengeful end must be brought to her adultery.

Three other writers allot their characters little or no specific punishment. Closest to Chekhov amongst the novelists is the Zola of *Thérèse Raquin*, who uses the mechanism of an adulterous affair to study the crime of murder and the guilt resulting from it. The latter entails a remorse which cripples the lovers' lives, while the adultery bothers them not at all. Given that Zola did however write other novels in which adultery is regarded as a grave, even devastating, sin, one is led to interpret this dichotomy as a tendency to see moral delicacy in terms of class. Thérèse and Laurent are relegated to a very low shelf in their creator's mind, and Zola simply does not expect them to have a conscience about sexual immorality. This is a point to which we shall return; but certainly *Thérèse Raquin* is evidence for it, as is *Pot-Bouille*, in which Zola clinically dissects the motivations of lower-class adulteresses with a tolerance which is almost insulting. At this level of society Zola simply does not bother about punishing his miscreants. Thérèse and Laurent suffer for having committed murder, it is true; but the *Pot-Bouille* creatures will continue to stew, as the name implies, in their own *misère* until, perhaps, they are hooked out by the claw of the Welfare State.

Yet this complicity with the vices of the lower classes is a far cry from the true indifference of Chekhov : in the interests of impartial realism Zola forswore emotional judgements on his characters, but one does not have to read his talk of taking a 'fer rouge' to society to cauterise 'une plaie où s'est mise la gangrène', to grasp the social intent behind his portrayal of vice and lust. What life offers these people is punishment in itself; the role of the writer is here accomplished not by condemnation but by exposure.

In this he is joined by Maupassant whose 'soif d'idéal' drives him to execrate a society 'repue, gorgée de plaisirs', but who does not in either *Bel-Ami* or *Mont-Oriol* visit his wrath upon the heads of his characters by any overt form of retribution. No one is upset by the rife adultery except the law and, indirectly, the child. Such moral criticism as the book arouses must be evoked in the mind of the reader, for when it closes Bel-Ami has succeeded in persuading the rich, young, and beautiful Suzanne to run away with him while he still maintains his relationship with Clothilde de Marelle; and so ambiguous is the message of the novel that many contemporary reviews, while praising its powerful realism, deprecated its picture of moral degradation. The characters in the book are *not* ashamed of themselves, and are more often crowned by success than disgrace. Is Maupassant then in danger of not getting his message over ? Or, indeed, are we wrong to assume, with his editor Gérard Delaisement, that the book is designed to be a 'searing portrait of the hypocrisy and injustice which thrive in the bosom of a disgusting social promiscuity'? I think Delaisement is correct in his appraisal; the clue to Maupassant's condemnation lies not in an outcome of death and destruction, but in the portrayal of growing despair. The poet Norbert de Varenne, Bel-Ami's friend, whom we quoted earlier in reference to the nihilistic theme of the novel – 'To whom shall we direct our cries of distress . . . ?' – continues his cry of anguish by a speech redolent of fear, anxiety and terror : 'Solitude now fills me with terrible anguish . . . I feel that I am alone in the world, unbearably alone, yet surrounded by intangible dangers, by terrible unknown things . . . I am overcome by a kind of fever, a fever of pain and fear, the silence of the walls terrifies me . . . It would be good, after all, when one is old, to have children.'[2] This is the message that Bel-Ami has not heard, but which will reach him with a clang of doom in the empty rooms of his old age, when his body is shrunken and paunchy, his hair thin and his cheeks sallow. The warning-bells are there, but Maupassant is too bitter to ring them loudly.

He is a whit more indulgent to Christiane, allowing her to learn her lesson in the course of the novel. That is, having been abandoned by her seducer and forced to face the facts of loneliness as well as near death through milk-fever, Christiane's solitary life in harness with an unloved husband is alleviated by the consolation of the child. She will continue to pay, but not too dearly.

The third and last to condemn adultery without strictly punishing those who practise it, other than by a life of unhappiness, is Barbey d'Aurevilly. Enough can be anticipated of Ryno's marriage during the many years ahead, filled as they must be with glacial constraint and silent reproaches, for us to understand that this will be punishment enough. And the lesson is drawn still more directly in *Ce qui ne meurt pas* : there the adulterous Allan, dragging out a life of conjugal misery, writes to a friend who has managed his marital concerns more wisely : 'Whenever I visit you, I cannot leave untroubled. There is in this union which is marriage, in the most fleeting contemplation of the surface of a happy love, something which speaks even to one who has been deceived with an eloquent and sacred language. It awakens one and tears at one, as if one were a new field to be conquered.'[3] A moment of bliss (in bed with his bride's mother) and a lifetime of sorrow, aggravated by the sight of domestic harmony not unlike the Augustin marriage in *Dominique* . . . and yet one can only suppose that this is a fate less than death.

For death is finally the most common wage of adultery.

Death by illness is probably the most merciful. Such is the fate for example of M. de Camors, who catches his death of cold making long nocturnal rides to gaze in the windows of the house where his wife is bringing up his son. But it would be unjust, I think, to see his death as a crude punishment for a man essentially the son of his eighteenth-century materialist father and 'une des physionomies les plus expressives de son temps et de son pays'; there is a deeper significance to be found in the delicate irony of the libertine's sentimental need to see his abandoned wife and baby. All men must die; but how much more edifying a death it will be if the scapegrace has learnt his lesson first. Camors' demise is almost a happy event, for it is accompanied by a softening of his cynical heart and an acknowledgement of noble sentiments. It is only a pity that in this novel the author needed to contrive the story in order to make the point – that there is no substitute for family happiness. Feuillet rather went out on a limb when he insisted upon the charm of Camors' set-up – a mistress for *volupté* and a wife for stability – for, once having committed it all to paper, he found himself caught with a situation he could not approve, but which had much appeal and no inbuilt way of escape. The night rides are a credible way out – but they are nevertheless a device used to introduce a 'proper' ending that might otherwise have proved elusive.

Zola takes fewer pains to dispose of Nana. The threat she poses to society by her enslavement of Muffat, her deliberate gestures of defiance to the social system when she makes him crawl the floor in his chamberlain's outfit, are unequivocally revenged by her solitary, ghastly death and the smallpox which encrusts her face. Zola says quite explicitly : 'It was as if the virus she had caught in the gutters and from the corpses, that ferment with which she had poisoned a whole people, had now recahed up to her face and made it rot.'[4] He is of course talking of the pox she has spread; but is he not also castigating the prostitute who, by degrading a male hitherto presumed to be morally and socially superior, defies the hierarchy upon which society rests and thus portends a shifting of class structures all the more menacing in view of its not being localised in the Nana–Muffat situation? Nana's resentment of Muffat's position and her exploitation of his pathetic need of her is a microcosm of female oppression and female emancipation – hardly a ground-swell in 1880, when the novel was written, but blowing strongly enough in the wind to demand immediate male retaliation. Nana – and Proust's Odette – are representative of a generation of women subconsciously aware of the possibility of emancipation, but not yet part of a politically active movement. The battleground of embittered sexual warfare was where Nana really caught smallpox, as well as the gutter in which she was made to die.

The final victims of illness are the crippled husband in *The Forgotten Question*, and also his widow who, after marrying her lover, dies in childbirth. There is no doubt that the author is concerned to multiply the tragedies (the death of the child of the first marriage has been remarked already) in order to bring home his point; but it is clear that Markevich's concern for the child is not simply the excuse for an opportunity to censure the unfaithful mother but is more significantly a genuine example of the Russian concern for children. Liubov Petrovna is certainly not whitewashed; but the overwhelming impression is that it is not the adultery which is being punished, but the neglect of the child.

The death of Carter *(Miss Ravenel's Conversion)* on the battlefield is yet another revelation of the way so many authors of the nineteenth century manipulate the fate of the characters in order to bring down a judgement. A battlefield death is always an arbitrary choice for the writer; and Carter's death is in no way demanded by the story. The real reasons for his demise must be sought below the surface; but they are not very deeply buried. De Forest was daring in his theme, as we know from its rarity. But the boldness of his inspiration appears to fail with the setting-up of a relationship – between Carter and Mme Larue – which could not be allowed to flourish. There was no doubt that the affair must be curtailed – but why can it not be done by mere repentence?

Two possible objections to the turning over of a new leaf present themselves : firstly, it is doubtful whether mere repentence, without punishment, is sufficient to atone for either the enormity of the crime or the telling of it in an American story; and secondly, an inner repentance, without any justification for the change of heart, is not very convincing. The most likely alternative was discovery by Lillie, and what could only be called a show-down, followed *then* by repentance and happy-ever-after. But apart from the difficulties always inherent in this situation (compare the question of forgiveness in *Une Vieille Maîtresse*) there seems to be every likelihood that de Forest was constitutionally incapable of facing the issue of what happens between a wife and husband when adultery is discovered and must be discussed. If Lillie could only tell her husband she was pregnant in the dark, how could she dream of discussing the details of a sexual liaison? How could a clean-minded American author describe it? No. There are certain things better left veiled; and if the death of a rather dubious husband was the price to be paid, then de Forest was at least handsome enough to let him die in battle.

So, we have seen the novelists punish their errant victims by illness and the sword. But are there no characters permitted to take the law into their own hands?

In spite of the sympathetic understanding accorded the *crime passionnel* in France, particularly when the offender is avenging a case of wifely infidelity, few novelists portray murder as a likely outcome of adultery. With *Thérèse Raquin* must be grouped Zola's other novel of the seamier orders, *La Bête Humaine*, in which the adulterous passion of Jacques and Séverine is directly related to the violence of the dénouement.

Séverine's husband, it will be remembered, was a *mari* not so much *complaisant* as impassive; Jacques plans to kill him, but the attempt fails.* Life goes on as before, except that the Roubauds' move to a new flat enables Jacques and Sévérine to see each other with greater ease. However, this very facility takes some of the spark out of their affair : when they find they can see each other any old time they also find they have exhausted their mutual interest in each other. Their relationship loses its intrinsic value, and comes to symbolise escape to a new life; at heart weary of each other, they nevertheless cling together because only with the other does departure seem possible, and the start of 'l'autre vie'. All depends on the killing of Roubaud, and since Jacques failed the first time, Sévérine begins to lose faith in him. She reproaches and nags him; when they plan a new attempt it is not Roubaud whom Jacques kills, but Sévérine. Jacques himself dies in a train crash.

Why the deaths? Sévérine's is psychologically convincing, while Jacques' is purely accidental. But neither is inevitable. While it might be argued that even in 1880 realism had its limits, and could not entirely do without a dose of melodrama, it nevertheless would appear to be Zola's desire not to grant a reward to a couple whom he regarded as criminal – and criminal this time not just for their murder-plans, but also for their adultery. Jacques and Sévérine are out of a drawer just slightly above the level of Thérèse and Laurent, consequently Zola is relatively more judgemental. In so far as they ought to have known better, so they must be punished – not by God, for their class prevents their being the stuff of tragedy – but by the inevitable rage which accompanies the inefficiency of their squalid affair, and by the symbolic heralding of the break-up of the old order by the forces of industrialisation and the steam locomotive.

It may seem surprising that amongst the novels under discussion the only case of an outraged husband killing either his faithless wife or her lover occurs not in France but in Russia : but given that this is indeed the case, it is certainly not surprising that the incident is found in a work of Tolstoy's, and specifically in one of his latest stories, *The Kreuzer Sonata*. This is a strange piece of literature, for interwoven amongst a powerfully realistic account of the breakdown of a marriage are many weird, extravagant and absurd arguments which are consonant with Tolstoy's own beliefs – beliefs which so evolved over a period of years that *The Kreuzer Sonata* positively contradicts his early writings. A fairly lengthy account of this development now follows, so that the separate contribution of each work to Tolstoy's view of marriage and adultery may be properly understood.

Family Happiness (1859) was written at a time when Tolstoy ap-

* For an analysis of Jacques' thought processes, and the reasons for which he kills or fails to kill, see Chapter 12 of F. W. J. Hemmings's *Emile Zola*.

peared to believe in a form of family love similar to the ideals of *Dominique* – that is, a quiet secluded life in the country spent in giving service to the peasants and neighbours. Unlike *Dominique*, however, he dares to explore the possibility that these pleasures may pall on a girl considerably junior to her husband. He creates a situation in which a young wife is saved in the nick of time from a false step in order that she may truly repent and develop a new relationship with her husband, consisting not of 'being in love' but of a steady affection nourished by common parenthood. Thus Tolstoy is here already rejecting romantic love, but still believes in conjugal harmony; adultery is not faced as a real possibility (he introduces the hackneyed ploy of the unexpected interruption to escape the dangerous eventuality) but used as a fate-worse-than-death alternative.

By the time he had written *War and Peace* ten years later, Tolstoy had considerably crystallised his views on love, women, marriage, wives and infidelity. Love is depicted as an emotion likely to blind man to a woman's real character, and hence should be treated as nothing more than a dangerous indulgence. Evidence of this attitude can be found in André's experience with Lisa, and Natasha's almost disastrous passion for Anatole. But it seems as though Tolstoy's anxiety to communicate his message blinded him to the need for audience-awareness. Before her marriage Natasha is slim, lively, always glowing with animation, sometimes burning with fire, apt to burst into song, and altogether charming. After her marriage she is broad, stout, robust, motherly, calm and serene, with no visible trace of fire or even of soul – except on Pierre's return from Moscow. To cap it all she is uninterested in dress or appearance to the point of being almost slovenly, and pedestrian in her manner. Tolstoy explains that 'all of Natasha's outbursts had been due to her need of children and a husband'; now she has a total relationship with Pierre, 'to whom she had given herself utterly from the first moment – that is, with all her heart, not keeping any corner of it from him. She felt, having taken him for a husband, that she bore towards him not those poetic feelings that had drawn him to her, but something indefinite but very firm . . .'[5] Strong indeed was his faith in the message, if he was willing to sacrifice the early Natasha to the later one *and* persuade his reading public to prefer the version who was Pierre's wife.

Further evidence of Tolstoy's convictions can be found in Henri Troyat's biography; describing Tolstoy in 1870 he writes :

He was delighted with a study Strakhov had just published in *The Dawn* on the position of women. According to its author, woman was entitled by her physical and moral beauty to be considered the queen of creation, as long as she did not forsake her mission. Born to give delight and bear children, she became a monster the moment she turned aside from the path God had traced for her. Feminism was a crime against nature and it was man's duty to see that his helpmeet did not succumb to this temptation . . .[6]

The evidence of this kind of comment (the choice is wide) plus the convictions expressed in the novel lead to the conclusion that Tolstoy held not only the theory that marriage and conjugal happiness depended entirely on family life, but also that wives should emulate only nuns or wet-nurses. Nicholas accepts his nun-wife because he respects her and because he is passionately happy doing the estate-work; Pierre accepts Natasha's demands for total devotion to family life because these demands 'flatter' him and because he has in exchange the right to completely regulate his home life and be treated as lord and master. To the modern reader the lesson is anachronistic; both sets of lives appear eccentric and unappealing, and the doctrine itself – that marriage must not be based on romantic love, that it should follow certain defined spiritual axioms (like population above copulation), that it must be lived in the country, that it must provide enough children to keep the wife thoroughly occupied even in a servanted household, and that the husband should stay at home, either working on the estate or pursuing intellectual studies – all this seems narrow and dogmatic. The saving clause is that quite clearly Tolstoy saw the correct balance as difficult to achieve and easy to upset.

A little less than ten years later *Anna Karenina* appeared, in which three more marriages are examined : the Kitty–Levin union, presented as the marriage most likely to succeed; the Dolly–Stiva example of the continuing but shaky marriage; and the break-down marriage between Anna and Karenin.

The first is a love-match, taking place after some wild-oat sowing on Levin's part and an unhappy first passion on Kitty's. Levin divides women into two classes, the pure and the impure, the good and the guilty, the sexually uncontaminated and the sexually initiated. The reasons for this appear to be threefold : half-memories of his mother, whom he endows with qualities of sacredness, holiness and exquisite ideality (Tolstoy at the age of seventy-two still spoke of his own mother in similar terms); shame for his earlier debauches; and an idealised notion of sexual purity which he tended to identify with young virgins, and which he was able to discern in Kitty, who charms him with her childlike serenity, her goodness, gentleness and honesty.

When he thought about her he could imagine her very vividly, especially that charm, that expression of childlike clearness and goodness, that small fair curly head, so lightly positioned on her stately but girlish shoulders. The childlike expression of her face in conjunction with the delicate beauty of her figure gave her special charm that he wanted to recall : but what always illuminated her, as if unexpectedly, was the expression of her eyes – gentle, peaceful, and true, and especially her smile, always able to transport Levin into a world of magic where he felt himself to be both clever and capable, where he could remember the rare days of his earliest childhood.

In fact the entire feminine half of the Shcherbatsky family shares an aura which is mysterious, poetic, full of lofty sentiments, and thus provides the answer to his dreams. 'All the members of that family, especially the feminine half, appeared to him to be veiled in some kind of secret poetry; he not only could see no faults in them, but under this poetic, hidden veil of theirs he perceived the most elevated feelings and the highest form of perfection.'[7]

Kitty turns out to have several more good points, which practically put her in the Natasha–Mary class; after their marriage she displays many domestic accomplishments, really enjoys life in the country, and, by her motherhood, raises her relationship with Levin to new heights of non-sensual bliss. It is a charming picture; and it symbolises, with the rest of the book, the crystallisation of Tolstoy's attitudes to women, summed up in the terse message of Chapter 40 of his essay, *What Then Must We Do?*, that mother is the only woman entitled to the respect of God or man.

For in the girl who must exist before Kitty has attained what de Forest called 'the apotheosis of womanhood', Tolstoy confronts his own attitudes to women who are not mothers, and finds himself severely inhibited. Kitty as a young girl is in fact deprived of sexuality, and her engagement period, normally a time when a prospective couple take long hard looks at each other, is glossed over completely. Tolstoy avoids the period between girlhood and motherhood because of the unredeemed sexuality of womanhood. The undeveloped personality of the girl-child poses no threat; nor does the sublimated personality of the mother. But womanhood equals the female personality on the rampage, a threat to everything, but especially to the self-doubting, self-hating, guilty and inadequate Russian male.

Tolstoy's fear of the sexual female is also evidenced in the episode of Kitty's visit to Levin's sick brother, who is being looked after by his mistress. Levin does not want Kitty to go, claiming it would be improper for his wife to associate with a woman of ill-repute; the real reason is of course that their proximity would make it harder to keep up the assumption that they are not sisters under the skin, that they are two different breeds of woman occupying two separate worlds. When Kitty wins her point and accompanies Levin, Tolstoy allows her to do her ministering angel job with due respect for this approved feminine role, but even so he jealously plays her for a fool in the last scene, where the brother reveals his death-bed repentance to be a sham and returns to his real comfort, the bottle. Tolstoy is only able to handle Kitty when motherhood has changed her relationship with Levin from one of sensual bliss to that of united parental responsibility – a role to which Kitty docilely knuckles down, smiling in the process.

However, the sequel to the Kitty–Levin story is *The Kreuzer Sonata* to which we now return. The preliminary conversation between Pozdnyshev and the other train travellers produces loose discussion about the value of marriage; weak on both sides of the case, the arguments produced pale before the revelation of the man who tells his own vividly personal story. His account presents the standard sexual experiences of an upper-class youth : boyhood homosexual relationships, an early visit to a brothel (claimed to spoil his relationship with women permanently) and a dissolute pre-marital period. Excited by the combination of too much food and a girl't tight jersey, he falls in love and embarks upon an engagement period, during which they find it dreadfully hard to find things to talk about, and a honeymoon which is horrid, shameful and dull. The marriage is finally seen as a union of 'two egoists quite alien to each other, who wished to get as much pleasure as possible from each other', but which not only produces no happiness, but becomes a heavy burden. Even the advent of children proves a regular torment instead of a blessing; the couple settle down to a *status quo* consisting of periods of physical love alternating with bursts of loathing – two convicts hating each other while chained together, as live 'ninety-nine per cent of all married people'. When the wife at last learns to avoid pregnancies she blooms, and anxious to make up for the last ten years she takes a lover, whom the husband kills. The story makes perfect sense; but objectively it appears as a projection of a highly individual personal experience, from which we can only draw the unsurprising moral that anyone seduced into marriage by a tight jumper, ignoring the warning-signs of an embarrassed and uncomfortable engagement, and aware that he does not know his wife, but thinks of her 'as an animal', can expect trouble ! But from this rather selective story-situation Tolstoy draws ill-based universal laws, intellectual propositions and emotional arguments which do little more than establish him as the Compleat Misogynist.

The arguments, summarised, state : that feelings of love are always impermanent and rarely mutual; that the notion of spiritual affinity is negated if the two concerned also wish to go to bed together; that once aroused, men's sexual desires override and destroy 'natural' relationships with all women; that women are equally lustful and have no other real interest (proof lies in the similarity of dress between society ladies and prostitutes); that men have made women into objects of sensuality, and because women resent the inequality of the roles played by both parties in sexual relationships they use man's sensuality to subdue and dominate him (proof : the enormous quantity of merchandise produced for the use of women); than nine-tenths of those who marry do not believe that marriage entails any obligations and that forty-nine out of fifty women are preparing to be unfaithful to their husbands; that the sex act is unnatural (proof : ask any child or unperverted girl); and that women are nervy and hysterical because they are forced to have sexual relations with their husbands even while nursing babies, whereas this should be a period of continence. The story-teller's bricks are still sound, but the moralist's mortar appears almost useless, in the modern age at least. However, *The Kreuzer Sonata* does explain the motivation behind the only *crime passionnel* to be found amongst the novels.

The erring husband does not escape Tolstoy's attention any more than the unfaithful wife. In *The Demon* he recounts how the happily married Irtenev cannot refrain from feeling tempted by the peasant-girl Stepanida. Irtenev does not fall, but only because he takes extreme measures. Not even Tolstoy was exactly sure what these should be – he gives alternative endings, the killing of Stepanida and Irtenev's own suicide. But the implication is the same in either case – that in Irtinev's situation something must be done, no matter how drastic. And in either case Tolstoy states that Irtenev was acting sanely – more sanely than many others who are supposed to be sane but are clearly deranged. He carried to its ultimate interpretation the biblical injunction to pluck out the eye that offends – or the apple of that eye.

Family Happiness, the Levin–Kitty marriage, *The Kreuzer Sonata*, and *The Demon* all develop out of each other, being studies of romantically based marriage; *Anna Karenina* differs, as we have seen, in observing the adultery that arises from an arranged marriage. She is the first of many adulteresses whose fate is suicide; and if we appear to have derided some of Tolstoy's statements and indeed his general view of females, it must be said here that nothing is more totally convincing, at every level, than Anna's gradual spiritual, mental, and psychological breakdown, and her deeply pitiful death. The *vraisemblance* of her story however, goes further; it shows that the adulterous situation contains much of the source of its own destruction : the intolerable isolation experienced if the surrounding society is conventionally moral; and the abnormally intense and inward-directed emotionalism without reprieve. The seeds are there, and in Anna they grew into choking weeds, making her situation intolerable in the most agonising sense of the word.

But the brilliance and truth of the psychology does not mean there was no overriding moral intent in Tolstoy's story; and while his contempt for society made him despise those who were no better than Anna and yet ostracised her, he himself remained to judge her on his own standards. Anna's adultery with Vronsky contravenes the law of the family far more than it contravenes the religious or social law. (Although Anna says once, 'God, forgive me', it is clear from the placement of the comma as well as from the rest of her behaviour that she is little affected by religious contrition; and it is also clear that society would have condoned her had she conducted the affair with more discretion.) But in abandoning her family she strips herself of the wherewithal to sublimate her sexuality; she epitomises Woman in all her seductive potential, and *therefore* she must be destroyed. This is why Tolstoy insists that she does not love Ani, though she continues, ineffectually, to love Seriozha, the child of her purer past; this is why Dolly notices that Anna does not even look after the housekeeping of the home she shares with Vronsky, but leaves to him all the domestic arrangements. Anna must not be allowed any straw of salvation, she may not redeem herself in even the most trivial things. Certainly she must not be divorced and remarried, for if this course of action was to be seen as a viable alternative to indissoluble marriage society would before long be thoroughly undermined. (Hélène's unsuccessful divorce arrangements and suicide are an example of a really unconvincing Tolstoyan manipulation of character for a preordained end.)

Troyat sees Tolstoy's personal ambivalence towards woman as a repulsion arising from extreme but suppressed attraction; he points out that in the earlier drafts Anna was a lecherous man-eater while Karenin and Vronsky were both warm and kind, and argues that Tolstoy fell in love with Anna, turned her into the creature of infinite charm she became, and debased her husband and lover in order to justify her. He thus created a fallen woman who earns universal sympathy, and an upright husband who makes us shudder. Is it surprising then that he punished all the more harshly the creation he loved for her allure and hated for her power over him?

It has been my suggestion throughout this section that Tolstoy was unique among the Russian writers in his stern opposition to adultery; but if this is true, Anna should be the only heroine to be punished by her author – yet there are two other suicides arising out of cases of adultery which must be considered.

The message of *In the Whirlpool* is both complex and gloomy. The Prince, as has been partly seen, is a confused man, half taken up with new ideas of Darwinism, free love, and the irrationality of religion, and half a product of his conventional upbringing. Not only does he find that he cannot accept after all the idea of his wife's taking a lover, but he is also thoroughly shocked when his mistress refuses to have their baby baptised. He finds it more and more difficult to accommodate Elena's ever more radical political activities, and she finally leaves him to take up with a Polish agitator. The Princess having returned from her voyage abroad, in the company of her lover, is taken back into the Prince's house, but there is no renewal of affection. When Elena, reduced to utter destitution, agrees to marry an unloved admirer, the Prince kills himself, and Elena also dies, though of illness (galloping phthisis). The novel is aptly named, for a whirlpool is not caused by any clearly directed wind of change; and indeed all the characters are swept into a maelstrom of conflicting ideals and confused loyalties. They finally die because there is no satisfactory solution. The Prince and Elena are punished during their lifetimes through the anguish of his divided love, and the misery of her material distress. The author is careful not to blame Elena, except perhaps for her political intriguing, since this is on behalf not of Mother Russia but of her own fatherland, Poland. No one could deny that two deaths do not add up to a dismal ending; but neither death is psychologically inevitable (though they are both credible). The most that can be said is that the characters were in fact victims of a windstorm of new ideas rather than of the sport of the immortals.

A similar confused ambivalence is revealed in the outcome of *What's to be Done?*, for in spite of the perfectly clear concept of male–female relationships between the New Man and the New Woman, human nature fails to live up to the rational ideal. Even love, supposed to be reduced to an entirely manageable emotion, is still, romantically, a law unto itself, striking when least expected. (Vera's cry, 'I cannot live without him . . .' is scarcely a very controlled remark.) And while marriage in the new society is essentially dissoluble, and almost platonic, replacing intimacy by courtesy and scorning all jealousy, Lopukhov's apparent generosity when Vera becomes attracted to Kirsanov, is, it comes out later, due to his declining interest in Vera. Further, the gravest doubts are cast on the much vaunted notion of the free union, *à deux* or *à trois*, when Lopukhov pretends to commit suicide. The author makes it into an act of generosity, based on two difficulties encountered by Vera in her new free union with Kirsanov : firstly, she is inhibited in the relationship by her old attachment to Lopukhov; and secondly, she is embarrassed by social considerations! This is certainly not what is expected from the New Woman, and one is greatly surprised that Chernyshevsky could not find a more equable and rational solution to a minor problem than killing off his hero. It seems that both the New Woman and the New Author fall short of their ideals; Chernyshevsky balks at the free union and has Vera and Kirsanov marry as soon as Lopukhov is out of the way; and Vera resorts to special pleading to explain why the *ménage à trois* did not work. She now denies that social considerations influenced her, and argues (somewhat confusingly): 'Our situation was unusual in that all three participants involved in it were of equal strength . . . its failure was not the result of weakness . . . I saw myself in a situation of dependence on his good will, and that was why it was so hard for me, that was why he saw that the only possibility was what he decided nobly to do – to kill himself . . .'

Not only do the New Man and the New Woman get married and live happily ever after, but they preach the extraordinary benefits of conjugal love: 'The longer they live together, the more does the poetry of their love glow and warm them, until the evening of their lives, when the care of their growing children preoccupies their thoughts too strongly. Then this care, sweeter than personal enjoyment, becomes more important than anything else . . .'

Still, what appears to be a variation on a theme by Tolstoy turns out to have one very unTolstoyan but necessary condition: 'Look at your wife as you looked on your bride, and know that she has always the right to say: "I am not content with you, leave me." Look at her in this light and in 9 or 10 years after your marriage she will arouse in you that same romantic feeling as she did when she was a bride. No – more romantic, and more ideal in the best sense of the word . . . This is how the husbands and wives of the new generation live . . . There is only one regret: for every new person these days there are ten of the old sort . . .'[8]

Kirsanov's personal testimony adds that the continuous, strong, healthy excitement of conjugal love necessarily develops the nervous system and improves the intellectual and moral forces to such an extent that he can now hold more facts in his head and his deductions are larger and more complete. The conjugal life of the New People seems to be rosy, naïve and muddled in the extreme; and one cannot forget that it was bought at the price of Lopukhov's faked suicide, the real significance of which is simply not faced by Chernyshevsky or any of his New Characters.

In France there was no such naïve confusion; the agonising suicide of Emma Bovary, while perfectly prepared by her desperate need for money and triggered by Rodolphe's refusal to help her – this last rejection being the final straw – is nevertheless a judgement as deliberate as Tolstoy's and a great deal more hard-eyed. Enid Starkie writes:

He [Flaubert] chose the subject because he wanted to study the clinical disease of Romanticism. He knew, from the effects on himself, its deliquescing nature, how it prevented any clear thinking, any clear and objective view of self, and how it led to senseless

dreaming which impeded all action. . . . Romanticism had idealised adultery – as had Flaubert also when he had been composing
Novembre – and all the authors he had read in his youth, whom
Emma was also to read, had glorified it – and the supreme rights of
passion had been set forth in the novels of George Sand – *Indiana*
and *Lélia.* Flaubert now wished to puncture this theory and show it
in all its sordid reality; he wanted to strip it of its glory and put it
in its place.[9]

Emma's ghastly death and the aridity of her love-affairs drive the
point home with savage contempt. Yet the novel managed to offend
public morality – to the point of its being banned. When Flaubert
was brought to trial the public prosecutor defined four areas of
offence : Emma's glorification of adultery in her affair with Rodolphe;
her religious phase, during which the adulterous woman goes to communion; the affair with Léon; and her death, in which the fallen
woman receives the last rites. He argued that a major defect was that
there was no character in the book who condemned Emma in the
name of Christian morality, whereas adultery must be stigmatised –
not because it was imprudent, or led to disillusion, but because it was
a *crime against the family* (my italics). He also claimed that realist
literature in general went too far beyond the bounds of public decency
– like a woman taking *all* her clothes off.

The defence was argued in detail, making the following points :

1. Flaubert's seriousness as an author;
2. the realism of the subject;
3. Flaubert was not so much vaunting adultery as attacking the
   education of country girls, educated beyond their station and
   married below it;
4. the book could just as easily give a young girl a horror of adultery;
5. much of the blame should fall on Rodolphe;
6. Emma's delight in being seduced by Rodolphe is natural but it is
   just as natural that this delight should be followed by remorse
   and shame;
7. adultery was always a torment to Emma and led to a dreadful
   death;
8. the absence of lascivious detail, because of the innate chastity
   of the author's mind;
9. Lamartine liked the novel;
10. many mothers had expressed gratitude that such a warning
    book should be written;
11. it attacked the encouragement of religious fervour in the young,
    based solely on pious practices without understanding;

12.   a passage from a Montesquieu work received as a school prize
      was far more erotic.

If the modern claim is true, that pornographic reading does not
lead people to commit sexual crime, then it is arguable that the reading of a warning novel will have as little effect in turning people away
from adultery. But I do not think it is possible to argue that Professor
Starkie and the Counsel for the Defence are not correct in insisting
that whatever the practical effect of the novel, Flaubert's intention
was certainly to castigate Romanticism by offering Emma as its foolish,
wilful, and wretched victim. Romantic passion drew Emma to the
door of death by the power of its attraction for her; but the arousal
in her of animal lust would just as surely have destroyed her through
the insatiability of her appetites. Earning her creator's profoundest
contempt, Emma is not so much punished as ground under the heel
of his boot.

Some less retributive writers allow their characters a second chance.
Amongst the Anglo-Saxon writers, the half-way ground between the
doomed adulterers and adulteresses who constitute the vast majority
of the sample, and the one supreme example of *The Golden Bowl* in
which a marriage is redeemed *through* adultery, is occupied by Hawthorne, Meredith and James's earlier novels. Hester Prynne returns
of her own free will, after taking Pearl to England, to the derelict
cottage she had always lived in, and voluntarily wears for ever after
on her breast the scarlet letter. But it has ceased to be a stigma; it is
now a sign of sorrow, and reverence; and Hester's wisdom attracts
people from all around, but especially women, who come to her for
comfort and counsel. So the scarlet woman lives to redeem her sin by
service and self-imposed solitude – though the sin still prevents her
from becoming the prophetess she had once imagined she might be.
It seems that although Hawthorne wanted, in a moment of youthful
daring, to contrive for Puritan America a heritage of the knowledge
that comes through passion alone, it was after all only an exercise.
His timidity is revealed both by the obscure language of the romance,
and by the fact that he eschewed the theme forever after. Even
though Hester is not allowed to expiate totally her sin, Hawthorne
comes dangerously close to seeing such a sin as necessary – and is
thoroughly scared off.
    His compatriot James was also chary of imputing too much good to
adultery, particularly before he came to write *The Golden Bowl*. While
he was disinclined to judge the act on its own demerits alone, but
quick to regret the other vices it entailed, the ending of *The Ambassadors* shows his judicious nicety. Strether has acknowledged every-

thing that Europe – wicked, experienced, knowing Europe – has been able to do for Chad; and he has even, after the severe shock of the truth, admitted that there was no other way Chad could have come by this formation except through his liaison with Marie. Strether's own (very proper) relationship with Mrs Newsome is over, for he now sees her with his new, half-European eyes, for the raw, tasteless, uncomprehending New England prig she is. Maria Gostrey, his friend since he landed in Europe, invites, even entices, him to stay, holding before his descaled eyes the 'selection ruled by beauty and knowledge' which is the quintessence of Europe. But Strether, sorely tempted though he is, and half-irritated at the stupidity of his own obstinacy, resolves to return to America. The price he must pay for his new understanding, for the loss of his New England innocence, is 'not, out of the whole affair, to have got anything for himself'. Thus, with exquisite delicacy James defines Strether's position : to *see* good arising out of adultery is to have come far enough; to engage in it himself is more than he can accommodate.

In Meredith too there is still a lingering ambivalence, for all his courageous grasping of nettles. Victor escapes the awkwardness and social stigma of his *de facto* marriage simply by being an insensitive man. Nataly, as we know, suffers. Victor's legal wife asks to see them, and on her death-bed forgives them all; but shortly afterwards Nataly dies, and Victor, demented by grief, soon follows her. The end is not tragic, for Nesta marries the man she loves, and her parents are well on in years; but there is an aura of sadness which hangs over both the ending and the parts of the book dealing with Nataly. It was a plank of Meredith's philosophy that the framework of law is detrimental to the play of nature; and while Victor and Nataly's adherence to nature was a stamp of their nobility, they were still, in some sense, the victims of society. There may be honour of an unconventional sort in refusing to live in defiance and contempt of nature, but there is little joy, for society itself is Law.

With Matey and Aminta too, it is not just a question of leaving England in order to be happy and together; like Strether, they must *prove* their selflessness. There *is* something to atone, no matter how right they feel in the eyes of God, how disdainful of worldly judgement. Their insistence on service is their justification and their expiation – their attempt to satisfy both Nature and Law.

Thus, Henry James stands alone in ascribing a truly redemptive role to adultery. Inspired simultaneously by desperation and integrity, Maggie in the end not only wins her husband back again, and commands his admiration and respect, but also leads him to an understanding of her own moral sense, which gives birth in him to one of his own. She further touches him to deep love and passion for her by showing how ardently these emotions act in her own self, for him. They enter a new, full relationship, based on the three elements James sees as essential to a marriage : aesthetic pleasure, erotic satisfaction and moral sensibility. Adam Verver and Charlotte consolidate their less perfect union by dedication to their chosen role in America. Charlotte still retains her moral insensitivity, but has learnt through her torment not to deviate from the committed path. The two marriages, which were both less than they should be when the story began, are remade.

During the course of the novel, James does not gloss over the degradation of adultery, in terms of its lustfulness, deceit and in particular the pain it causes, but he clearly has an ideal marriage in mind, which is equally betrayed by inadequate, albeit faithful, relationships. Because he is willing to use adultery as the necessary shock to arouse Maggie's comprehension of where she has gone wrong, he implies that there is nothing so intrinsically, absolutely immoral about adultery that it cannot have a good end. Self-realisation for James depends on full self-knowledge, which must come through experience of good and evil – though the evil is ultimately to be discarded. He does not say 'you should not have', but only 'understand more, and do better'.

It is evident that James takes marriage seriously, as a form or institution of our civilisation, and he nowhere questions its right to exist. As a form, however, it can be expressed in varying degrees of integrity to *itself* – not to any superimposed moral order. The signs of this integrity include honesty, loyalty, full sexual richness and, ideally, aesthetic refinement. Deviations from these virtues are deviations from an ideal : but it is an ideal which must not be held naïvely – it only becomes truly worth while when comprehended fully.

Thus an essential component of James's system of morality is intelligence; his main characters approximate to the 'high personages' of classical drama, through their sensitivity, delicacy, insight and moral earnestness – not to speak of their freedom from material want. But activating, sharpening and highlighting these qualities is their intelligence. Mrs Assingham, a minor character in *The Golden Bowl* says, 'Stupidity pushed to a certain point *is*, you know, immorality. Just so, what is morality but high intelligence?' Thus the Prince tries to justify himself by claiming 'not to understand' Maggie and her father – and precisely this failure to understand *allows* him to be immoral. Fanny Assingham commits the unintelligence of trying to organise other people's marriages, and her meddling nearly turns out to have created a disaster. The Prince unintelligently pretends to believe that the situation with Charlotte can remain static, only to find himself in it deeper and more damagingly. Adam marries for the wrong reason; his misguidedness – a form of unintelligence – leads to his betrayal.

Both he and Maggie are for a time *culpably* innocent, unwilling to be sharp enough to see what is required.

On the other hand, Maggie's entire handling of things after she understands what is happening is highly intelligent, as well as deeply loving; and thus her final accomplishment is to restore the moral order of things as they should be. (Isabel is equally unintelligent in marrying Gilbert, and betrays her own ideal of marriage.)

The reason for being moral, however, is simply to establish a more perfect form of living. So, while the components of morality – honesty, commitment, selflessness – are to be prized as ideals of human behaviour, they are not enough in themselves, at least for the more exquisite of James's characters. For they must have not only the added refinement of intelligence, but also fidelity to aesthetic standards in all things. Though the 'touchstone of taste' is in itself an insufficient and sometimes dangerously seductive guide, cultivation of it enhances the life already validated by adherence to moral integrity.

Adultery for James causes an impairment of this more perfect form of living, which he records precisely and without sentimentality. His attitude sets him apart from the other novelists in that he is indifferent to the kinds of moral imperatives they are unable to dissociate from the act. Meredith must yet defend, even champion, those whose adultery is committed for the sake of 'true' union; the rest will punish their faithless creations in the name of a morality they unconsciously use to support their own infirmities. We shall in fact see that, with only few exceptions, there is often no difference in the nineteenth-century novel between the end of the affair and the wages of sin. But amongst those exceptions remains one more writer, whose disenchanted and unattractive hero provides a major clue to the differences between the idealism of the Anglo-Saxon and the despair of the French.

The outcome of *En Ménage* is a relatively happy one, since Berthe and André are finally reunited. But the author's *penchant* towards nihilistic cynicism makes him anxious not to make anything too sentimental or idealistic of the happy reunion. André has a friend, Cyprien, who lives with a *de facto* wife; after a long discussion the two decide that 'le concubinage et le mariage se valent', since in neither is one free from 'préoccupations artistiques' and 'tristesses charnelles'. Perhaps the book argues a little more solidly the value of marriage, since it is more surely a savings account in which one accumulates a debt of care and support in one's old age – the right to find relief from one's cares by putting them on someone else's shoulders – the right to complain at will, and occasionally to be loved. Thus Huysmans argues, not on moral grounds, but from the fruit of sour experience, the advisability of a permanent union. Although the word is misleadingly ambiguous, the French nihilist and the Russian have here something in common : while they both wrench marriage out of the hands of the Church, and entertain no absolute objections to illegal unions, they nevertheless find themselves arguing – languidly or fervently, it is only a difference of style – for a permanent conjugal relationship.

In Huysmans' case it appears to be *faute de mieux*; but behind his weary determination that everyone will have to put up with it, but that no one must set any store by it, lies something much more important. His cynicism veils a well-hidden but desperate attempt to rationalise man's dependence on woman.

Bitter experience has brought home to André the humiliating truth that he cannot live without a woman; the grudging reluctance with which he comes to accept this fact is the burden of the action of the novel. But it also is a revelation of one of the most profound but dissimulated features of nineteenth-century France : the innate, unacknowledged, but mounting fear of the immanence of a matriarchal society. The Frenchman argues to himself that psychological dependence on a woman (of the sort André experiences) infers male inferiority. Unable to countenance such a situation, he fights back – by attempting to prove the baseness of every female. This he does normally by seducing her – unless, of course, she is deemed to belong to that small band of women whose existence is the only safeguard against total depravity, the *honnêtes femmes*. For the *honnête femme* is of course a wife, potentially one's own wife; *her* virtue, as revealed by her fidelity, poses no threat of moral superiority, for a husband is by definition and in law her superior. The wife in the home is a tame domestic animal, menacing no one. But *out there*, disguised by smiling lips and girlish waists, is a horde of Nanas cracking whips over their degraded masters, of Hermangardes gazing with marble-faced implacability upon their grovelling deceivers . . .

Can we really be surprised that in the majority of nineteenth-century novels – the woman is *made* to pay?

5 The Justification of the Order

The pattern of death and destruction which, with the significant exceptions that have been noted, encompasses the act of adultery must raise the question of the validity of its own compulsion. One way of trying to answer such a question is to ask, more simply, whether the reader of the novels, having seen the issue raised and resolved by the various authors, feels the given outcome to be justified or not; and in either eventuality to try to ascertain at what level the justification operates, or fails to – whether the grounds for the punishment of the nineteenth-century adulterer/adulteress arise out of relativities like convention or economics, or out of more profound psychological, religious, or even mystical imperatives.

The emergence of certain important themes throughout the novels provides some guidance in these matters; it will be noted that the major part of this 'positive' or head-on approach to the role of adultery is to be found in the French novels, as opposed to the evasion or lack of interest of the other literatures.

The family

Although the family is not always an explicit feature of the novel of adultery, it is often of implied importance to the anti-Romantic school especially, and particularly to Barbey d'Aurevilly, whose novels are based on the premise that the preservation of society depends on the stability of family life. Hence their insistence of the unhappiness of the divided marriage. In some of his non-fictional writings, Barbey specifically compares the breakdown of family life in the 'instables républiques romaines' with the experience of the nineteenth century, and reveals a deep-seated fear of the disintegration of the society around him. He was speaking for numbers of his contemporaries who saw themselves as inheritors of the Romantic generation, whom they took to be in turn inspired by the Revolution, whose chaos and destruction many still recalled with horror. For these people the family was the model (in both senses) of society; its perpetuation was a political, social, and psychological necessity.

Barbey writes in a context where marriage is assumed to be of itself a stable structure (as he wanted the State also to be), threatened only from the outside by the external temptress (here the exact analogy breaks down, since France feared not an invader from the outside, but a crumbling from within). But the parallel goes far enough for Barbey to speak for a generation to whom all women who were not transformed by marriage into submissive wives were potential temptresses, marriage-breakers and symbolic threats to society.

While the stable marriage is in this context supposed to be guaranteed by its religious basis, its indissolubility is argued on the grounds of the future of the children. But since Barbey makes even a childless marriage (as was Marigny and Hermangarde's) subject to the same strictures, one concludes that he was in fact more anxious to allay his personal fears regarding the subversion of marriage than to produce convincing arguments of either a social or a theological kind. In short, child welfare was less his concern than irregular sexuality, and to judge by the number of novels in which the question of the child of the unhappy marriage is ignored, or where there is no child, he was not alone in placing the emphasis where he did. However, the small number of novelists who do see the child as a major factor are united in putting him or her first in any conflict situation; the peripheral characters who fail to do this earn sideways glances of heavy disapproval from their authors.

Thus an instinctive and ubiquitous concern for the child may appear to be one of the few factors working *for* the stability of marriage, but this concern frequently masks a fear of instability whose object is not the child but the society – just as concern for the marriage was not attached to the happiness of the spouses but to the preservation of the institution.

Romanticism and romantic passion

The equation between family and political stability appears strong in the French tradition, and unimportant in the others. This may be in part explained by the greater influence in France of the French version of Romanticism, which in the middle and latter part of the nineteenth century was identified in the minds of the bulk of the people with political anarchy in public life and uncontrollable passion in private.

There is no simple answer to the question of whether passion is in fact uncontrollable, and certainly a study of this kind would not provide one. The question here is rather whether the novelists saw it as such, and the significance of their viewpoint. Zola, Barbey and France write as though it were; Fromentin is determined to show it is not; Flaubert confines himself to warning of its dire consequences. Perhaps the most one can say is that the concept of uncontrollable passion has been familiar to the French mind since Racine, and that whatever its cause it is an accepted, though not necessarily a self-justifying, fact of life. In its most extreme fictional form, that is in the case of Emma Bovary, romantic passion conforms to the de Rougemont theory that it is essentially destructive. Thus there is a very strong implication in Barbey. Fromentin and, more obscurely, Flaubert, that passionate love is to be avoided even within marriage because it is inflammatory, dangerous and of itself evil.

Among the Russians, as Renato Poggioli has also pointed out, Tolstoy stands alone in his vituperative rejection of romantic love, pursuing instead activities characterised by their contempt for women : promiscuity, uxoriousness and asceticism – 'whereas "l'amour-passion" derives from a profane apotheosis of the Eternal Feminine'.[1] While Turgenev balks at it, and Dostoevsky practically ignores it, Tolstoy thrashes passionate love to death in a fury of disgust. The elsewhere feeble and short-lived 'take' of Western Romanticism in Russian literature makes Tolstoy's stance the more striking.

The reasons for it can only be postulated, but they appear to add up. Firstly, Tolstoy shared the normal Russian reverence for motherhood, but carried it to an extreme degree. Both his diaries and his autobiographical *Childhood* support the notion that he made womanhood synonymous with motherhood, with the result that even normal sexual relations had for him an un-spelled out, indeed unconscious, taint of oedipal perversion. His adolescent sexual life was thus from the beginning compounded by guilt, especially as his urge for sexual activity was both powerful and promiscuous. Marriage to Sonya Behrs did not solve the situation, for he was so extremely sexually dependent on her that he suffered from severe feelings of humiliation and a resentment which he directed towards his wife, but cast upon all women in general, until he had talked himself into an abhorrence of all, including legitimate, sexuality.

Beyond this personal attitude, Tolstoy inherited and shared his class's feelings of inadequacy and guilt over social issues – their inability to right the wrongs of the Tsarist régime, their conviction that they were, in the famous phrase, superfluous men, failing utterly to redress the ills of society, unable to provide a lead when by birth and education they were the only possible leaders. But side by side with this sense of guilt and inadequacy was the awareness in the Russian male mind – and in Tolstoy's in particular – of the tradition of the strong Russian woman. And thus was born a fear that she would rush in and fill the void, taking to herself the power over society that the Russian man found himself unable to wield. Thus the male would be humiliated anew – and his hold over the female would be lost for ever.

Such feelings were only exacerbated by the exterior forces at work in the society – the instability caused by the industrial revolution, the feminist ideas imported from France, and the championing of the social revolution by the Nihilists and their ilk.

All these factors combined to imbue Tolstoy with a fanatical desire to keep woman in her place, that is, in the family circle, and to preach at all costs the stifling of passion even in marriage – for he feared the exterior temptress, evil though she might be, less than he feared the terrible hold that his own wife had over him by the simple and basic fact of her sex. He never ceased to feel threatened by the mere existence of female sexuality, and the fear grew with age. Hence his early acceptance of love as a prelude to marriage, as we saw in *Family Happiness*, and the final rejection of all male–female relationships in *The Kreuzer Sonata*.

Idealism and nihilism

Tolstoy's refuge from passion lay in asceticism – at least in a would-be fashion – and here the posed opposition is quite plain. In the French scene however it seems firstly that the alternatives to passion are not asceticism, but either idealism or nihilism, and secondly that neither of them is nearly as distinct from passion as is asceticism. Moreau's romantic passion for Mme Arnoux contains a streak of idealism that demands that she remain an *honnête femme* in order to satisfy his need for a feminine, unattainable quasi-mystical ideal – a reaction against the world-embracing disgust and nihilism expressed by the Flaubert of *Novembre*, and almost identical to the idealising of Madeleine engaged in by Dominique and his reaction against the corruption of a world given over to the excesses of Romanticism. But Fromentin's horror of romantic self-indulgence leads him to imbue Dominique with a kind of secular quietism which uses the terminology of nihilism – a nihilism not of despair, but of withdrawal from the world at large (though not from the life of the family circle).

This oxymoronic 'positive nihilism' contrasts strongly with the nihilism of despair which overtakes Emma, as each successive role fails, and the impossibility of attaining her impossible ideals, which for a while actually sustains her longing for an ideal, finally turns to dust and ashes in her mouth.

However, in the latter part of the century the left-over impulse of unstructured idealism fades, leaving only a nihilistic materialism which proclaims, as in *En Ménage*, that life holds nothing worth idealising, that marriage and concubinage are the only alternatives available to what is merely a physical need with a few psychological overtones, and that either of the two is worth putting up with for the sake of domestic convenience.

Maupassant sees society in similar terms, but relates adultery directly to nihilistic despair via the argument that the 'what does it all matter'? attitude poses a threat to the underpinnings of life (culture, education, morality, etc.) – that is, society in fact needs its structures, and among them the structure of marriage. Therefore, anything that threatens marriage, as adultery does, works towards a valueless society which Maupassant finds unacceptable. Marriage ought to be a stronghold of affection and solidarity; but adultery, he seems to be saying, causes breaches in it through which emptiness and hopelessness flow out into society at large.

Hardy, by contrast, uses passion as a counteraction to the personal nihilism he was prey to once he had rejected all religious beliefs. But his frustrating of every attempt to perform this substitution indicates either an ultimate fear of passion, or an unwillingness to believe that there can in fact be in passion a replacement for God. His efforts to explore the mutual workings of each drew down upon his head the wrath of many critics who imagined he overstepped the limits of Victorian respectability, and this treading of new ground by an English writer was not without its reaction across the Channel. A French critic wrote after Hardy's works started to be published : 'Ce n'est plus en Angleterre que les mères françaises pourront s'apprivoisonner, en toute confiance, de romans pour leurs filles.'

As for the Russians, the fact that passion was a concept that the Russian nihilists viewed with distaste is an indication of the extraordinarily varied meanings attached to this word in different parts of the world in the nineteenth century. The Russian nihilists were so named because of their desire to sweep away existing institutions, but there is no hint of romantic passion or despair in their movement. And although there is some idealism in their hopes for the future of relations between the sexes, it is an *applied* idealism which stops far short of the disgust for the corporeal and the embracing of the unreal associated with the ultimate French idealism. Wa are here dealing with two different worlds, and the Russian one has nothing to say to us about the kind of nihilism which afflicted French society – or Hardy.

Class differences

While it would be going too far to suggest that the principle of *noblesse oblige* actually demands that the members of the upper classes are required, in order to conform to the *mores* of their social group, to engage in adultery, there is nevertheless an assumption on the part of the writers that the practice of adultery will be found most commonly amongst the highest and lowest levels of society, but that it actually matters more when it is the former.

Factually, it is simply the case that the servanted classes enjoy greater freedom from domestic chores, preoccupation with children and the need to earn a living, and thus for them affairs are not difficult to conduct. This freedom is evident in *Une Page d'Amour, Bel-Ami, Anna Karenina, The Golden Bowl* and so on. Even Emma Bovary, though scarcely aristocratic, has enough home help to enable her to slip off to Rouen without worrying about who is minding the baby. In Emma's case we also see an eminent example of the enervating boredom endured by women with little occupation and even fewer personal resources. As far as the erring husbands are concerned, the presence of servants eases the male dependence upon a wife for the daily requirements of life, and thus makes marriage less of a necessity, and marital break-ups not so terrifying. (André manages with a servant for a little while after Berthe's departure, and sees the solution as quite pleasant in the short term.)

However, several novels leave the impression that this practical facility is in conflict with a sense of class consciousness; they seem to promote the idea that adultery is not more *wrong* (or more right) when practised by the upper classes, but somehow more socially significant, more likely to cause philosophical doubts and despair. Thus Maupassant is more mordantly critical of the Bel-Ami set, who are extremely influential in the moulding of public opinion through journalism and controlling the finance of the country, than he is of the more private characters in *Mont-Oriol* and *Fort Comme la Mort.* The unconvincing, or at least not inevitable, death of M. de Camors suggests that the author quite definitely thought he *ought* to be punished, and that he would be setting too bad an example altogether if he were to escape with impunity. First punished by remorse, Camors still fails to mend his ways and is therefore struck down by his wrathful creator, with the message writ plain for all who have eyes to read it. Dominique, on the other hand, takes on his exemplary marriage and local duties as a 'devoir de position'; such a performance by a less notable person would be edifying, but insignificant. However, it should not be forgotten that the majority of writers were of middle-class origins, so that a tendency to be both hypercritically sensitive, as well as somewhat enviously admiring of aristocratic 'immorality', coupled with righteous attacks upon lower-class 'depravity', may be unconsciously inherent in their attitudes.

Henry James, in England, is outstanding for his supreme indifference to the minions who bring in the tea or run the shops where the golden bowls are bought; his interest only lies with the 'high personnages' who are most likely to breed the qualities of mind he was concerned to explore; and it is just as impossible to imagine Anne Karenina in anything but an aristocratic setting. She was born to grace ballrooms, attend race-meetings, read and talk – to have the *time* to allow full play to her emotions.

On the other hand, for those at the lower end of the scale the assumption seems to be that of course they do it, and why not? Zola's series of lower-middle-and-working-class people practise adultery with little or no moral guilt; *Thérèse Raquin* suggests that concealed adultery hurts no one in any practical way – only the educated can be distressed by an *idea*. Relationships, it is implied, may be damaged, but relationships are rare in lower-order marriages; and those leading a life of grinding *misère* have neither the time nor the inclination for moral issues.

Even Hardy, for all his sensitivity to the tortuous impulses of intimate behaviour between the sexes, is not free from assumptions about the lower order of loose women, whose promiscuity is simple, straightforward and, it is implied, of no real significance. (It is certainly true that his main characters are not aristocratic, but they are often well-off, independent and educated beyond their peers.)

It even began to appear at times during this study that jealousy was assumed by the writers to be a class-based emotion. The sophistication of the upper classes produced a good number of *maris complaisants*, whereas absence of jealousy was regarded amongst the lower bourgeoisie as abnormal, even shameful. On the other hand, the supposedly sophisticated André *(En Ménage)* gives proof that his armour of cynicism is not a sign of real detachment at all, when the confrontation comes, and he finds himself feeling jealous on behalf of a wife he does not even love; and there are in any case quite different factors affecting other cases, like Charles Bovary's utter (or was is wilful?) stupidity and Moreau's anxiety for Mme Arnoux not to lose her married status, which enabled him to be perfectly friendly towards her husband.

Nevertheless, there does appear to be an assumption which argues that the lower classes, owing to their lack of education, also lack the ability to rationalise situations (e.g. of the sort 'what's good for the gander is good for the goose', as long as she's discreet) and tend to react more instinctively – that is, to adopt a more primitive approach which involves strong feelings of possession and fear of the ridicule of other males if the female escapes. So, while it would appear that jealousy is an emotion occasioned by threats as varied as loss of spouse, fear of ridicule, and blows to self-esteem, some general class-lines hold true

F

because of the greater facility amongst the upper classes for both husband and wife to even up the situation, and because of their ability to override intellectually the irrational impulses of feeling.

Less elusively than jealousy, aestheticism also appears to have a class-based bearing on the practice of adultery. Neither Zola nor George Moore encourage the reader to feel shocked by the adultery of their lower-order characters – in fact Zola goes so far as to seem to condone it, which has the desired effect of highlighting the absence of moral delicacy in the seamy underworld. But this must be seen in contrast to the upper-class novels, where aesthetic repugnance to adultery becomes a recurrent theme. Even the structure of *Dominique* has a Racinian symmetry and controlled form which imply an approval of all that is firmly under the rule of a proper authority. The classical composition imposes restraint on romantically unquenchable passions and modes of life, as well as on undisciplined structures. Mme de Camors nourishes a self-satisfying taste for virtue so ardent that she abhores wrong doing as if avoiding a blemish rather than obeying an injunction. Her self-image is completely bound up in self-approval and lady-like taste. In fact it seems that not only is M. de Camors the true son of his eighteenth-century *philosophe* father (as the author makes a point of noting), but Madame is also a direct inheritor of certain eighteenth-century ideals. While one must go back to Plato and the ancients for the original exposition of the essential harmonies attained by the proper, and natural, juxtaposition of happiness and moderation, of pleasure and virtue, there is no doubt that the eighteenth century took up these ideas with a spontaneity they could only regard as commendable, since the result was so happy! To choose one amongst many writers of that century who were concerned to establish these relationships, Levesque de Pouilly insists that 'Le plaisir naît au sein même de la vertu',[2] and that personal happiness depends on the balancing of two elements : desire for our own perfection, and the judicious use of our faculties in pleasure. But since the greatest pleasure is that born of virtue, we can see very well why Mme de Camors was so inordinately admirable.

Other writers also throw light upon the matter, especially those who, like Remond le Grec, distinguished between '*plaisir*' and '*volupté*', defining the latter as 'l'art d'user des plaisirs avec delicatesse et de les goûter avec sentiment'. Thus the sense of refinement, and the aesthetic basis of Mme de Camors' self-esteem, are both traceable to another eighteenth-century notion, that the ideal image of man (or woman) will not lack either refinement of taste or delicacy of feeling; and naturally these virtues will not be found in 'âmes vulgaires'.

Flat assertions in the field which is characterised by the phrase 'ce je ne sais quoi' are naturally to be avoided, and I do not propose to elaborate any further what the eighteenth century had to say. But if the claim is true that reforms are more often made in reference to a better past than to a creative future, then the self-image of Mme de Camors is not to be underestimated.

By a similar token, the Parisian adulteresses of Bel-Ami's society are accused of letting down by their behaviour their aristocratic side, the last refuge of *goût* (seen also in the willingness to let *nouveau-riche* Jewish financiers into their salons). There is again the complex, difficult to justify, but very much existent association of the aristocracy with the maintenance of moral appearances and aesthetic taste, and the similar association of the *nouveau-riche* bourgeoise and brutish lower classes with lack of taste. What this particular *goût* consists of is no easier to define, but certainly one element of it is discretion and the keeping up of appearances – presumably partly on account of the nobility's obligation to set a good example to their inferiors. The code of acceptable behaviour for top people seems to be ingrained into their way of life in each of the three countries.

It suggests however another argument relating to more primitive needs : the female primitive need for protection as the weaker of the species requires that she be able to attract the male. To do this she needs to be, or feel confident that she is, beautiful – a feeling which is sublimated into a self-image of moral beauty when physical beauty becomes suspect through being associated with unchannelled, possibly destructive, sexual arousal (hence the Mme Arnoux and Mme de Camors of the world we are dealing with). This female self-image is paralleled by the aristocrat's need to maintain an image of himself as superior in everything, including *goût*, which embraces both moral and aesthetic standards – and hence the public attitude of condemnation of adultery, colluded with by the writers, in despite of private practice.

If this argument is valid however, it also explains more simply and perhaps more truly than any other Anna's course of self-destruction – and the gulf between her suicide and Emma Bovary's. Until her fall Anna's beauty is not just physical; her capacity to heal wounds, to comfort the distressed, to inspire the young with ardent adoration – all this betokens a moral beauty of which she is not unaware. When Vronsky seduces her she feels she has killed a part of herself – or rather a part of the self-image that was necessary to her own self-esteem. This is the first and greatest loss that she sustains; the subsequent loss of psychological equanimity is a result of the imbalance affecting her whole psyche. When both these two are gone it only remains for the body, useless without its other elements, to be destroyed too. Emma, on the other hand (because of her peasant origins?) never had a self-image dependent on moral beauty – in fact her life was spent in seeking an image for herself. The search was doomed to frustration because no earthy role of herself or of her love could satisfy her; but she in no sense died of loss, as Anna did, for what Anna lost, Emma never found.

Inequality of the sexes

In spite of the fact that adultery is essentially the coming together of the male and female of the human species, it is always seen against a background of an essential disparity, disequilibrium, and even disaccord between the two sexes in general. Fear of a matriarchal society rears its frenzied head in more places than one. It is unfortunate that Barbey d'Aurevilly, its most explicit exponent elsewhere than in his novels, is not its most convincing advocate. Holding firmly to the belief that marriage is so important to society that the happiness of the individual should be sacrificed to it, he argues that the alternative to marriage – divorce – is worse than polygamy, since it allots the woman to the highest bidder and 'necessarily' leads to polyandry, which in turn creates a state of amazons, in which there is child massacre and 'la pulvérisation sociale'.[3] The only possible explanation of this extraordinary argument would have to involve the preservation of the primitive male ego, with its assumption of established virility and superiority over the female. This lurking fear would certainly explain the shattering effect on the husband who has a stake in the confidence he feels in his wife when he finds she is unfaithful (André, Muffat, Karenin, Angel) while indicating that the opting out of the more sophisticated *mari complaisant* simply means that his self-image is not bound up in a relationship he regards as merely a legal contract.

The Barbey–Fromentin attitude is amplified to some extent by more immediate causes such as the dominating and influential role played by women in the salons of the Revolutionary era and after, the sway of the courtesan in previous French history and later under Napoleon III, the enthusiasm aroused by George Sand and other Romantics who preached the death of marriage, the still significant influence of the rationalist philosophers of the eighteenth century, and perhaps even the fear that society might be taken over by rich Jewish matriarchalists.

Yet how extraordinary it is that this fear should be so paralysing when in every sphere – economic, political, and religious, and most clearly in the area of sexual freedom – the dominance of the male is what is in fact visible at every turn. In *En Ménage* the wife is turned out, although the husband indulges in adultery with impunity; in *L'Education Sentimentale* Arnoux's concept of marriage entails his freedom to take a series of mistresses, while the wife must remain faith-

ful for fear of being shown the door, quite penniless, and with no hope
of supporting herself financially – except perhaps by prostitution. In
Une Page d'Amour the adulterous husband is hardly affected by the
drama surrounding him. (There is one and only one exception to this
list of male power-figures; it is Mlle Vortnatz in *L'Education Sentimentale* who is embryonically emancipated, financially independent
and who manipulates men and women through her funds of capital.
But she is a lone figure; and Flaubert does not allow her to get much
pleasure out of her power.)

The obvious benefit to the male to be obtained from keeping the
female in her place at a time when there were signs of a feminine dissatisfaction – if not revolt – need hardly be stated. But a related point
which emerges very clearly from the novels is that the male thought
not of a woman's place, but of her places; the hierarchy of women he
set up so that all his needs might be catered to had also the happy
side-effect of dividing and enfeebling woman herself. This hierarchy
is most clearly seen in *L'Education Sentimentale* where there is a
descending order of women, all of whom must stay in their appointed
stations : Mme Arnoux must remain the *femme honnête*, symbolising
the ideal of purity and honour to an irreligious society; Mme Dambreuse represents the ethos of the upper classes – unfaithful but discreet, elegant and nearly intellectual, she runs a kind of salon; Rosan-
ette is the middle-of-the-scale mistress, emulating a courtesan for lack
of other means of support, but yearning in her bourgeois little heart
for marriage and respectability; and Deslaurier's mistress is the
cheapest of all, grateful for what she can get – a *grisette* rather than
a *laurette*. Around these hovers Mlle Vornatz, disconcertingly un-
classifiable, the threat of things to come.

Muffat also supports the hierarchy in his contempt for Nana and
his respect for his unloved wife; when she cuckolds him he is wounded
not in his affections but in his assumptions. The problem which arises
when Muffat finds himself becoming *fond* of Nana is not just related
to the inter-class *status quo*, but more profoundly to the balance of
power between the sexes. Muffat fears above all becoming dependent
on Nana, and thereby acknowledging her superiority over him. He is
primarily a pathetic example of the male ego shattered by blow after
blow – the infidelity of his wife, his own loss of pride, the realisation of
his inadequacy to himself, his inability to live without Nana. His
degradation is rendered all the more acute by the fact that Nana is
a low-born slut, and certainly she manipulates their relationship to
satisfy her hatred of the aristocracy. But for Muffat she is woman first
and plebeian second, and terror of her sexual power over him is stronger
than the humiliation she causes to his rank. In fact, the end of the
novel shows Zola's awareness of impending social changes; but Zola

himself avoided looking at them too clearly. It is true that he was a realist, and that one click of the camera shutter cannot reveal change; but this limitation of literary style was also a protection against the imperative contained in his own work to relate social change to moral evolution. Nana and the Countess must not change places – not just to preserve the social order, but to ensure that neither step out of the roles man has appointed her to, the roles he has learnt to cope with.

The importance of the *femme honnête* is becoming increasingly clear now. We recall Augustin's wife in *Dominique* – so modest, simple, clean and devoted that she is almost a caricature. But she is intended perfectly seriously. Dominique's wife is herself a cheerful and industrious nonentity. Mme de Camors, though admirable, is passively virtuous; her determination not to nag, her consoling interest in her baby, and the support she finds in piety are splendid qualities, but they are of very limited interest to the reader, and, one suspects, to her husband. Mme Arnoux, whose motives are confused, as we have seen, between fear of her husband and fear of God, is utterly unadventurous.

Thus the French male is caught in a dilemma of his own making : he demands to marry nothing but an *honnête femme*; but she in fact betokens sheer dullness, sometimes veering on inanity. Marital constancy becomes associated with utter dreariness – but is necessary for the sake of security. That the husband should require fidelity from his wife is not a surprising notion; but what is really emerging is that the male in general, as represented by the male author, in his views and in the characters he creates, should uphold the notion of the necessity of a category of faithful wives in the community for the sake of his own mental security. (His anxiety to perpetuate the notion of the *femme honnête* allows the male to endow her with one form of superiority, in an area in which he does not compete, and which in fact guarantees his own self-preservation – the area of spiritual piety. There is no hint of male jealousy in regard to the moral superiority of Hermangarde or Madeleine, Kitty or Mary. Yet even here the arrangement may backfire, for as we saw, the barrier of forgiveness may prove insurmountable : the male is only ready to accept female piety in so far as it is of obvious benefit to himself; in the intimacy of married life there may be too much of a good thing.)

By contrast, the Russian male, no more secure than the Frenchman, is utterly different in his approach to women and to adultery. The importance of the strong woman/weak man tradition long before the middle of the nineteenth century presents us, when we look at the novels studied, with the *fait accompli* of the will-less hero preoccupied with his own guilt and anxious on the whole not even to tangle with the daunting female – still less to put her in boxes and tell her to stay there – for fear of coming off worst and sinking deeper into the depths of acknowledged inferiority. The overriding factor in many Russian male–female relationships, especially those described by Turgenev, Ostrovsky and Goncharov, is not illicit passion with its accompanying problems of conjugal jealousy, but this male inadequacy, exacerbated by class-guilt, *vis-à-vis* the strong blameless female who has nothing to reproach herself with. The nihilists were genuinely more concerned with the social emancipation of women and their rights to freedom because they were not bothered about retaining what they never had, that is firm authority over the female – even in the sexual sphere. Some of their most devoted adherents were, as we have seen, really able to sublimate all sense of personal ownership over their wives, and to be free of jealousy. Whether such emancipation was applicable to all men is still doubtful, as witness the mysterious 'suicide' of Lopukhov; and the existence even in Russia of the extreme opposite type is clearly apparent in the person of Tolstoy who, again as we have seen, began by defending the institution of marriage and family life against the new ideas and ended by becoming so personally involved in the issues that it is necessary to read his biography in order to fully understand the evolution of his thought.

The three great novels

Indeed, on the face of it, it might seem that it is only his utter Russianness which prevents us from lumping Tolstoy in with the French writers more easily than with his own compatriots. But the reason we do not do this – why, in fact, the very idea seems extraordinary – bypasses the mere accident of nationality. It relates to a more complex individuality, the unique result of the combination of three essential features of his work : its highly personal quality, its faultless psychological truth, and its almost terrifying sense of inevitability. These are the elements which make *Anna Karenina* stand apart both in stature and in essence from the French novels.

The three elements are puzzling, for the first ought to negate the second, and there is no reason why the first plus the second should contribute to the third, at least with that sense of inexorable doom that informs a Greek tragedy. Anna's loneliness, her insecurity, her loss of Seriozha – all these are convincing factors at the psychological level; and they are a necessary condition of her death. But are they sufficient? For all Hardy's ironic reference to the sport of the Immortals, we understand that Tess dies not by the hand of God, but by the pen of her author, who simply did not believe in the fulfilment of human happiness through the love of another person. Why then, out of all the novels, does one feel that Anna alone has not exactly incurred the divine wrath, but has tempted tragedy itself beyond its strength, so that its overtaking of her is not of her choosing nor of its author's? No doubt Tolstoy suggests this sense of destiny in part by the dreams Anna has and the recurrent symbolism of the train; but there is more to it than mere literary device. Steiner has touched upon the problem :

> Much of the perfection of *Anna Karenina* lies in the fact that the poetic form resisted the demands of the didactic purpose; thus there is between them a constant equilibrium and harmonious tension . . . The Pauline epigraph initiates and colours the story of Anna but does not utterly control it. Anna's tragic fate yields values and enrichments of sensibility that challenge the moral code which Tolstoy generally held and was seeking to dramatize. It is as if two deities had been involved : an ancient, patriarchal God of vengeance and a God who sets nothing above the tragic candour of a bruised spirit.[4]

Steiner's remarks are pertinent and helpful, but not final – because, in fact, there is no definitive answer, for a pluralist society, to the question of the nature of the laws transgressed by the adulterer or adulteress. Certainly they transgress the laws of many lands; but what was illegal in the nineteenth century will have changed in the twentieth, just as what society will tolerate will have been expanded. Already church teaching has evolved in the area of divorce and pre-marital sex, though so long as the Ten Commandments are invoked adultery ought to be considered a sin against the moral law. However, the point of these remarks is to indicate that the only question that can be asked about the justification of the Order in relation to the novels is not whether the justification is proved, which it cannot be, but whether the novelist had succeeded in convincing the 'spectator', that is, the reader at the time of writing *and* the readers of a later time, that his sanctions against adultery are any more than an ephemeral reaction against the infringement of temporal laws limited by the fact that they are reflective of a particular society. In this light, one must answer that Tolstoy – in spite of himself – *does* convince us that the Order broken by Anna moves on a higher plane than do the social sanctions operating in, say *En Ménage* (to take any one of the other works studied); and that only two other novels can approximate to this level of experience : *Emma Bovary* and *The Golden Bowl.* All three novels suggest an order which appears worth justifying even to the twentieth-century age of permissiveness.

In the second it is true that Flaubert punished Emma for her romantic folly, and that this was in one sense simply an expression of Flaubert's personal hatred of Romanticism, an attempt to paint its excesses in colours sufficiently lurid to make its dangers obvious to his reading public. But it is also the case that Flaubert was doing more than this; the greater significance of his onslaught on Romanticism is that it is also a focalised and contemporary spearhead of a more universal attack upon all attempts to base reality on insecure fictions. And this brings us back in a roundabout way to de Rougemont, for *Mme Bovary* can now be seen as a myth designed to contain the element, destructive to society, not just of passion, but also of foolish fancies and false notions – of unreality itself.

But de Rougemont's and Bataille's theses do not, by the above suggestion, lose any of their own importance. In spite of what both writers have done to expound their subjects, the relationship between passion and eroticism and death remains mysterious, as does the hidden way in which society works to contain in myths the elements it knows to be destructive to it. So the reader acquainted with 'l'amour-passion' may well see that beyond Emma's nonsense-filled head, her discovery of *la volupté*, and her financial worries, there is an inadmissible, inexplicable, and irresistible longing for death, which grows ever stronger as life's promises are seized, exploited and discarded because they proved to be mere husks. But this is no more than an explanation so consonant with the psychology of the novel that it cannot be ignored; it is not essential to the novel, and it does not impose itself on the reader's consciousness in the way that the certain fear of tragedy does with Anna.

However, it would be wrong to see the difference between the two novels as an implication that *Mme Bovary* is therefore a lesser work than *Anna Karenina*. Anna appeals to the intelligent and sensitive reader because she also shares these qualities; her problems and reactions are on the same plane as that of the reader. But Mme Bovary is both unintelligent and uneducated, so that the reader will consider her problems essentially from outside – and from above as well. Flaubert's genius lies in making the problems of a worthless person worth something to the reader, of rendering more accessible and real something he might otherwise pass over with disdain. The fact of course that Flaubert has continued to be hailed as a great writer in this century, when the immediate dangers of nineteenth-century romanticism have disappeared or taken another guise, makes him at least the equal of Tolstoy – with both on dizzying heights of achievement. And perhaps, if we have interpreted him properly, Flaubert may in fact be more relevant to ourselves, since while both Anna's and Emma's fate depends *partly* on the circumstances of their milieu, the emotional fictions on which our own society depends, via the film and the television in particular, would appear to be more significant than shibboleths proscribing illegal love.

Paradoxically, James, who allows adultery to play a redemptive role, alone persuades us of a concept of marriage which is so high as to be above ethics. In his very terminology he is Platonic; Maggie talks of the 'funny form' of her marriage, by which euphemism she means the wilful travesty it has become. It is not that after the closing pages of the novel Maggie and Amerigo will live happily ever after, but that through her achievement Maggie has succeeded in restoring their marriage to the 'form' it should have – a form existing primarily in James's mind, an ideal rarely if ever attained in practice, and one which the events of *The Golden Bowl* are merely a preparation for, not a state now reached, through the regularisation of an erring husband. We have seen, of course, that James was able to lay down his necessary conditions – the intelligence, honesty, selflessness and commitment at work in Maggie and betrayed by Sir Charles; but as with Tolstoy, the necessary conditions are not the whole story. The ideal form of marriage exists even before there are spouses, and some characters – Isabel is one – assume it and pay homage to it irrespective of the conjugal situation in which they find themselves. Maggie's awareness of it *as a good* was what impelled her to wrest her husband back from Charlotte's toils; and for all the growth Chad received from his relationship with Marie, it is overwhelmingly clear that their liaison was a shadow-dance compared with the reality sensed by the Princess.

But what James is also saying, of course, is that even though marriage is an ideal form of human commitment, adultery is not at all the same kind of absolute. It is a flaw, just as the dishonesty and selfishness that lust entails are flaws. There is no negative counterpart to his ideal; there is only absence or ignorance or failure to live up to the ideal, and thus none of his characters is punished except in completely human terms. Charlotte lives on to lie in the bed she made when she contracted marriage with Adam Verver, and that in itself is her penance.

To some extent James is a high form himself of the English attitude to marriage and adultery. For amongst the English novelists are many who appear to take marriage seriously, but who have not been treated in this study because they did not dare to approach adultery at all. We know that the repressive forces of Victorian England forced the golden image of marriage into two distorted halves – the paterfamilias with his lady-like (i.e. sexually restrained) wife leading their exemplary children to church or chapel on Sunday morning and reading aloud to them on Sunday evening from the bowdlerised books dedicated to the perpetuation of the model family; and the 'secret-lifers' whose patronage maintained huge numbers of brothels and supported a vast pornographic industry. And we also know that while Paterfamilias and Secret-lifer were frequently the same person, it was normal for the former not only to pretend ignorance of his intimate relationship with his alter ego, but to deny its very existence.

This said, it still remains that James writes in a tradition which frequently upholds a golden ideal of marriage, which at its best is seen as a happy and fruitful partnership sparked by romantic love but settling into a steady flame of enduring affection. When the picture comes out wrong, the novelists tend to retain their ideals of love and marriage and blame the infelicity of the arranged (though not forced) marriage, or the too-hasty and thoughtless choice of partner.

So, by way of the more dominant patterns standing out from the basic fabric of the novel of adultery, we are finally led to our ultimate consideration.

Concepts of lasting relationships

Both the cursory survey of the background to marriage and adultery in the civilisations under review, and the assumptions implicit in the novels themselves, indicate that the ancient historical prevalence of the notion of a lasting exclusive and personal relationship between man and woman is a basic fact in West European tradition; it appears to have weaker emotional surrounds in Russian society, but nevertheless provides both now and in the past the norm of social structure as much in Russia as in the West.

The original development of pair-bonding amongst the primate hunting apes ensured fidelity on the part of the female when the male was away hunting, reduced sexual rivalry between males, and finally benefited the offspring.[5] Since then the pattern has been strengthened by the need to propagate the species and provide for the offspring. Church and State have codified the rules, posing and imposing them as the sophistications of civilisation have threatened an arrangement which visibly contributes to a stable, hierarchical, and authoritarian system.

All the civilisations have seen the system challenged, mostly by the unselfconscious example of the common man and woman who simply find themselves drawn by lust, love, or a combination of the two, to a relationship with a person other than their legal spouse, for a period which may vary from half an hour to half a lifetime. Challenge in the form of a whole movement came in the eleventh century from the cult of romantic love; and later from the intellectual convictions of seventeenth-century utopians, eighteenth-century *philosophes*, and nineteenth-century Romantic and social reformers. The experiments of, in particular, the reformers and Romantics provoked a reaction in favour of marriage; and it is this dual pressure which gives the nineteenth century its essential character.

I believe that if we stand far enough away from the particular, the generalities I have just sketched hold true for the Anglo-Saxon, the French and the Russian situations. The opposition between George

Sand and Barbey d'Aurevilly, between the Nihilists and Tolstoy, and between the life of Marion Evans and the novels of George Eliot, all testify to an ambivalence in human thought and behaviour that is expressed in terms of our dual needs for security and stimulation, stability and novelty, order and change. Unfortunately, the side on which the angels are to be found is not crystal clear. Moreover, any attempt to examine the duality more closely does seem to throw up national divergences in the way the ambivalence is both expressed and solved.

In the tradition of the French novel, marriage as an institution basically fails to appeal since the wife is so essentially a non-person. Either she is the proffered partner in some contractual arrangement in which mutual liking is not even a consideration, or she is carefully chosen for her virtues of docility, devotion and dullness. On the other hand, the exploration of adulterous relationships has revealed a contrasting concept of vital interpersonal encounters between lovers, which goes beyond simple physical desire. It would be fatuous to embark on a definition of the word love; but when Muffat discovers that he has begun to love Nana 'réellement' we understand that by this he means something involving enjoyment and need of her as a person, out of bed as much as in it, as well as a need to see their relationship as a continuing one. M. de Camors experiences real conflict when he begins to relate to his virtuous wife as a person, but cannot give up his voluptuous mistress. He is unable, even ultimately, to make the choice between two distinct kinds of attraction. Bel-Ami and Mme de Marelle sustain a lasting relationship in spite of their quarrels and mutual infidelities; and the categorical exploration of non-lasting liaisons in *En Ménage* leads both hero and anti-hero to opt for a lasting relationship whether or not there is a wedding-ring. The last argument is one of the very few, in the novels of the 1880s and 1890s, in favour of marriage; and even they are weak. Marriage is perhaps marginally better than concubinage if considered as a 'caisse de'épargnes'; just as fear of solitude may also foster thoughts of grandchildren playing at one's feet. Neither argument could conceivably be called compelling.

Thus, while the need for durable relationships is admitted, even in the paradoxically fleeting glimpse offered by an affair, it is not thought that marriage will provide a really satisfactory answer. Zola and Maupassant may castigate a sick society, but they provide no positive solutions; Fromentin provides a solution as ineffective as it is unattractive. And yet no writer gives open approval to the alternative of the mistress, since adultery is always punished, if not by death, then at least by disillusion and despair.

French society at the end of the nineteenth century was truly on the horns of a dilemma in regard to marriage. The established institution was a failure due to the determination not to associate marriage with sexual or emotional love and to the fixation not to allow women equal freedom. But no writer is willing to abandon marriage altogether, with its seldom realised but potential promise of a lasting personal relationship. The Frenchman is caught, in other words, between two mutually exclusive and *parallel* relationships, neither of which is ultimately satisfactory.

The few English novelists who deal with adultery tend, on the other hand, to see it as the result of an erroneous first marriage – a rectifiable mistake if only society will allow a change of partner. The continuous triangle is not the way the problem presents itself, since the old union, once acknowledged as a mistake, ought to be shuffled off, while the new one is seen as quite permanent, though starry eyes should be lit only by a vision of self-sacrifice if the original fault is to be truly vindicated. The marriage ideal remains an ideal in this picture of society, but only if it lives up to certain standards of integrity and truth; and while Meredith is anxious to set up 'true' relationships in despite of false marriages, James's concern is to temper the image wrought in gilt into one of pure gold.

To the Russians, always more preoccupied with the relations between man and man, or man and God, than between man and woman, adultery is almost a non-question. While it does not have great appeal, it does not earn severe condemnation. To the Nihilists the term is almost pointless, since they at least believed, and many of them actually practised, a concept of freedom between the sexes which defied all notions of possession and commitment to one person. The liberation of the female as a socio-political entity got caught up in the bid for freedom for all mankind; but to Western eyes the ease with which the personal dynamics of the 'woman question' were put aside for the social ones is astonishing (as is, paradoxically, the extreme reaction this attempt to remove marriage aroused in Tolstoy). Billington sees a parallel between the two in these terms: 'Always the egocentric lover, he [the aristocratic intellectual] embraced both men and women and ideas with a mixture of passion and fantasy that made a sustained relationship almost impossible . . .'[6] The hope for sustained relationships lay in the future brotherhood of man, not in the bed of the strong Russian woman who ridiculed the male by her very fortitude and saved her own soul through her motherhood.

However, the century or so which has passed since the publication of *Anna Karenina* has seen the assumptions on which it is built questioned consistently and widely, with increasing impatience, both mindlessly and intelligently, by men and by women. There are many who simply reject marriage in order to take up free unions, long or short term, in love nests *à deux*, or in communes of like-minded peers, many of which allow free-ranging sexual relations within the group, even though there may be couples in it who see themselves as permanently married. Clearly, to talk of adultery in such an arrangement would be almost meaningless – though this is not to assume that emotions like insecurity and jealousy will also be irrelevant. Just as clearly, such a commune will not be persecuted by society unless its members commit a genuine crime or unless they offend an ordinary member of society on whom they are dependent – such as the landlady. Its members will argue that not only will the children born to the community not suffer, but they will be a great deal better off than the child of the nuclear family.

If such groups were to proliferate to the extent of becoming the norm, then the concept of adultery would become anachronistic to modern society The dramas of the nineteenth century would have (possibly) the same literary merit and the same remoteness of social identification as *Le Cid*. The ethics which inform them would simply be irrelevant, though if they were well enough written we should still be able to appreciate the values they debated. But whether this will come to pass remains unproven. When the debris of vested male interest in authoritarian hierarchies, in their sexual and social domination over women, and in the maintenance of the *status quo* is cleared away, we still seem to be left with some universals.

On the basis of his research with animals, Robert Ardrey has claimed that the needs of both animal and man can be reduced to three basics – the need for identity, stimulation and security. These needs can be met in marriage, though of course they often are not. They can also be met in a totally secure lasting relationship, though here the commitment would have to be explicit and trustworthy at least to the degree that these qualities can be found in marriage. It is significant that those who do not believe in divorce often argue that the absence of an escape clause induces a deeper loyalty to the marriage as well as to the spouse, and a firmer determination to 'make it work'. On the other hand this argument is not admitted by those who see no point at all in making something work imperfectly. However, the essential point remains. *If* human needs are those three basics postulated by Ardrey, and if marriage or its imitation is capable of fulfilling them, then the future of monogamy is assured. It will be up to the commune people to prove their system better, or to provide for the inclusion of monogamous relationships within a larger set-up.

But a monogamous relationship, even if it is only one of a series, is still a different proposition from the notion of taking a mistress as well as a wife, the escape pursued primarily by a race of divided men – divided because the organisation of their women into a hierarchical system symbolised by the gulf between the *femme honnête* and the mistress rebounds in the division of the male who seeks both quarries. The process is not unlike a form of dualism in which the person is split into body and soul. (France was after all not only the seat of the passionate love cult but also the land which produced Descartes.)

The adulterous situation which results in a *ménage à trois* cannot then supply either identity or security, though there is no denying that stimulation may be there in abundance. The adultery that leads to a change of partner may still presume an idealism about lasting personal relationships if error, ignorance or constraint had any part in the first marriage; on the other hand if concepts of honour, loyalty and truth are part of the individual's identity or self-image, then the commitment to fidelity may override even these considerations. As so many of the novelists pointed out, it is difficult for the adulterer to keep his integrity free of attendant vices no matter how guiltless he may feel about the act itself.

Does this mean then that the tragic treatment of the adultery theme *is* out of date? Is not just *Le Cid* but *Phèdre* also irrelevant to the twentieth century except in historico-literary terms? Is the long-faced novel wrong in its perspectives and the comic tradition more accurate and apposite when it sees adultery in terms of the ridiculous cuckold, the bedroom farce, the lunacy of taking marriage seriously, the all-out romp of Restoration comedy?

These questions only seem to be the ones to ask : they are thrown up by a false understanding of tragedy – or rather by a confusion of the two levels on which tragedy operates. Of course it is not entirely misguided to label 'tragic' a work which ends with the death of one or more of the main characters (assuming we are not in the realm of farce, melodrama or detective stories). But we also recognise that M. de Camors is not a tragedy at the same level as *Anna Karenina*, that the two deaths at the end of *In the Whirlpool* are less tragic than the tortured survival of the characters in *The Return of the Native*. And certainly we also acknowledge that when we read *Phèdre* we have touched the apotheosis of tragedy. We are simply realising that death has only enough sufficiency to qualify for tragedy if it is accompanied by other circumstances such as supreme injustice, inexorableness or prematurity. The peaceful death of old age or the release that means the end of disease may well not be tragic at all – otherwise we should never have the phrase 'a happy death'. But *Phèdre* is tragic because she is committed to a destiny which arouses the rage of the gods. There is a quality of fatality not just about her death but about the passion which seizes her – and no glib account of genes and environment can dispel the onlooker's sense of impending doom, of the unleashing of forces beyond human control, of the defeat of reason by chaos and destruction. This is the tragedy which demands death as its penalty, but of which death itself is only a part; it is a recognition of the forces which myth seeks to contain, but terrifies us with in the telling.

The history of the decline of tragic drama has been told by George Steiner in *The Death of Tragedy*. The Romantics, he says, failed to restore to life the ideal of high tragedy, and thus prepared the ground for the 'separation between literature and the playhouse, and the radical change in the notion of the tragic and the comic brought on by Ibsen, Strindberg, Chekhov and Pirandello'.[7] Believing, in the dawn of their existence, in Rousseau-esque hopes for the perfectibility of man in the natural state, and freed from the weight of the conviction of original sin and the displeasure of the gods, the early Romantics were also able to attribute crime to the corruption of society or even non-culpable ignorance; guilt for them became a relative thing. But, says Steiner,

> such a view of the human condition is radically optimistic. It cannot engender any natural form of tragic drama. The romantic vision of life is non-tragic . . . to argue that Oedipus should have been excused on grounds of ignorance, or that Phèdre was merely prey to hereditary chaos of the blood, is to diminish to absurdity the weight and meaning of the tragic action . . . Where a tragic conception of life is in force, moreover, there can be no recourse to secular or material remedies. The destiny of Lear cannot be resolved by the establishment of adequate homes for the aged.[8]

But it is not at all certain that most of the problems of the novels under discussion could not have been eased by a visit to a marriage guidance counsellor, a good lawyer, or by the establishment of a sounder education for girls. Wives like Christiane are caught in a trap, certainly, but it is not of the gods' creation. It is a man-made snare resulting from the wilful and short-sighted determination that marriage should be a contract based on property. In the end, only Anna – by a quite incredible paradox, when we think of the Tolstoy of *The Kreuzer Sonata* – wears the true mask of tragedy. There is something utterly inevitable in her story which operates *in spite of* as well as because of psychological accuracy – something terrifying and awesome and immutable. It is partly to do with her extreme beauty, her intense vitality, her complete hopelessness – nothing about Anna, not even her jealousy, is trivial or ordinary. It also has something to do with the absoluteness with which she gives herself up to passion, abandoning even her child; it has something to do with the symbolism of the train – for by throwing herself under it she was simply finding a suitable altar on which to let her fate catch up with her. 'Verse', says Steiner, 'is the prime divider between the world of high tragedy and that of ordinary existence'.[9] In general he is perfectly correct, and that is why *Anna Karenina* is so extraordinary an exception.

The authors who most nearly approach this peak are Hardy and Flaubert. But Hardy's sense of irony comes between him and it. He allows Tess to endure a fate as painful as that of Iphigénie, but he cracks the mysterious crystal ball of destiny by his sardonic comment about the President of the Immortals, and the mockery of the jibe ('Justice was done'). Forces had acted upon Tess, it is true; but Hardy allows them no grandeur, no lordliness, no inevitability. Nothing more or less than unlucky coincidences, stupid men and human weakness dog poor Tess; and though her fate was cruel and stark and undeserved, it is still possible to believe it was not inevitable.

Flaubert, on the other hand, plots Emma's downfall from the opening sentence onwards, and leaves no room at all for the wistfulness of the 'if only . . .' But Emma is basically a little person. The very mistranslation of her name confuses the issue, for one has only to think of her as 'Mrs Bovary' rather than Madame to recognise her essentially bourgeois origins, the mediocrity of her education, the sordidness of her affairs. She is not tall enough for the gods to strike down – and in any case they do not need to act. In her own self-determined embrace of romantic passion she traces her own path to destruction; but in doing so she moves us not to pity or terror, but simply to horror (which is not a tragic emotion since it invites the escape of turning away our eyes. Tragedy by contrast compels us to fix our gaze upon the awful workings of fate – and we dare not turn away).

However, this is not to say that the remaining authors did not think they were writing tragedies. Taking upon themselves the divine powers of the creator, they set up characters only to cut them down; the moral must be preached, the lesson be made clear. The transgressor must perish, the law must be maintained. 'In what name?' asks the modern reader, conditioned to reject any proposition which is not immediately self-justifying. Well, there is no name to be automatically invoked any longer; almost all the tenets are in the process of being challenged : the role of the family, the male-given hierarchy of women, the docile wife, the authoritarian father-figure, the structure of class, the repugnance of extramarital love, the right of society to interfere with the private life of the individual. But sweep all these things aside, and we are still left with three works : *Madame Bovary, Anna Karenina* and *The Golden Bowl.* In the last we know – ironically by the kinds of touchstone of which James himself was doubtful – that we are being shown an ideal, a platonic form, a good. We may all tell lies from time to time, but we should be sorry if there were no example of shining truth left in the world; society may or may not give itself over to the multiple divorce, the 'ultimate compliment', the group marriage; but we should still want to hear the story of Héloïse and Abelard, and indeed of Maggie Verver. It is one thing to fail, or even to reject standards, another to have no concept of an ideal form at all.

So, what of Anna? Does she then become a warning finger, a cautionary tale decked out in the trappings of tragedy? Far from it. Even brave new man is still mortally afraid of disorder. He makes his rules in the light of his own necessity, and when he breaks them he chastises himself. When the rules become uncomfortable he tries to bend them and even change them; but he does not completely eliminate them. Anna is simply a restatement of the rules. Without her – all is chaos.

Notes

Chapter 1

1. F. Henriques, *Love in Action* (Panther ed., 1965) p. 190.
2. B. Malinowski, Article on Marriage, 14th ed. *Encyclopedia Brittanicus*, vol. 14.
3. See *Household and Family in Past Time*, ed. Peter Laslett (Cambridge, 1972); also G. P. Murdock's article, 'The Universality of the Nuclear Family', in Bell and Vogel (eds), *A Modern Introduction to the Family* (New York, 1968).
4. Bell and Vogel (eds), *Modern Introduction to the Family.*
5. E. Schillebeekx, O.P., *Marriage: Secular Reality and Saving Mystery* (London, 1965), vol. 2, pp. 3–32.
6. The source of this quotation, and of the information contained in the whole section, is *The New Catholic Encyclopedia* (New York, 1967) pp. 803–13.
7. *A Short History of Women* (London, 1948) p. 156.
8. Henriques, *Love in Action*, p. 82.
9. C. S. Lewis, *The Allegory of Love* (New York, 1958) p. 3 et seq.
10. Gérard Duplessis-Le Guélinal, *Les Mariages en France* (Paris, 1954), p. 11 et seq.
11. Andrée Michel and Geneviève Texier, *La Condition de la Française aujourd' hui* (Geneva, 1964) t. 1, p. 74.
12. Duplessis, *Les Mariages en France*, p. 37.
13. Quoted by Ernest Cadet, *Le Mariage en France – Statistiques, Réformes* (Paris, 1870) p. 8.
14. D. G. Charlton, *Secular Religions in France* (London, 1936) p. 8.
15. Ivy Pinchbeck and Margaret Hewitt, *Children in English Society* (London, 1969) vol. 1, p. 13 et seq.
16. C. S. Lewis, *Allegory of Love*, p. 37.
17. Ibid., pp. 173–97.
18. G. Rattray Taylor, *Sex in History* (London, 1959) p. 192.
19. Leslie Fiedler, *Love and Death in the American Novel* (London, 1970) p. 15 et seq.
20. Quoted by S. Marcus, *The Other Victorians* (London, 1964) pp. 31 and 188.
21. Duncan Crow, *The Victorian Woman* (London, 1971) pp. 23 and 52.
22. Ronald Pearsall, *The Worm in the Bud* (Pelican ed., 1971) p. 252.
23. Milton Rugoff, *Prudery and Passion: Sexuality in Victoria America* (London, 1972) p. 38 et seq.
24. Andrew Sinclair, *The Better Half: The Emancipation of the American Woman* (New York, 1965) p. 118.
25. Ibid., p. 261.
26. G. P. Fedotov, *The Russian Religious Mind* (New York, 1960) p. 13.
27. S. S. Shashkova, *Istoria Russkoi Zhenshchiny* (St Petersburg, 1879) p. 12.

28 Maxime Kovalevsky, *Modern Customs and Ancient Laws of Russia* (London, 1891) p. 36.
29 Elaine Elnett, *The Historic Origin and Social Development of Family Life in Russia* (New York, 1926) p. 63.
30 T. A. Bogdanovich, *Liubov liudei shestidesiatykh godov* (Leningrad, 1929) p. 13.
31 James Billington, *The Icon and the Axe: An Interpretative History of Russian Culture* (New York, 1968) p. 311 et seq.
32 Geoffrey Gorer and John Rickman, *The People of Great Russia: a Psychological Study* (London, 1949) p. 140.
33 N. K. Gudzy, *History of Early Russian Literature* (New York, 1949) pp. 57 and 77.
34 Paul Miliukov, *Outlines of Russian Culture: Literature* (Philadelphia, 1948) pp. 13–15.

Chapter 2
1 G. de Maupassant, *Mont–Oriol* (Paris, 1887) p. 21.
2 E. Zola, *La Bête Humaine* (Bruges, 1960–7) p. 1193.
3 L. Tolstoy, *Anna Karenina* (Moscow, 1955) p. 150.
4 L. Tolstoy, *War and Peace* (Moscow, 1967) pp. 254–5.
5 H. James, *The Golden Bowl* (Penguin ed., 1966) p. 267.
6 H. James, *What Maisie Knew* (London, 1947) p. 110.
7 Ibid., p. 128.
8 G. Flaubert, *Madame Bovary* (Paris, 1961) p. 63.
9 Ibid., p. 180.
10 Ibid., p. 198.
11 T. Hardy, *Jude the Obscure* (London, 1963) p. 290.
12 G. Meredith, *Lord Ormont and his Aminta* (London, 1914) p. 299.
13 Quoted by N. Berdiakov, *The Russian Idea* (London, 1947) p. 79.
14 Tolstoy, *Anna Karenina*, p. 125.
15 G. Meredith, *Diana of the Crossways* (Westminster, 1902) p. 98.
16 E. Fromentin, *Dominique* (Paris, 1966) p. 151.
17 J. Hillis Miller, *Thomas Hardy: Distance and Desire* (Harvard, 1973) p. 182.
18 Ibid., p. 154.
19 R. Freeborn, *Turgenev, the Novelist's Novelist* (London, 1960) p. 40.

Chapter 3
1 Alfred C. Kinsey *et al.*, *Sexual Behaviour in the Human Female* (New York, 1965).
2 Meredith, *One of Our Conquerors*, p. 96.
3 James, *The Golden Bowl*, p. 233.
4 Tolstoy, *Anna Karenina*, p. 163.
5 E. Zola, *Nana* (Bruges, 1960–7) p. 1267.
6 L. Tolstoy, *The Kreuzer Sonata* (Moscow, 1947) p. 212.
7 B. d'Aurevilly, *Une Vieille Maîtresse* (Paris, 1964) p. 406.
8 James, *The Golden Bowl*, p. 285.
9 Tolstoy, *Anna Karenina*, p. 390.
10 d'Aurevilly, *Une Vieille Maîtresse*, pp. 432–501.
11 Ibid., p. 486.
12 James, *The Golden Bowl*, p. 304.
13 Ibid., p. 337.
14 James, *What Maisie Knew*, p. 158.
15 Meredith, *One of Our Conquerors*, p. 298.

Chapter 4

1 A. F. Pisemsky, *Collected Works* (Moscow, 1959) vol. 1, pp. 208–9.
2 Maupassant, *Bel-Ami*, p. 134.
3 B. d'Aurevilly, *Ce Qui ne Meurt pas* (1884) p. 663.
4 Zola, *Nana*, p. 1485.
5 Tolstoy, *War and Peace*, vol. 3/4, p. 696.
6 H. Troyat, *Tolstoy* (Pelican ed., 1970) p. 452.
7 Tolstoy, *Anna Karenina*, pp. 35–6.
8 N. Chernyshevsky, *What's to be Done?* (Moscow, 1962) pp. 322–4 and 354–6.
9 E. Starkie, *Flaubert: The Making of the Master* (London, 1967), p. 297.

Chapter 5

1 R. Poggioli, *The Phoenix and the Spider* (Cambridge, Mass., 1957) p. 70.
2 And passim: references taken from Robert Mauzi, *L'Idée de Bonheur au dix-huitième Siècle* (Paris, 1967) pp. 240ff and 417ff.
3 P. J. Yarrow, *La Pensée politique et religieuse de Barbey d'Aurevilly* (Geneva, and Paris, 1961) p. 169.
4 G. Steiner, *Tolstoy or Dostoevsky* (Peregrine ed., 1967) p. 256.
5 D. Morris, *The Naked Ape* (Corgi ed., 1968) p. 35.
6 Billington, *Icon and the Axe*, p. 350.
7 Steiner, *Death of Tragedy*, p. 124.
8 Ibid., p. 128.
9 Ibid., p. 241.

Bibliography

(Dates in brackets denote date of writing, unless otherwise specified)

THE NOVELS USED AS PRIMARY SOURCES

Barbey d'Aurevilly, *Oeuvres Romanesques Complètes,* 2 vols, textes presentés, établis et annotés par Jacques Petit. Bruges: Bibliothèque de la Pléiade, 1964. Vol. 1, cont. *Une Vieille Maîtresse* (1851); vol. 2, cont. *Ce qui ne meurt pas* (écrit 1833, publié 1884).

A. P. Chekhov, *Collected Works (Sobranie v vos'mi tomakh).* Moscow, (1970).

N. G. Chernyshevsky, *What's to be Done? (Shto deliat'?)* (1864). Moscow, 1962.

F. M. Dostoevsky, *Crime and Punishment (Prestuplenie i nakazanie)* (1864). Leningrad, 1962.

Octave Feuillet, *Monsieur de Camors.* Paris: Calmann-Lévy, n.d. (set 1860).

Gustave Flaubert, *Novembre* (1842), avec une préface de Henri Guillemin. Collection du Sablier, Neuchâtel: Ides et Calendes, 1961. *Madame Bovary* (1857). Paris: Gallimard, 1961. *L'Education Sentimentale* (1869). Livre de poche, Gallimard et librairie générale française, 1965 (set 1840).

John William de Forest, *Miss Ravenel's Conversion* (1867), ed. and with an introduction by Gordon S. Gaight. New York: Holt, Rinehard & Winston, 1968.

Eugène Fromentin, *Dominique* (1876), introduction, notes et appendice critique, avec les variations du manuscrit original par Barbara Wright. Paris: Librairie Marcel Didier, 1966.

Thomas Hardy, *The Return of the Native* (1878). London: Macmillan, 1961. *The Woodlanders* (1887) London: Macmillan, 1920. *The Mayor of Caster-bridge* (1888). Papermac ed., 1965. *Tess of the d'Urbervilles* (1891). Papermac ed., 1965. *Jude the Obscure* (1893). London: Macmillan, 1963.

Nathaniel Hawthorne, *The Scarlet Letter* (1850), foreword by Leo Marx Signet. New York, Toronto: New American Library, 1959.

Joris-Karl Huysmans, *En Ménage* (1881) dans *Oeuvres Complètes,* t. 4. Paris: C. Grès et Cié, 1928.

Henry James, *Portrait of a Lady* (1881) introduced by Graham Greene. London: Oxford University Press, World Classics, 1947, 1952. *What Maisie Knew* (1897) London: John Lehmann, 1947. *The Awkward Age* (1899). London: Bodley Head, 1967. *The Ambassadors* (1903). New York: Dell, 1964. *The Golden Bowl* (1904). Penguin Modern Classics, 1966.

B. M. Markevich, *The Forgotten Question (Zabytyi Voproc)* (1875) vol. 1. St. Petersburg, 1885.

Guy de Maupassant, *Bel-Ami* (1885), texte établi, avec introduction, notes et relevé de variantes par Gérard Delaisement. Paris: Garnier, 1959. *Mont-Oriol* (1887). Paris: Victor-Havard, 1887. *Fort Comme la Mort* (1889). Paris: Paul Ollendorff, 1889.

George Meredith, *The Ordeal of Richard Feverel* (1859), introduced by Robert Sencourt. Everyman ed., London: Dent; New York: Dutton, 1954. *Diana of the Crossways* (n.d., set 1825–6). Westminster: Constable, 1902. *Lord Ormont and his Aminta* (1894). London: Constable, 1914. *One of Our Conquerors* (1897) rev. ed. London: Constable, 1914.

A. F. Pisemsky, *Boyarshchina* (1845). Moscow, 1959. *In the Whirlpool (V Vodovorote)* (1871). St Petersburg, 1911.

A. S. Pushkin, *Evgenii Onegin* (1837). Moscow, 1970.

George Sand, *Indiana* (1831), texte établi, avec introduction, notes et relevé de variantes par Pierre Saloman. Paris: Garnier Frères, 1962. *Jacques*. Paris: Calmann-Lévy, 1834.

L. N. Tolstoy, *The Demon (Diavol)* (1889). Moscow, 1948. *The Kreuzer Sonata* (1889–90). Moscow, 1947. *Family Happiness (Semeinoe schaste)* (1859). *Voina i mire* (1868–9) v 4 tomakh. Moscow, 1957. *Anna Karenina* (1878). Moscow, 1955.

L. S. Turgenev, *Collected Works (Polnoe sobranie sochinenii i picem v dvadstati vos'mi tomakh)*. Moscow, 1965.

Edith Wharton, *The Age of Innocence* (written 1920, set 1870). New York: Signet Classics, 1962.

Emile Zola, *Les Rougon-Macquart: Histoire Naturelle et Sociale d'une Famille sous le Second Empire,* edn, intégrale pub. ss. la direction d'Armand Lanoux, études, notes et variantes par Henri Mitterand. Bruges: Bibliothèque de la Pléiade, Gallimard, 1960–7. t. 2, *Une Page d'Amour* (1878), *Nana* (1880); t. 3, *Pot-Bouille* (1882); t. 4, *La Bête Humaine* (1890). *Thérèse Raquin* (1867), nouvelles ed. Paris: Bibliothèque Charpentier, 1916.

WORKS OF LITERARY CRITICISM

Dmitry Čiževskij, *History of Russian Literature* (1960) 's Gravenhage: Mouton and Co., 1962.

Leslie A. Fiedler, *Love and Death in the American Novel* (1967). London: Paladin, 1970.

Richard Freeborn, *Turgenev, the Novelists' Novelist.* London: Oxford University Press, 1960.

N. K. Gudzy, *History of Early Russian Literature* (1941), translated from 2nd Russian ed. by Susan Wilbur Jones, introduced by Oleg Struve. New York: Macmillan, 1949.

F. W. J. Hemmings, *Emile Zola,* 2nd ed. London: Oxford University Press, 1953, 1966.

J. Hillis Miller, *Thomas Hardy: Distance and Desire.* Cambridge, Mass.: Belknap Press, 1970.

Louis James, *Fiction for the Working Man: a study of the literature produced for the working classes in early Victorian Urban England* (1830–50). London: Oxford University Press, 1903.

C. S. Lewis, *The Allegory of Love: A Study of Medieval Tradition.* New York: Galaxy, Oxford University Press, 1958 (first published 1936).

Mirsky, *Pushkin.* London, 1926.

Renato Poggioli, *The Phoenix and the Spider.* Cambridge, Mass.: Harvard University Press, 1957.

E. Starkie, *Flaubert: The Making of the Master.* London: Weidenfeld & Nicolson, 1967.

George Steiner, *Tolstoy or Dostoevsky* (1959). Peregrine ed., 1967. *The Death of Tragedy* (1956). London: Faber, 1968.

Patricia Thomson, *The Victorian Heroine: a changing ideal, 1837–1873*. London: Oxford University Press, 1956.
P. J. Yarrow, *La Pensée Politique et Religieuse de Barbey d'Aurevilly*. Génève: Libraire Droz; Paris: Libraire Minard, 1961.

HISTORICAL, RELIGIOUS, AND SOCIOLOGICAL WORKS CONSULTED

Robert Ardrey, *The Territorial Imperative* (1967). London: Fontana, 1970.
Georges Bataille, *L'erotisme*. Paris: Ed. de Minuit, 1957.
Norman W. Bell and Ezra F. Vogel (eds), *A Modern Introduction to the Family*. New York: Free Press, 1968.
Nicolas Berdyaev, *The Russian Idea*. London: Geoffrey Bles, 1947.
James H. Billington, *The Icon and the Axe: An Interpretive History of Russian Culture*. New York: A. A. Knopf, 1968.
T. A. Bogdanovich, *Liubov' liudei shestidesiatykh godov*. Leningrad, 1929.
Paul Bohannen and John Middleton (eds), *Marriage, Family & Residence*. American Museum Sourcebooks in Anthropology, New York: The Natural History Press, 1968.
Ernest Cadet, *Le Mariage en France – Statistiques, Réformes*. Paris: Guillaumin, 1870.
D. G. Charlton, *Secular Religions in France 1815–1870*. London: Oxford University Press (for University of Hull), 1963.
Duncan Crow, *The Victorian Woman*. London: George Allen and Unwin, 1971.
Georges Duby and Robert Mandrou, *A History of French Civilisation*, translated by James Blakely Atkinson. London: Weidenfeld & Nicolson, 1955. (Originally published in French as *Histoire de la Civilisation Francaise*. Paris: Max Leclerc & Cié, 1958).
Gérard Duplessis-Le Guélinal, *Les Mariages en France*, avec préface de Paul Gemaehling. Paris: Armand Colin, 1954.
Elaine Elnett, *The Historic Origin and Social Development of Family Life in Russia*. New York: Columbia University Press, 1926.
G. P. Fedetov, *The Russian Religious Mind* (1946). New York: Harper & Row, 1960.
Geoffrey Gorer and John Rickman, *The People of Great Russia: a Psychological Study*. London: Cresset Press, 1949.
René Guerdan, *La femme et l'amour en France*. Paris: Plon, 1965.
Fernando Henriques, *Love in Action: The Sociology of Sex* (1959). London: Panther, 1965.
Initiation Théologique, par un groupe de théologiens, T. IV, *L'économie du Salut*. Paris: Les éditions du Cerf, 1961.
Alfred C. Kinsey *et al*, *Sexual Behaviour in the Human Female* (1953) New York: Pocket Book 1965.
Maxime Kovalevsky, *Modern Customs & Ancient Laws of Russia*. London: David Nutt, 1891.
John Langdon-Davies, *A Short History of Women*. London: Watts & Co., Thinkers Library no. 72. (First published 1926, first issued in Thinkers Library. Revised and abridged, 1938, 2nd imp., 1948.)
Suzanne Lilar, *Aspects of Love in Western Society* (1963) tr. with a preface by Jonathon Green. London: Thames & Hudson, 1965. (First published as *Le Couple* by Editions Bernard Arasset, Paris, 1963).
B. Malinowski, *Sex, Culture and Myth*. London: Rupert Hart-Davis, 1963.
Steven Marcus, *The Other Victorians, a study of sexuality and pornography in*

mid-nineteenth century England, sponsored by the Institute for Sex Research, Indiana University, Bloomington, Ind. London: Weidenfeld & Nicolson, 1964, 1965, 1966.

Robert Mauzi, *L'idée du bonheur dans la littérature et la pensée française au XVIII᷾ siècle* (1960). Paris: Armand Colin, 1967.

Andrée Michel et Geneviève Texier, *La Condition de la française aujourd-hui,* 2 tomes. Genève: Editions Gonthier, 1964.

Paul Miliukov, *Outlines of Russian Culture,* ed. Michael Karpovich, trans. Valentine Ughet and Eleanor Davis. Philadelphia: University of Pennsylvania Press, 1948.

Desmond Morris, *The Naked Ape* (1967). London: Corgi, 1968.

Ronald Pearsall, *The Worm in the Bud: The World of Victorian Sexuality* (1969). London: Weidenfeld & Nicolson, 1919; Pelican ed., 1971.

Ivy Pinchbeck and Margaret Hewitt, *Children in English Society, Vol. 1, from Tudor Times to the 18th Century.* London: Routledge & Kegan Paul; Toronto: University of Toronto Press, 1969.

G. Rattray Taylor, *Sex in History.* First published in Great Britain by Thames & Hudson, 1953; rev. ed., 1959.

Denis de Rougemont, *L'Amour et l'Occident* (1939), ed. remaniée et augmentée. Paris: Plon, 1956.

Milton Rugoff, *Prudery & Passion: Sexuality in Victorian America.* London: Rupert Hart-Davis, 1972. ·

E. Schillebeeckx, O.P., *Marriage: Secular Reality & Saving Mystery,* vol. 2, *Marriage in the History of the Church,* trans. N. D. Smith. London, Melbourne: Sheed & Ward, 1965.

S. S. Shashkova, *Istoria russkoi zhenschiny,* 2nd ed. St Petersburg, 1879.

Andrew Sinclair, *The Better Half: The Emancipation of the American Woman.* New York: Harper & Row, 1965.

Edith Thomas, *The Women Incendiaries,* translated from the original *Les Pétroleuses* (1963) by James and Starr Atkinson. New York: Brazillac, 1966.

Transliteration: *A.L.A. Cataloguing Rules for Author & Title Entries,* prepared by the Division of Cataloguing and Classification of the American Library Association, 2nd ed., ed. Clare Beetle. Chicago: American Library Association, 1949.

Henri Troyat, *Tolstoy* (1965). Pelican ed., 1970.

Index